Teaching to Live

Black Religion, Activist-Educators, and Radical Social Change

ALMEDA M. WRIGHT

OXFORD
UNIVERSITY PRESS

Oxford University Press is a department of the University of Oxford. It furthers
the University's objective of excellence in research, scholarship, and education
by publishing worldwide. Oxford is a registered trade mark of Oxford University
Press in the UK and certain other countries.

Published in the United States of America by Oxford University Press
198 Madison Avenue, New York, NY 10016, United States of America.

CIP data is on file at the Library of Congress

ISBN 978–0–19–766342–4

DOI: 10.1093/oso/9780197663424.001.0001

Printed by Sheridan Books, Inc., United States of America

For activist-educators everywhere

Contents

SECTION III: RADICAL LOVE, CITIZENSHIP, AND EDUCATION

SECTION IV: RADICAL BLACK RELIGIOUS EDUCATION: POST-CIVIL RIGHTS MOVEMENT

Acknowledgments

Like all intellectual work, *Teaching to Live* would not exist without the generous support of myriad people and institutions. I must begin by acknowledging all of the teachers who shaped me and helped me to see the truly revolutionary power of *activist-educators*. In particular, I want to acknowledge the almost twenty Black teachers I had from elementary school to doctoral work: Mrs. Helen Henderson, Ms. Audrey Arrington, Mrs. Mary Miller, Mrs. DeBerry, principal of Dewitt House, my differential equations professor at MIT, my analog circuits laboratory teaching fellow, Dr. Cheryl Giles, Dr. Peter Gomes, Dr. Robert M. Franklin, Dr. Ronald Ferguson, Dr. Joan Martin, Dr. Griffin, Dr. Abraham Smith, Dr. Dianne Stewart, Dr. Alton Pollard, Dr. Thee Smith, and Dr. Emmanuel Lartey. This list also includes those outside of formal education like Sunday school and Baptist Training Union (BTU) teachers and mentors. I revel in what they taught me and how privileged I was to have so many teachers invest in me at critical points in my life (the half can never be told).

Along with my teachers, I am grateful to fellow religious educators and public school teachers who are continuing this work. In particular, I owe a tremendous debt to Akosua Lesesne and SIEC (Sisters in Education Circle), for the monthly gatherings where I was surrounded by Black women (and educators), learned from our elders, and felt the spirit of our ancestors. I learned so much and was loved in so many different ways. My soul is grateful.

I am grateful for the community of scholars, teachers, and learners at Yale Divinity School (YDS). Support for research, writing, and travel for this book was made possible through the generous junior faculty leave policy at Yale. Dean Gregory Sterling went above and beyond to support faculty through course releases, through editorial funding, and by simply understanding what it meant to be both a faculty member and a parent during a pandemic. The Practical Theology teaching group has been a source of tremendous advocacy and mentorship—helping me to navigate institutional culture and writing with grace. I am deeply indebted to the entire YDS *Village* of Black faculty and staff. I am grateful to Professor Willie Jennings for advocating for

Black faculty in amazing ways and for the sisterhood of Black women faculty at YDS (for Yolanda Smith who paved the way and for Awet Andemicael, Sarah Farmer, Donyelle McCray, and Eboni Marshall Turman, who showed up *just in time* to remind me that I was not alone).

Several writing groups helped keep me accountable and focused on finishing this project. Tisa Wenger and Melanie Ross helped me through several writing hurdles during our early on-campus writing groups (and became genuine friends and confidantes in the process). AnneMarie Mingo and the SisterScholars™ writing group helped me carve out space to write—particularly during the pandemic. The virtual writing group was a life raft when I didn't fully understand that I needed one. Likewise, Nicole Turner organized a virtual writing group and gently pushed us to write even on Fridays.

Conducting research for this book would have been much more difficult without the support of innumerable archivists and research librarians at the Avery Research Center, University of Charleston; Vanderbilt University, special collections; the Manuscripts, Archives, and Rare Books Division of the Schomburg Center for Research in Black Culture; Emory University Manuscripts, Archives, and Rare Book Library (MARBL); the Manuscript Division, Library of Congress; and Howard University Digital Collections. Tremendous thanks go to the staff and librarians for the ways that they pivoted during the pandemic and graciously scanned documents so that the work could continue—even as in-person research halted.

Many people took time to read drafts and offer critical feedback. Tisa Wenger and James Logan read early drafts of the book proposal and helped me clarify what I was trying to do. Professors John Swinton and Evelyn Parker read drafts and offered wise and encouraging feedback. My personal editor, Ulrike Guthrie read every word carefully and pushed me to write both quickly and clearly. My research assistants Mary Inge and Abigail Barrett offered critical bibliographic and editorial support. Likewise, I am grateful for the amazing staff at OUP, including Cynthia Read, who believed in this project early on and even as she was retiring passed it on to the careful stewardship of Theo Calderara.

I offer gratitude for many conversations and opportunities to share this research and get feedback. Thank you to the organizers of Maryville College's Cummings Conversations; Candler School of Theology, Anna Julia Cooper lecture; and the gathering of High School Youth Theology Institutes hosted by the Forum for Theological Exploration. My amazing students in the Black

Religion and Radical Education seminar also patiently read primary and secondary source materials with me as I began wrestling with the questions that shaped this book.

I have been blessed with a community of extremely close friends and family who have been the source of unwavering support and encouragement. For over twenty years of friendship and reality checks, I thank Monique Moultrie, James Logan, and Laura Everett. They are the embodiment of friendship—always pushing me to be great, to get out of my own way, and to celebrate. For believing in me even before I knew how to write my own name, for playing school with me, and for showing up without questions or reservation I thank my sisters: Angela, Aletha, and Anita. My sisters collectively embody the excellence and resourcefulness of Black women. They epitomize the best of "Black aunties," who love fiercely and daily help me parent and be a scholar. For being my first teachers, I am grateful to my parents, William and Lula, who even as ancestors are still encouraging me to dream big and change the world. For being my newest teacher (and colearner), I am grateful to Amani. She has taught me how to stay in the moment and why this work is so important. Finally, but most importantly, I am grateful to God for the calling to teach and the freedom to learn.

Introduction

Religion, Education, and Radical Social Change

Educator Rita Pierson's seven-minute TED Talk went viral (with almost 12 million views) with the simple message that "Every child deserves a champion." She told stories of working with students whom others had written off. When Pierson encountered classes of students who were academically deficient, instead of giving up on them she gave them mantras to say as they walked through the school hallways: "I am somebody. I was somebody when I came and I'll be a better somebody when I leave. I am powerful and I am strong. I deserve the education that I get here." Pierson described how she'd apologize to students when she had made a mistake; how she'd deliberately shop and visit in the neighborhoods where she taught to run into her students and their families; and how she'd keep crackers at her desk for students who came to school hungry—all to connect and build relationships with her students. Pierson's brief and passionate talk, which captured the imaginations of so many people, also reminds us that she stands in a long line of radical activist-educators. She is in a long tradition of teachers who are working to educate students and who know that their particular work (of educating children) connects to the much larger task of transforming the world.

At first glance, the TED Talk by Rita Pierson appears to be primarily a secular education talk. But as I researched her life, I began to uncover the ways that Pierson's faith also informed her commitment to her students and to her work as an educator and activist. Pierson was a committed church leader, a gifted singer, and a pastor's wife. When her community and family mourned her death in 2013, they remembered her love of God and her tireless work to educate students and to train teachers to work with children across a range of backgrounds.[1] As I explored Pierson's religious background, I wondered which other educators, particularly Black women, were doing similar things. How did *their* religious formation shape their educational activism on behalf of others? Often the religious lives of educators and activists are

Teaching to Live. Almeda M. Wright, Oxford University Press. © Oxford University Press 2024.
DOI: 10.1093/oso/9780197663424.003.0001

not explored, even ignored. But here I foreground other twentieth-century African American activist-educators and wrestle with how—and perhaps why—we have erased or ignored the specifically religious foundations of their activism.

Pierson embodies the many ways in which the radical, activist education tradition intersects with religion, but she is neither alone nor the first in this tradition. This line of activist educators includes figures like Anna Julia Cooper, who found that there was little support for the educational efforts of an ambitious Black girl like herself and instead had to commit her life to advocating for women's education and for the rights of all Black students to choose the types of courses (either classical or industrial) that they wanted to take. And while Black feminist scholars have more recently embraced Cooper's work, few have engaged her religious life and theological writings.[2]

These activist-educators also include figures like Septima Clark, an educator in rural South Carolina and the architect behind the *Citizenship Education Program* of the Southern Christian Leadership Conference. Septima Clark, along with Dorothy Cotton and others, worked tirelessly to train teachers and develop ways of teaching literacy to adults to help them register to vote, to become full citizens, and to improve the lives of Black people across the country. Their cohort also includes educators like James Lawson, a young minister and activist who had the daunting task of teaching nonviolent resistance and social change strategies to college students at the height of the civil rights movement, and Olivia Pearl Stokes, a pioneering religious educator who sought ways not only of caring for the spiritual growth of children, but also of helping them to understand the liberating work of God in their lives.

Each one of these teachers, some well known and others not, inspires the imaginations of generations. Each emphasizes the ways in which teachers can become leaders of change and transform their communities and the larger world. This book explores the ways in which these twentieth-century educators and others like them exemplify what it means to be an activist-educator, but also what it means to be activist-educators in conversation with larger religious traditions and communities of faith. It asks: How did the faith formation of such educators prompt and shape their activism? What was it about their own upbringing that made the activist life so urgent to them? What can we learn from religious, activist-educators about the ways that religion, education, and social change intersect?

Certainly not all Black teachers became activists or even regarded their work as participating in a revolutionary cause. Likewise, not all people of faith were inspired to work for change or to enact their faith in ways that benefited others. However, this book pays close attention to the educators who were doing what often looked like simple interventions on behalf of students and children and doing it in ways that left a legacy far beyond what they could have imagined or planned.

Starting Places

Black Religion, Young Adults, and Activism?

Like most practical theological research projects, this one began with and in communities of practice. It began in conversations with and about the practices of Black youth and young adult *religious* activists. After decades of teaching and researching young people, I was still wrestling with how to inspire in young people a larger sense of the work that many of them felt called to do, and how to help them stay grounded or have some religious grounding for their activism and ways of thinking about the world. Likewise, in the last decade, many conversations have (re-)emerged regarding how Black young adults are participating in social change movements and the often-erroneous assertions that more recent movements are not religious or are even antireligion—as opposed to the legacy of the Black church–centered civil rights movement.[3]

At first I was both fatigued and annoyed by the assumptions about contemporary Black youth and young adult activists and the role of religion in the civil rights movement, and thus I wanted to explore more directly some of those connections. However, to me what was more pressing than responding to contemporary critiques was the urge to explore how Black people (young and old) had been educated or trained to work for change in relation with religious communities.[4] In this sense, this work expands on a conversation started in my previous research on Black youth spirituality by turning to religious activist-educators and exploring the pedagogies of religiously inspired social change.

Yet researching the pedagogy and religious practices that undergird social change movements also requires challenging many assumptions about a natural, positive, or even predominant connection between Black religion and

radical social change. The interconnection between faith, religious organizations, and social change is often messy and inconsistent (and sometimes negatively correlated). Scholars such as Barbara Savage and Kenneth Hill point
out that Black religion has never, or even primarily, been characterized by
its support of or connection to positive, political, and social engagement.[5]
Instead, Savage notes the early intellectual consensus among Black scholars,
such as W. E. B. Du Bois, Carter G. Woodson, and Benjamin E. Mays, that
African American churches had failed as a political institution (or as a consistent source for social change).[6]

This complexity pushed me to delve deeper into how people come to participate in radical social change, inspired or at least connected to their faith life.
I had to ask if there was or if there could be traced a historical thread between
religiously inspired social change and different ways of educating or training
people—a line to formal and informal education (religious, communal, and
secular). For example, recent Christian activist Bree Newsome, with her
seemingly conservative theological language and practices, challenges the
assumptions that the theological convictions undergirding modern social
change emerge only from liberal theologies or churches that value human
rights or freedoms as the highest ideal—above and beyond orthodoxy or a
fervent belief in the movement of the power of God. In truth, many of the
theological claims of Black Christian activists do not fit neatly into categories
of a liberal theology or social gospel. Instead, they emerge from strong (and
often conservative) understandings of a powerful and sovereign God who is
empowering people to resist oppression and oppressive regimes. And it is a
radical belief in this type of powerful God and the Spirit to move through this
God that Newsome spoke of enlivening her faith and her activism. Newsome,
and others like her, also prompted me to ask and explore how she was educated and trained both theologically and for social change.[7]

But how does that help us to theorize about the types of religious activist-
educators that we see across history? Do we see Black religious communities
educating and leading people in methods of social gospel reforms? Or do
we see visions/practices of education, which wed faith in God with action in
the world? Yes and no. Any wholesale integration of religion and education
or religion and social change in African American churches (at any point in
the last two centuries) does not exist. Instead, there are many case studies
or exemplary educators who help us explore the contours of how religious
education and social change might connect or have connected in African
American Christianity. Therefore, what began as an exploration of how

religious organizations educate participants in and for social change grew to become a celebration of Black teachers who exemplify commitments to religion/faith, education, and social change. I was able to see the widest diversity by looking at individual educators and exemplars, and these in turn helped me to theorize about how we might move forward in empowering future generations to integrate faith and action, or to educate/be educated in transformative faith and social change.

Religious Activist-Educators

I collectively refer to the teachers in this book as *religious activist-educators*, pointing to the long intersecting history of activism among educators within African American communities and looking at the role of religion for these educators.[8] Included in this volume, however, are not particularly obscure or new figures. For the most part, I am reviewing the life and pedagogy of well-known African American leaders (and for this some readers may find fault with this text). Why? To help us understand and reclaim the ways in which these leaders were also serving as *religious educators* and religious social activists and intellectuals—as leaders who were influential in shaping how we think about Black religion and figures who from their faith convictions chose to act and educate in ways that transform society.

I am indebted to historian and educator Audrey McCluskey's careful discussion of Black women educators and school founders in her book *A Forgotten Sisterhood*.[9] While McCluskey does not offer a precise definition of activist-educators, she shows how activism and education intersected in early twentieth-century educators. McCluskey notes that the idea of combining activism and education does not originate with the school founders she researched (Lucy Craft Laney, Charlotte Hawkins Brown, Nannie Helen Burroughs, and Mary McLeod Bethune). Instead, she emphasizes the unique ways in which Black educators (particularly women educators) saw their work as deeply connected to freedom. McCluskey argues that activism and education were interwoven because of the societal structures and contexts in which the pioneering women educators were coming of age. She writes, "Being among the first of their race and sex to receive formal education, the school founders were collectively committed to education as a counteroffensive to racial degradation and an instrument of uplift for themselves and their race."[10]

McCluskey describes the "constancy of activism and organizing among women who began their professional lives as teachers and followed that path into a more public arena."[11] She remarks on the widely held view that "Teachers were considered 'the best organizers.'"[12] In my own research, I likewise note the ways that radical educators *become* movements and begin to work for change through and beyond their individual classrooms and schools.[13] Other scholars, like bell hooks, also note the revolutionary and anticolonial work of Black teachers throughout the mid-twentieth century. hooks's reflections on her education in the apartheid American South show that her experiences of education were very different in her segregated, all-Black schools because the teachers there were on a mission: they were participating in a type of countercultural project to educate and empower Black children to learn as a strategy of resistance to racism and colonization.[14]

McCluskey argues that women educators and school founders were an often-forgotten "subset of clubwomen whose response to the world of disadvantage and danger that African Americans inherited from enslavement was to place faith in God and themselves and bring about change by building institutions of learning."[15] McCluskey's description resonated with me because of her inclusion of the essential intersecting of faith in God and self with education and responding to social injustices. Inspired by and building upon McCluskey's description of these school founders, my definition of activist-educators (or more specifically of religious activist-educators) takes shape.[16] Throughout this work, I explore the ways in which different teachers help us to nuance and further define activist-educators. For example, building on McCluskey's foundational emphasis and examples of these Black teachers' faith in God and themselves, I note the added faith that many of these educators placed in the students and communities whom they felt called to serve.

Defying Categorization: Learning from Religious Activist-Educators

Exploring the lives of Black teachers pushes beyond the often-rigid boundaries in discussions of religion, education, and social change and helps us to see the myriad and complex intersections of these ideas.[17] Also, in considering the lives of religious activist-educators across the twentieth century, I came to realize and appreciate the reality that there is no definitive, unified, or simple definition of religion, education, or even activism or social change. Instead, each of the teachers explored in this book helps to expand our understanding of these categories and point to the ways in which contemporary activist-educators are expanding this work yet further. Therefore, one of the tasks in this book, in addition to analyzing the narratives of activist-educators, is to learn from these teachers and to see how they expand our understanding of each of these categories (and practices) as well. Therefore, at the outset of this work, I start with some preliminary contours of how I am approaching each of the categories of *religion* and *education* in conversation with social change.

Religion

For starters, I had to assess how the category of religion operated in the lives of African American activist-educators. I looked broadly at how each of the teachers included in this volume defined, practiced, and attempted to live in relation to their understanding of faith, spirituality, and religious convictions. For the vast majority of the activist-educators I explore, their primary religion and religious practices were Christian, or associated with Christian denominations in the United States. There are, however, both exceptions and variations even among this small group of activist-educators. In particular, I include the likes of Du Bois, who evolved from attending a predominantly White Northern Congregational church to more agnosticism over the course of his lifetime, but who never lowered his expectations of what churches could and should do, or even his interest and rigorous study of how religion operates in the lives of Black people. I also include activist Ida B. Wells, whose faith and approach to religion skew much more conservative in some regards than Du Bois in that she was a faithful participant and teacher of Christianity and attempted to live a Christian life, attending revivals and religious services throughout her life and adhering to rigid moral codes and expectations for herself and those around her.

I also began to place the activist-educators' religious practices and beliefs in conversation with scholars of Black religion both to situate their practices/faith and to see how these activist-educators defy categorization. In writing this book, I could have traced the development of African American religious groups and the many educational and publishing endeavors that were and are connected to the establishment of free Black churches and denominations in the United States. And I appreciate such work by Kenneth Hill, Raboteau, and others that chart the history of religious groups.[18] Yet their attention to the formation of official bodies and institutions often overlooks and undervalues the daily practices of ordinary people or even of lay leaders (and often women) within these organizations. Therefore, in this work the emphasis on religion shifts from official stances and officially sanctioned and supported doctrines to exploring how individual educators and leaders negotiated and lived out their personal faith convictions in and for public and communal ends.

I began placing these activist-educators in conversation with the idea of religious and social radicalism—exploring the radical strand of Black religion. A primary work in defining and framing the radical tradition in Black religion is Gayraud Wilmore's *Black Religion and Black Radicalism*. Wilmore coined the positive view of radicalism among Black religion. He did so at the height of the Black Power movement and in line with the emergence of formal articulations of Black theologies of liberation. For Wilmore, one of the characteristics that distinguished Black Christianity from White Christianity was this radical and liberationist bent. He writes in the preface to the second edition that

> This bubbling, meandering stream rises somewhere in the dim history of the black worshipping community. Over the years it has taken on sharpened definition in the black church and its affiliated organizations, so that it is possible to say today . . . that there are three characteristics of the radical tradition in black religion: (1) the quest for independence from White control; (2) the revalorization of the image of Africa; and (3) the acceptance of protest and agitation as theological prerequisites for black liberation and the liberation of all oppressed people.[19]

However, even as he articulated these distinctive characteristics, Wilmore also wrestled with the imprecise nature and "ebbs and flows" of radicalism in Black religion. Wilmore wrote about the struggles of many to understand a positive interconnection between Christianity and social change.[20] Thus, Wilmore continued to write and revise works about Black religious radicalism, in part because of the ongoing demand for

> the kind of scholarship that . . . deal[s] honestly with facts, uncover[s] truth, and lead[s] the reader toward a religious commitment to help remake the

world and not be satisfied to simply dissect it. . . . It is [his] opinion that some persons are still searching for historical foundations within the heritage of black religion to undergird the continuing struggle for justice and liberation.[21]

This acknowledgment points to the reality that religion in African American life is not simply or easily characterized as primarily radical. As I explored the lives of Black activist-educators further, I saw religious values and practices that stretched across theological and denominational lines and still somehow served as a catalyst for their efforts to work for change and remain faithful to improving the lives of those around them.[22] In fact, the majority of the activist-educators I explore in this text are laypeople and with few exceptions would not have been classified as theologically liberal or progressive. Most were not participating in the type of Afrocentric Black religious radicalism Wilmore explored. However, their religious practices were no less significant in shaping their efforts toward change or their convictions about the rightness of their causes based on their beliefs that God was in it or calling for it.

As a womanist practical theologian and religious educator, I was also attentive to the ways that, even though I was studying individual activist-educators, their faith and activism were calling them to work and act on behalf of their communities. They were charting paths toward freedom and even in moments of harsh criticism of institutional churches, they were seeking to help Black people live into a liberative vision. Therefore, in addition to Wilmore's work, I began to place the religious lives of these activist-educators in conversation with the larger canon of Black religion—the Black liberation and womanist theological tradition and particularly the work of Delores Williams and Linda Thomas. Williams and Thomas offer not only womanist theological content, but also methods through which to center the agency, activism, and religious experiences of African American women and communities.[23]

Even before the official emergence of Black theology and Womanist theology as academic disciplines, the radical communally oriented threads of interpretation and reflection on the lived realities of Black people, their encounters with God, and the call to struggle for freedom were present in the lives of ordinary Black people and in these activist-educators. And while none of these early exemplars would have self-identified as womanist or Black liberationist, their work helped to create the canons out of which these later disciplines developed. Likewise, a womanist theological interpretive lens helps us to connect what might even be seen as conservative religious teachings of these early activist-educators with their undeniable faith in God to help them fight for freedom and against oppression in the United States and globally.

I also relied upon Peter Paris's *Social Teachings of the Black Church* and *Spirituality of African Peoples* and Evelyn Brooks Higginbotham's explorations of the religious practices and institution building of Black Baptist women (and theorizing about the Black church that went far beyond the dichotomies outlined by Lincoln and Mamiya to emphasize the heteroglot nature of Black churches and Black religion). More recent scholarship on Black religion helps us to recognize and situate the messy and complicated relationship between Black religion and social change that we see exemplified in the lives of these religious activist-educators. Throughout each chapter of the book, the conversation between the lives of religious activist-educators and theories of Black religion pushes beyond any single set of criteria as defining their religious lives. There is no singular way of being religious and activist. Instead, collectively their lives help underscore the wide-ranging ways that religion and social change have intersected in the lives of Black people during the twentieth century.

Education and Religious Education

Likewise, each of these teachers approached education in different ways and came to teaching under different circumstances. In each chapter these activist-educators therefore remind us of the diversity and complexity of education and who or what is included in education—and what is at stake both for teachers, their students, and the communities in which they are educating. As such, the lives of these religious activist-educators defy unilateral categorization in educational arenas as well.

I open each chapter with a description of the teaching of the activist-educator. In part, I begin with a teaching vignette to recenter the importance of the praxis of teaching, of holding together the practice and theorizing about education that was central to the work of these activist-educators. I focus primarily on their personal reflections on their teaching in order to capture their self-understanding as teachers, the ways that they struggled, and for what they yearned in the teaching exchange. However, in starting with their personal reflections we also learn much about schools and the politics of teaching and learning during their lifetimes. For example, when I explored Ida B. Wells's journals and autobiographic descriptions of her struggles as a young teacher, I found that they reveal as much about her perceived lack of preparation as they do about the daunting multidimensional nature of rural education for Black populations post emancipation.

The experiences and reflections of these activist-educators stand in stark contrast to the writings of early twentieth-century progressive or liberal educators, in part because of how often the experiences of African Americans, as educators or students, were excluded from these conversations, or, if included, their insights did not extend beyond their potential impact on/in Black communities.[24] Somewhat naively, I wanted to situate the work of these activist-educators within popular dominant philosophies of education—but here again they defy the earlier categories, not simply because they were not included in the creation of these educational theories but also because the work of many of these teachers reveals something deeper or more urgent to their educational work throughout the twentieth century.[25]

Looking more specifically at religious education as a practice and a discipline, I also see these religious activist-educators pushing several boundaries within the field. Their lives and writings remind us that, like religion, religious education has an equally complicated history and imprecise definition, particularly in relationship to African Americans. In this book, I am not focusing narrowly on religious education as formal religious instruction or education for religious growth and formation. For in truth only one or two teachers in this book would have self-identified as a religious educator in terms of the guild and profession. Instead, I push beyond the guild to explore the ways that Black educators throughout the twentieth century were also participating in a type of religious education and expanding how we might understand the early and long-lasting connections between religion and education, particularly within African American communities.

Religious education as a vocation and academic discipline is complicated and often marginalized. This marginalization stems in part from the narrow perceptions of religious education simply as *techniques* for how to teach the theologies or belief of particular religious communities or that other scholars have already created. And while part of religious education does indeed focus on how to teach religion and how people learn and are formed in faith, religious education is much more than this. Religious education scholar Mary Boys helps to show the complex history and growth of religious education by mapping four "classic expressions" of it in the United States. Her four classic expressions include evangelism, religious education, Christian education, and Catholic education.[26] Boys constructed these classic expressions as a result of wrestling with the foundational questions of "What does it mean to be religious?" and "What does it mean to educate in faith?"[27] Her schema helps show the breadth of questions that are part of religious education, from the beliefs and values of communities to what is considered knowledge and how people are expected to engage culture or in society. Alongside Boys's typology are many other attempts to outline the landscape of religious education in the United States. Of particular interest to this work are the scholars who point to the ways in which religious education and social change have intersected.

Religious educator Allen Moore, in *Religious Education as Social Transformation*, called for a social theory of religious education by returning to some of the earlier work at the start of the academic discipline of religious education in the early twentieth century.[28] Drawing upon early religious education scholars George Albert Coe and Harrison S. Elliot, Moore pointed to the way in which religious education was understood to be a force for social transformation. Coe and Elliot stood in an early tradition of combining liberal theology with progressive education and wrestling with the ways in which the work of religious education included the need to transform society and not simply individuals. Recounting this early thrust in religious education, Moore thus argued for a definition of religious education that moves far beyond indoctrinating or forming persons in faith. Moore instead defined religious education as

> an ethical way of life that serves to transform religious platitudes into concrete social structures that are just and serve the welfare of all people. . . . Radical human learning is moving from theories of a better society to human activity on behalf of that society.[29]

Moore's definition, like Boys's typology, is helpful in pointing to the more complicated understandings of what is included in the scope of religious education. However, neither Boys's classic expressions nor Moore's emphasis on the social thrust in religious education fully addressed the practices of religious education enacted by individual teachers or communities. Likewise, neither one's works significantly (if at all) engaged the work and ideas of African American religious educators or thinkers.[30] African American religious education scholars such as Kenneth Hill consequently had to offer correctives to these "classic" views of religious education in the United States. Hill charted the development African American Christian religious education, noting that prior to 1974 the academic study of religious education among and by African Americans was not systematized.[31] Hill points to the early scholarship of religious educators like Grant Shockley in the formalizing of scholarship about African American religious education, while also identifying earlier figures such as W. E. B. Du Bois and Carter G. Woodson as laying the foundations of a scholarly study of religion and education among Black people. Hill's work is helpful in correcting the lacuna in historical overviews of religious education in that it looks specifically and carefully at the work of Black people. It is also invaluable in offering a broad sketch of the field of African American Christian religious education. As such, his work serves as a backdrop to the ways in which Black religious education developed and continued to evolve.

In this work, I attempt to analyze more carefully religious educators' lives, practices, and commitment to social change. Intentional self-identification as a religious educator, among Black scholars and teachers, was a much later phenomenon. Earlier and most often there were religious people who were also educators, and at most points in African American history prior to the mid-twentieth century there was no separation of education and religious instruction, even in institutions of higher education.[32]

In this book I consequently expand the category of religious education by attending to the variety of exemplars of religious activist education. I focus on figures who had significant religious leanings, based on their writings, church activities, and even what they chose to research and study—this is in part because I define Black religious education as both education within Black religious communities (with a goal of shaping more faithful community members) and as education that includes the academic study of the religious experiences of Black people. In early twentieth-century terms there was no official African American religious studies department or curriculum; the emergence of such study was the result of the work of religious activist-educators. Black theology pioneer James Cone even credits part of his inspiration for creating his first academic Black theology text to the encouragement of a religious educator, Grant Shockley. Cone wrote,

> As one of my teachers at Garrett Theological Seminary, Grant Shockley challenged me to do theology out of the black religious experience. Without his challenge and encouragement, I do not know whether I would have

developed the intellectual courage and self-confidence to articulate my perspective in black theology.[33]

However, prior to the mid-twentieth century, there were many schools that were started by missionaries (Black and White)—with both a mission of Christianizing the newly freed Africans and of helping to advance their development in basic literacy and much more. Thus, there emerged Black religious schools that took up the charge of teaching Black people theology and philosophy as well as basic literacy as a sign of the ability of Black people to engage in this type of intellectual work. Many of the early twentieth-century radical educators were products of such missionary schools and efforts.

Book Overview

The book explores three primary ways that religion, education, and social change intersect in the lives and work of activist-educators. These include (1) religiously inspired, activist-educators, or educators (in the public or private sector) who were guided by their faith convictions to educate in revolutionary and radical ways; (2) radical religious scholars, or educators who stretched the canons and methods of studying the religious lives and practices of Black people, both as a form of activism and as a way of inspiring other African Americans to embrace their own religious history/heritage; and (3) radical religious educators, or religious educators who were working to transform how we educate and form people in African American Christian faith so that Black people would better understand the connection between their faith and their liberation or freedom struggles. These categories did not emerge suddenly at one point in history or in one neat place all. I have therefore chosen to organize the book more chronologically as a way of indicating that these models were developing and overlapping during the twentieth century.

Thus, the first two chapters begin with a discussion of some early religious advocates for both freedom and the education of African Americans. Although early independent denominational leaders and educators of the eighteenth and nineteenth centuries were often involved in the establishment of schools or publishing houses for Black people, here I focus on the published work of educators at the turn of the twentieth century, work that foregrounds and systematically studies Negro life in the United States.

I center the published writings of Anna Julia Cooper (chapter 1) and W. E. B. Du Bois (chapter 2) on what Black people had accomplished in the years since slavery, as well as their scathing critiques of the education and religion of Black people up to this point in history.

The next two chapters explore the lives of Ida B. Wells and Nannie Helen Burroughs and pay specific attention to the early twentieth-century radical activism and organizing of Black women. Wells and Burroughs pursued related, but drastically different, projects. In part due to the ongoing patriarchy and sexism of religious and educational institutions in the United States, Burroughs (and other women) established schools for educating Black women and girls in the United States. Others, like Wells, began teaching in segregated rural schools out of financial necessity, only to be fired when she increased her activism and protest. These chapters highlight the significance of the communal organizing and club movements of these women. Though different from the establishment of academic disciplines, this work was equally influential and radical in its impact on the lives of their students and on the organizing of Black women for generations to come.

Next, I delve into the lives of religious leaders and educators at the center of large-scale movements for change, particularly the civil rights movement itself. While Martin L. King Jr. is often lauded for his charismatic leadership and sermons, which inspired and expressed the religious and moral grounding of the mid-century civil rights movement, here I focus instead on the educators and organizers who put into practice King's visions (and created some others of their own). Chapter 5 centers the pioneering work of Septima Clark and the way that her faith was inspiring her to effect change in the South Carolina public schools even before she helped launched the Citizenship Education program. In chapter 6, I explore the work of Rev. James Lawson, who became the chief strategist for nonviolent direct action during the civil rights movement. Their work reflects the radical vision and tactics of nonviolent social change as well as the power of religious ethics to call for mass social reform. It foregrounds nonviolence and a love ethic, as well as student-centered learning, and improvisational teaching as part of a radical religious program.

The civil rights movement prompted unprecedented models of religious activism as well as questions from religious and nonreligious groups about how to reconcile one's faith with one's commitments to freedom and liberation (particularly in Christianity). As a result of these challenges, activist-educators began speaking up in new and different places and ways, and consequently examples of radical religious education began to emerge in theological education in seminaries and universities, as well as in churches. Similar to earlier radical assertions of the humanity and dignity of Black people, which resulted in the creation of systematic projects to study Black life, the emergence of Black liberation and womanist theologies represented a radical move at the intersection of religion, education, and social transformation. Thus, chapters 7 and 8 focus on the work of religious educators Olivia Pearl Stokes and Albert Cleage Jr., as a way of mapping both the development of new theological discourse for Black people and attempts to develop models of teaching Black theology in Black churches.

I conclude the book by reflecting on the ways in which Black educators (religious and nonreligious) are still living into the legacy of these pioneering radical Black activist-educators. I draw on Cynthia Dillard's reminder that Black educators are called to (re)member as a means of wrestling with what these religious activist-educators teach us and how their actions offer a renewed vision and hope for what is possible for the future of radical Black religion and education.

SECTION I
TELLING OUR OWN STORIES

At the turn of the twentieth century, African Americans were still wrestling with the ongoing quandary of affirming to themselves and to the outside world their capacities and identities as a people. This quandary was not simply an individual pursuit, with one person struggling to see their own worth, but a collective wrestling with centuries of dehumanization and systematic erasure/dismissal of the contributions of their people and their stories. African Americans' responses to the questions and the practices of self-affirmation were multidimensional and often included attempts to research and catalog the achievements of Black people since the end of slavery in the United States and to affirm through collective forums and critical and creative exchanges the ways in which Black people not only appreciated but also themselves contributed to the arts, culture, religious life, and politics and were otherwise engaged citizens. *Racial uplift* was often the term used to describe this practice of affirmation and progressing the collective standing of Black people.[1] At its best, racial uplift was an attempt to improve the lives of the masses of Black people and to remind educated Black people of the collective work that must be done in order to help all Black people succeed. Each of these responses (and so many more) were part of the radical educational work emerging at this point in history.

Both Anna Julia Cooper and W. E. B. Du Bois contributed to the project of racial uplift, frequently writing on this theme and working tirelessly to *tell their own stories* and the stories of other Black people. In the next two chapters, we explore these two exemplars of activist education among African Americans. Cooper and DuBois advocated for freedom and for the transformative education of African Americans. We look closely at the radical work that these educators undertook, first as teachers committed to their individual students and communities, and then to the impact of their teaching, advocacy, and scholarship on the wider debates and practices of education. The debates included battles over who should be educated (among

Black people) and what types of courses they should be able to take (women's only, industrial, and so forth).

I choose to focus on Cooper and Du Bois because they were among the vanguard of Black educators and scholars who published both reflections on what Black men and women had accomplished in the years since slavery as well as scathing critiques of how Negroes were being educated. Each also gave considerable attention to the religious life of African Americans in the early twentieth century, but in very different ways. The differences I note between Cooper and Du Bois have to do with their personal histories and social location, and with how they understood themselves and defined their projects or callings. However, they also interest me because they lived much longer than the early 1900s and evolved and grew as scholars, teachers, and activists. Thus, it is the long arc of their lives that I see as having the greatest impact on our current discussions of what radical religious education and religiously inspired activist-educators might look like.

1

Anna Julia Cooper

August 10, 1858–February 27, 1964

Teaching the Voiceless: "Sketches from a Teacher's Notebook"

Anna Julia Cooper's "Sketches from a Teacher's Notebook," an essay that remained unpublished during her lifetime, tells a vivid story of her efforts to teach a family that had been cut off from society and education. Cooper describes encountering the children as they sneaked onto the playground she was supervising during WWI as the director of War Camp Community Service in West Virginia.[1] They piqued Cooper's interest because they did not come to the playground along with the rest of the children, but only after its gates were locked. Though these children rarely spoke to anyone, Cooper had a chance encounter with the younger girl, "a frightened little creature,"[2] whom she coaxed into playing on the swings. Cooper describes how the young girl ran off as soon as her older brother appeared and with just a glance indicated that it was time for the young child to go home. Cooper, never one to back down from a challenge, took the older brother to task right there on the playground for not speaking to his sister, for not introducing her to the world through language, and more. Cooper also described the interactions she had with another brother from this family, and her attempts to engage their mother during a home visit. Though as a linguist Cooper's primary intention in "Sketches" was to outline the importance of language for education and socialization, what she conveys more fully is a picture of who she was as a teacher and advocate for Black women's and youths' access to education.

Only after leaving the War Camp position did Cooper learn why this family had become cut off and isolated from their community: their father had been lynched, and their mother, in an attempt to protect herself and her children, had withdrawn from the community. Cooper wrestled in this essay to make sense of what a typical school might do for such a family. She "wondered what our brand of education, what our smug injunction that the

Teaching to Live. Almeda M. Wright, Oxford University Press. © Oxford University Press 2024.
DOI: 10.1093/oso/9780197663424.003.0002

home 'is expected' to cooperate with the school will find or create for the help and guidance of such a home."[3] She wondered too whether isolation would really solve the family's problem but empathized with the mother (and so many Black mothers) in making this choice.

While "Sketches from a Teacher's Notebook" is not the essay or set of writings that most often comes to mind when we think about Anna Julia Cooper's legacy, for me it nonetheless paints one of the most significant pictures of her as a teacher and advocate for Black women and children. She enacted radical pedagogy inspired by her faith in trying to connect with this mother and these children. She initially thought she knew best and could help them, but she respected the mother's position and articulates in her essay the complicated relationships that Black women and children have with even the most well-intentioned educational systems.

This essay contrasts with her better-known work, *A Voice from the South*, which she published in 1892. That book made her one of only a few published African American women and set the stage for a long career as an educator and advocate for the education of Black people, particularly Black women. Cooper had already gained recognition through her lectures and her work as the women's editor of the *Southland* magazine[4] by the time her book was published.[5] Of course, one has to wonder how Cooper, a daughter of an enslaved woman and her enslaver, came to be invited to lecture about women's education, to write about it, to be educated, and later to learn to be the type of teacher that sought out the most recalcitrant of students and attempted to invite them out of their experiences of *voicelessness* into the world that she believed transformative education could offer.

Even though Cooper was a contemporary of Du Bois and published her signature work more than a decade before Du Bois's *Souls of Black Folk*, until recently her contributions to Black life, culture, education, *and* religion have been largely overlooked and undervalued. Though Cooper is now esteemed as a pioneering Black feminist, as a scholar of religion and education I am surprised and often confused by the ways in which her religious views and positions have been marginalized or ignored, even as more contemporary readers and scholars embrace her. There are a few exceptions to this. I think particularly of the work of womanist theologians and other religionists such as Karen Baker-Fletcher, whose research on Cooper has helped us to understand the breadth and import of Cooper's complex legacy and theological views, as well as her contributions to Black religion and religious education. However, Baker-Fletcher remains one of only a few scholars who have

carefully considered Anna Julia Cooper's contributions to religion and theological thought in a book-length or other sustained treatment.

The lack of engagement with Cooper's religious life is surprising. Not only
was Cooper fluent in religious ideas thanks to the religious nature of education during the nineteenth and early twentieth centuries, but she also wholeheartedly embraced her religious convictions and used her understanding of
Christianity as justification for many of her social and political activities. Her
early collections of writings about womanhood directly connect Christ's role
to the work of eradicating suffering and advocating equality, work I discuss
more closely below.

Cooper's religious life and educational journey were intricately connected.
Cooper was educated primarily in religious schools, from primary school to
Oberlin College. It was in these settings that her religious understandings
were shaped (including her somewhat elitist preference for the quiet, and
what she called the *refined*, worship of her Episcopal denomination). These
religious educational spaces were also where she experienced firsthand the
challenges of patriarchy and sexism in education. Cooper noted the multi-
farious ways in which the studies of men toward becoming clergy were always given more attention than the strivings of (even the brightest) women
students to learn and be educated. It was here that her activism and her
calling as a religiously inspired activist-educator emerged.

Cooper's Early Background

Anna Julia Cooper was born in Raleigh, North Carolina, in 1858, as Anna
Julia Haywood. Her mother, Hannah Stanley Haywood, was still enslaved
at the time of Anna's birth, and from all indications Cooper's father was her
mother's enslaver—but her mother never spoke of this.[6] Given that there are
no records indicating otherwise, we can assume that Cooper and her family
were only set free by the Emancipation Proclamation; the first census record
of her family (her mother and her brothers) is from 1870.[7]

Cooper's educational history is one of the most remarkable parts of her
early life. Cooper was able to attend St. Augustine's Normal School beginning
in kindergarten, when she was around the age of eight or nine.[8] She recounts
her "good fortune" at being selected to attend during her most formative
years and was grateful to the founder Dr. J. Brinton-Smith.[9] St. Augustine's
Normal School was established in 1868 by the Executive Committee of the

Board of Missions of the Episcopal Church with the goal of educating persons to teach "freedmen." Historians recount that even at such an early age, Cooper was not only learning to read herself but was also teaching others to read.[10] Indeed, part of the scholarship that Cooper received to attend St. Augustine's included a job as a "peer-teacher." It is amazing that Cooper was teaching and tutoring others from such an early age.[11] Among those she was helping learn to read and write was her own mother.[12]

Her early educational period in North Carolina was one of "self-assertion"—a time in which many of the newly emancipated Black people in North Carolina were organizing to reobtain voting rights as well as pursuing education and "manhood":

> No longer supplicant slaves in the house of bondage, Blacks in North Carolina—as elsewhere—turned to the schoolhouse to remove vestiges of slavery. They believed that once Black people were armed with benefits of education, full citizenship and manhood rights would be forthcoming. It was this climate of self-assertion, with awareness of full citizenship rights, that nurtured Annie Haywood in her formative years.[13]

Clearly, for her and for others the quest to become educated was intricately tied to the quest for citizenship and equal rights—as it continued to be for much of the early twentieth century.

Even as Cooper was grateful for the opportunities afforded her at St. Augustine's, it was also there that she experienced inequitable education and learning opportunities for boys and girls. She recounted some of her experiences in her essay "The Higher Education of Women":[14]

> I had devoured what was put before me, and, like Oliver Twist, was looking around to ask for more. I constantly felt (as I suppose many an ambitious girl has felt) a thumping from within unanswered by any beckoning from without. Class after class was organized for these ministerial candidates. . . . A boy, however meager his equipment and shallow his pretentions, had only to declare a floating intention to study theology and he could get all the support, encouragement and stimulus he needed, be absolved from work and invested beforehand with all the dignity of his far away office. While a self-supporting girl had to struggle on by teaching in the summer and working after school hours to keep up with her board bills, and actually to fight her way against positive discouragements to the higher education; till one such

girl one day flared out and told the principal "the only mission opening before a girl in his school was to marry one of those candidates." He said he didn't know but it was. And when at last that same girl announced her desire and intention to go to college it was received with about the same incredulity and dismay as if a brass button on one of those candidate's coats had propounded a new method for squaring the circle or trisecting the arc.[15]

Cooper noted that her struggles to gain an education were hardly unique. In her appeal to give girls a chance to learn, Cooper reveals a great deal about her own experiences as an "ambitious girl" who struggled not for lack of ability or even desire to learn, but for lack of financial wherewithal. Most of the girls had to work to support themselves and their educational endeavors, while there was all manner of support for boys and men who professed even the slightest interest in becoming ministers, even if they were not studious or particularly gifted. Cooper argued against the de facto practice that women's development and educational achievement were limited to marrying one of the male theology students. However, Cooper did marry one these students, and this afforded her a modicum of privilege, especially after his untimely death, to continue her education and career as a teacher.

Cooper's critique of men receiving support to study theology did not mean she did not support theological education or having a learned clergy. She was simply pointing out the discrepancy of educating men[16] without also fully supporting the education of women and girls. Cooper argued that taking women and girls seriously and valuing their contributions in all fields, including theology, would drastically change the face of these disciplines. For example, she suggested that theologies that cast children into lakes of fire were implausible for women to write, and that it mattered for women to be included in the writing and creating of theology. She believed that many male ideals would not continue to hold sway if or as women's voices and perspectives were heard.[17]

It was only after the untimely death of her spouse that Cooper was able both to continue her education at Oberlin College and her teaching career. Consequently, our richest record of Cooper's intellectual thought is her early collection of essays and speeches, *A Voice from the South*, published just a few years after she had completed her education at Oberlin, had taught at Wilberforce and St. Augustine's (where she started her education), and had moved again to Washington, DC, where she served the longest on the staff of

M Street School, formally known as the Washington DC Preparatory School for Colored Youth.

Cooper ranks prominently among African American activist-educators in general and religious activist-educators in particular. Her life as an activist began with her advocating for herself and her own access to education and with her working as a peer-educator helping those around her to learn as well. However, Cooper used her access to wider publics and opportunities to speak and write about the significance of women's education in the larger project of uplifting Black people as a whole. She attempted to convince her audiences—typically of Black ministers or of other educators—of this need by employing and interweaving in her speeches religious ideals familiar to the majority of her audience, examples from her classical education, and stories from her experiences as a student and teacher.

Yet while the long history of Cooper's teaching and educational endeavors is expansive and fascinating, I agree with the need that Black feminist scholar Brittney Cooper identified to extol more than the accomplishments of great women, and to engage also her spoken words, her writing, and her intellectual work.[18] I therefore begin by exploring Cooper's writings on women and education.

Cooper on Women, Religion, and Education

Cooper's educational philosophy and core commitments are best elucidated through her actions, her long career as a teacher (primarily to Black high school men and women), and through her writing. It is in her early essays that she reflects on her struggles simply to be educated. There too she wholeheartedly affirms that the entire world would be better if women were educated and allowed to contribute to every arena of life. As with many early feminist writings, her essays include what we now consider to be problematic gendered dualities, such as contrasting the greed and acquisitiveness of men (businessmen) with the "sympathetic warmth and sunshine of good women."[19] However, even though today we might understandably want to challenge the idea that simply by being female women have the power to "bring a heart power into this money getting, dollar-worshipping civilization" and to challenge the undercurrent that women are morally good or better than men, Cooper's early essays unquestionably took a significant stand by not limiting women to merely one or two spheres of influence.

ANNA JULIA COOPER 25

Cooper named the possibility and necessity of women's influence in economics, global affairs, politics, and many other arenas as she built her case for
why women should be educated in each of these areas. She wrote,

> Fifty years ago woman's activity according to orthodox definitions was on a
> pretty clearly cut "sphere," including primarily the kitchen and the nursery,
> and rescued from the barrenness of prison bars by the womanly mania for
> adorning every discoverable bit of china or canvas with forlorn looking
> cranes balanced idiotically on one foot. The woman of to-day finds herself
> in the presence of responsibilities which ramify through the profoundest
> and most varied interests of her country and race. Not one of the issues
> of this plodding, toiling, sinning, repenting, falling, aspiring humanity can
> afford to shut her out, or can deny the reality of her influence. No plan for
> renovating society, no scheme for purifying politics, no reform in church
> or in state, no moral, social, or economic question, no movement upward
> or downward in the human plane is lost on her . . . no woman can possibly
> put herself or her sex outside any of the interests that affect humanity. All
> departments in the new era are to be hers, in the sense that her interests are
> in all and through all; and it is incumbent on her to keep intelligently and
> sympathetically *en rapport* with all the great movements of her time, that
> she may know on which side to throw the weight of her influence.[20]

Cooper encouraged both men and women to adopt her expansive view of
the expanding roles for women. She encouraged men to be open to this influence and women to be prepared to influence others by availing themselves
of opportunities as they arose. Cooper wrote with an exuberance and ex-
citement about the endless possibilities that could take shape with and for
women at the end of the nineteenth century. Her hopefulness and optimism
are somewhat surprising given her early struggles to be educated. But perhaps Cooper was simply one whose struggles did not harden or defeat her.
Instead, she wrote with gratitude for being alive and being able to participate
in society in that moment:

> She [the woman] stands now at the gateway of this new era of American
> civilization. In her hands must be moulded the strength, the wit, the states-
> manship, the morality, all the psychic force, the social and economic inter-
> course of that era. *To be alive at such an epoch is a privilege, to be a woman
> then is sublime.*[21]

In this bold statement that "to be a woman [at this epoch] is sublime," Cooper was proclaiming what we might describe as an early Womanist stand that even today pushes the boundaries of the ways that many scholars theorize about gender and racial inequities. For Cooper did not lament the "burden" of being a woman, or of being a Black woman. Instead, she was excited and energized by imagining the unique contributions that women could make if only they were given an opportunity. She was advocating for the rights and education of women not because they were destitute, but because they were capable and the world needed them. And in that moment, she was excited to see her students and other women flourish and lead.[22]

In her earlier essay on "Womanhood the Vital Element," Cooper offered a more explicitly theological case for women as essential to larger social work, and a celebration of women as part of this work. In many ways, Cooper's affirmation of women and womanhood pointed to a major radical intervention in Black religion and Black education; she started from the place of seeing the Black female body as a gift, not a burden. She boldly proclaimed the God-given ability of women to enhance the world around them, and she wholeheartedly pursued a life that supported women in doing so and that embodied this belief in women's capacity.

Graduate students reading Cooper's work often ask why or how her work could be so positive and hopeful during this era. Digging deeper, those remarks express wonder about the ways that being born in slavery, experiencing the hope of Reconstruction, and living in communities where large contingencies of newly freed Blacks were coming to political power, shaped her views and early writings in such a positive way. Recall, however, that most of her early writing was produced or published decades after the gains of the Reconstruction era were overturned. Her optimism consequently seems to have much less to do with the political and social climate of her time and more to do with her genuine belief in the power of God and the capacity of people, when afforded opportunities, to take advantage of them and to advance. Thus, she was contributing to a radical vision of Black humanity that pushes us to consider how one's beliefs about Black people—and women in particular—and their capacities shape the types of educational and social changes in which we participate. Her understanding of the gift of Black women pushed her to advocate for their ability to live into their gifts and to empower them to make contributions beyond the prescribed domestic and on occasion religious realms.

Cooper was making the case that women's influence and contributions would drastically transform all walks of life. Cooper started with the radical vision that Christ outlined for men and women, asserting that Christ had called all to the same "code of morality"—lives fully shaped and committed to the work that they were undertaking. She wrote,

> By laying down for woman the same code of morality, the same standard of purity, as for man; . . . throughout his life and in his death he has given to men a rule and guide for the estimation of woman as an equal, as a helper, as a friend, and as a sacred charge to be sheltered and cared for with a brother's love and sympathy, lessons which nineteen centuries' gigantic strides in knowledge, arts, and sciences, in social and ethical principles have not been able to probe to their depth or to exhaust in practice.[23]

Cooper pointed to Christ's esteem for women as equals and as helpers working together with men toward common goals. She built upon the biblical example of the woman caught in adultery whom Christ did not condemn; on the example of Mary and Martha, whom Jesus counted as friends alongside of their brother; and on Jesus's attention to and care for his mother even while he was dying on the cross.[24] Her description of the care that Jesus offered to these women and to the time that he shared with them when he could instead have opted to attend to his own needs speaks to the strength of Christ's love for and esteem of women. Her understanding of both theology and society draws on the radical, liberal, and universal teachings of Christ. Without a doubt, her theology was influenced by the liberal Christianity she experienced at Oberlin in the 1880s, but she applied these views in ways that connected with the particular issues she was facing as a Black woman in the United States, and she pushed far beyond notions of chivalry and respect for women that were contingent on rank or race.

Cooper also clearly noted men's inability to put Christ's ideals into practice during the many centuries since he modeled them. She indicted the church and larger society for this failure but remained hopeful about the vision Christ had shared and about the possibility that structures in contemporary society could afford women the chance to live into this vision. This vision and hope drove her own work and her critique of the Church and its leadership for its treatment of women and failure to support women's education. Theologian Karen Baker-Fletcher identifies Cooper as one of the harshest critics of the church, and indeed Cooper was not shy about naming the failings of the Church as a whole with regard to the education of women and to the needs, education, and abilities of Black people. However, in Cooper's speech "Women as a Vital Element," she more specifically addressed the ways in which White leaders in her Episcopal denomination had failed to fulfill its mission among Black people. Cooper described their efforts as a "halting progress," and she noted that even as they offered lip service in support of women's education and a more educated "Negro clergy" and leadership, their efforts in the area proved to be scant to none.[25] Cooper remained critical of the ridiculously low number of women graduates from the schools established by the Episcopal church, noting that they had graduated only "five young women" between 1868 and 1886, and five more by the time her book was published in 1892. As a result, Cooper took seriously her role as an advocate and activist in asking the clergy of color in her denomination to respond boldly to this startling failure to educate women. She notes that

> the number of indigent females who have here been supported, sheltered and trained, is phenomenally small. Indeed, to my mind, the attitude of the Church toward this feature of her work, is as if the solution of the problem of Negro missions depended solely on sending a quota of deacons and priests into the field, girls being a sort of *tertium quid* whose development may be promoted if they can pay their way and fall in with the plans mapped out for the training of the other sex.
>
> Now I would ask in all earnestness, does not this force potential deserve by education and stimulus to be made dynamic? Is it not a solemn duty incumbent on all colored churchmen to make it so? Will not the aid of the Church be given to prepare our girls in head, heart, and hand for the duties and responsibilities that await the intelligent wife, the Christian mother, the earnest, virtuous, helpful woman, at once both the lever and the fulcrum for uplifting the race. As Negroes and churchmen we cannot be indifferent to these questions.[26]

Yet in all her critiques of the church and church leadership, Cooper interestingly never challenged the church's position on the ordination of women. Perhaps that is understandable: she was already pushing and prodding the male hierarchy to support women's education and was attempting to make a case to support the new roles of women just entering the teaching professions during the late nineteenth century. I suggest that rather than simply letting sexism dominate, Cooper argued in a different way for the equal authority and valuation of women's ministry. As she attended to the essential work of women in evangelizing persons of African descent, Cooper pushed the church to honor teaching on par with preaching.[27]

So, this lack of direct challenge has to be held in tension with Cooper's long commitment to educating women and girls to contribute in all arenas, and not simply to prepare them for "women's spheres." In part we see this echoed in her disdain for single-gender education. Cooper was critical of *women's courses* because she thought they were sexist and limiting. She recognized that there were differences in the types of courses and the quality of education that women like her could access. Cooper herself likewise pushed against limiting women in the professions and resisted taking positions in which she would be in charge of teaching only women or girls. We see this in her initial decision to teach classics and Greek at Wilberforce after she finished her degrees at Oberlin, instead of accepting an offer to go back to St. Augustine's in North Carolina to teach girls.

Cooper's Commitment to Teaching Black Youth

A commitment to teaching defines Cooper's entire life, beginning when she was a childhood peer-teacher as part of the scholarship enabling her to attend St. Augustine's Normal School and continuing to her career of thirty years at M Street High School. In one of her later essays on education, Cooper writes that "Whether from force of circumstances or from choice and loving consecration, we [Black teachers] are ministers of the Gospel of intelligence, of moral and material uplift to a people whose need is greater than the average . . . by reason of past neglect."[28] In short, she saw herself as *called* to teach and lived fully into this role, herself teaching students, writing, and speaking in order to advocate for the work that her students were doing and for the support they needed in order to continue. This sense of divine calling and deep connection and commitment to teaching made Cooper stand out from many of her male counterparts in this era, even men like Du Bois and later Woodson to whose work we typically go in search of discussions on Black education or for the most pressing critique of the educational systems. Cooper's life, ideas, and work were also distinctive because she was actually engaged in the formal teaching of Black high school–aged youth for most of her life.[29] Even as she obtained multiple degrees, her *project* and *calling* remained teaching—the careful education of students.

Many of the struggles that persisted in Cooper's life, including her often precarious financial situation and the resistance she faced from her male counterparts, did so because she was committed to offering her students the best education possible. Cooper was a teacher committed to pushing students to excel and to be able to participate in society because of their education. Cooper knew for herself the transformative and emancipatory power of education—particularly of an education that was wide and open, what she would have called a classical education, or a liberal arts education today. Cooper was not opposed to industrial education; she simply did not want Black people or women to be limited in what they could learn. She wrote,

> The only sane education, therefore, is that which conserves the very lowest stratum, the best and most economical is that which gives to each individual, according to his capacity, that training of "head, hand, and heart" or more literally, of mind, body, and spirit which converts him [sic] into a beneficent force in the service of the world.[30]

Therefore, just as she protested and resisted teaching in women-only courses and tracks because she saw the inequities and limits placed on women's aspirations in these courses, Cooper also resisted industrial-only education. Throughout her teaching career, she instead tried to offer education that shaped the whole person; that, she said, was the "business of schools."

Her commitment to classical education set her at odds with emerging trends being supported by both White and Black leaders of DC school boards. Specifically, Cooper faced a great deal of opposition and censure as the principal of the M Street School when (from 1904 to 1905) she insisted on continuing both the "classical" education track as well as the vocational or *industrial* training programs instituted by her predecessor and made popular by Booker T. Washington and others. Cooper's school offered both tracks and wanted to be able to continue offering this variety of educational opportunities for students, and to do so in the face of myths and narratives of Black mental inferiority and the attempts to say that *all* that the Negro should aspire toward was skilled labor.[31]

Cooper fought fierce gender- and race-based prejudices by advocating for different educational models, by pushing her students to excel, and also by working with these students to help them secure admission to the country's premier universities, including Harvard, Brown, Oberlin, Yale, Amherst,

Dartmouth, and Radcliffe.[32] In many ways it was her success in the latter more than her ideals about how Black students should be educated that infuriated her opponents and persuaded them to limit her leadership at M Street and in Washington, DC, public education. She was ousted as the principal of M Street School on June 30, 1906, when the board of education opted not to reappoint her.

The newspaper accounts of the controversy are telling. They recount the ways in which her intelligence and tenure as a teacher could not be and were not challenged. Instead, her detractors criticized her on trivial grounds: "Those who question her efficiency as a teacher make no war upon her personally. But while they admitted that she may be a woman of unusual intelligence, they say her personality is not impressive and that she is incapable as a disciplinarian."[33] The vagueness of this statement and the gendered insults about her personality and inability to discipline the students seem too easy an excuse or perhaps even a fabrication to cover up larger issues at stake in her approach to educating Black students. Many M Street alumni rallied to support Cooper, as did many of the clergy of Washington, DC, but nothing was effective in countering the attacks on her leadership or in stemming efforts to move the education of Black youth into an even narrower set of opportunities.

Cooper, however, was not deterred by the M Street School controversy. She continued teaching as well as advocating for Black women and men to have access to education. Even years later, after she had completed her Ph.D. work, and after she was far past the age of retirement, Cooper continued to teach and push students to achieve. As president of Frelinghuysen University, Cooper continued her mission with even more urgency as she strived to help poorer students, both youth and adults, who because of lack of time or opportunity had not been able to gain access to education. Frelinghuysen offered a vast array of courses and learning opportunities, full and part-time, for both older and younger adult students, among the poorer and working-class Black population of Washington, DC. Cooper noted that even though the school did not have tremendous success, the need for this type of education persisted.[34]

While some scholars criticize Cooper's sense of respectability and her emphasis on classical education, in reality Cooper's vision of education and calling to teach were far more inclusive than this. She concluded an unpublished essay on education by emphasizing the reach of her educational vision and program:

Any scheme of education should have regard to the whole man [sic]—not a special class or race of men [sic], but man [sic] as the paragon of creation, possessing in childhood and youth almost infinite possibilities for physical, moral, and mental development. If a child seems poor in inheritance, poor in environment, poor in personal endowment, by so much the more must organized society bring to that child the good tidings of social salvation through the schools.[35]

Cooper's lifelong commitment to teaching Black people is both exemplary and paradigmatic of many of the activist-educators who came after her. She set a standard in her writing about the education of Black people broadly and in working tirelessly to focus her efforts on change and educational reform in her local community. Like many of the other educators this book explores, Cooper knew that teaching was not merely theoretical or philosophical, but something that touches individuals and communities and offers a type of *salvation* amid the inequities of life.

Contributions to Radical Black Religious Education

It is hard to summarize Anna Julia Cooper's many contributions to radical social change and the myriad ways she contributes to my understanding of the intersection of religion, education, and social change. But it is clear that her long-standing commitment to her students and to her calling to teach must always be explored in light of her unwavering faith and commitment to God and God's people. In reflecting on her one hundredth birthday, Cooper noted that what is important "isn't what we say about ourselves, it's what our lives stand for."[36] Womanist theologian Karen Baker-Fletcher expands:

Her life stood for unfailing, persevering commitment to Christian service and hope in a God of freedom and equality. Service was public and required participation in God's activity of reform. It required social gospel theology and ethics. It required the application of biblical principles to a wholistic analysis of racism, sexism, and classism.[37]

Cooper's contributions to her community were manifold, and her legacy to generations of scholars of both religion and education has yet to be explored. Cooper's life was marked by this intriguing combination of struggle and hope—an optimism that was grounded in her belief in the power of God. While never aspiring to ordained ministry herself, Cooper was well acquainted with clergy and had developed her own ideas on biblical inter-pretation.[38] Her theological ideas and understanding of scripture are evident in how she refers to the model of Christ as the great exemplar of progress and women's support (as noted earlier) and in how she identifies Black people as created in the image of God.[39] Moreover, Cooper taught Black people in ways that would help them live into their God-given abilities. The intersections of Cooper's theology with her radical vision of education for her students stands out.[40] Baker-Fletcher also makes a comparison between Cooper's rad-ical theological views and those espoused later in the twentieth century by Black Liberation theologians. She notes how radical it would have been for White people to wrestle with the idea of Black people being made in God's image—just as they later struggled with claims that God is Black. Baker-Fletcher's comparison is an attempt to help contemporary readers grapple with the radical nature of arguing for your humanity in the face of a system that only within your own lifetime has stopped treating you (at least in some ways) as chattel, property, and subhuman. And Cooper did just this.

Cooper wanted nothing more than for her fellow Christians (Black and White) to live into the ideals set out by the example of Christ, and in living into these ideals to begin to approximate the type of "liberal and universal ideas" that she saw in the Gospel of Jesus Christ.[41] Cooper contributes to our discussions of Black religious radicalism and activist education by the myriad ways that she attempted to live fully into the ideals she held about who Jesus was and how living like Christ would expand our most radical ideas.

Cooper also pushes us to expand how we study and theorize about Black religion and religious educators by modeling a tireless ethic not only to ed-ucate her students, but also to make sure that her voice (and the voices of people like her) are heard. Cooper's writings left a complex and nuanced record of her particular theological reflections on women and education. But they also document how she embodied the common early twentieth-century struggles of Black people, and especially of Black women, not only to be edu-cated but also to have their perspectives and thoughts valued and published alongside their White and/or male counterparts. Cooper's educational achievements are numerous, as are her writings. However, one wonders how much more Cooper could have accomplished had she not had to struggle constantly to get her writings published or take extra jobs to provide for her-self, her family, and even the many educational causes that she supported.

I place Cooper alongside other early twentieth-century educators who were also expanding the ways that we teach Black people and the content of that curriculum, because she too was pushing for the inclusion of women and women's voices in all efforts to *uplift the race*. While her intellectual projects look different (on the surface) from those of her male contemporaries—like Du Bois or even later activist educators like Woodson, who created projects that systematically studied Black people and their culture, history, religion, and lives—Cooper's project was one of sharing her voice and by example of encouraging others to share theirs, of living among Black people, and of consistently speaking out for Black women on local and national levels. Both in publishing her *A Voice from the South* and in her long life of teaching and advocacy afterward, Cooper expanded how we come to understand the intersectional nature of Black women's religious practices and how we create spaces to take seriously what Black women have to say.

Charles Lemert in his introduction to an edited collection of Cooper's writing notes that Cooper pioneered in pushing for the "acutely self-conscious understanding of the importance of the Black woman in American political and cultural life . . . [and in] inventing the discursive space of the Black woman."[42] Even as Cooper struggled for the rest of her life to publish her work, often living on the precipice of poverty, with some class benefits but never full financial security, she continued to write and to interject her voice into the wider discourse about Black people and Black people's education. I am drawn to Cooper both because she created what became the foundation for Black feminist thought and education, and because she held this together with her understanding of her call to teach. Thus, while we celebrate Cooper's contribution to Black feminist thought and even womanist theological discourse, I honor the way that she told her own story. And in telling her story, she summarized her life and her desires for how she wanted to be remembered at the end of her life, writing,

> No flowers please, just the smell of sweet understanding.
> The knowing look that sees Beyond and says gently and kindly
> "Somebody's Teacher on Vacation now.
> Resting for the Fall Opening."[43]

From her first book to this last couplet, Cooper told her own story first to advocate for the education of Black women and later to point to the sacred work of teaching. Cooper defined her life not by her myriad accomplishments, but by her calling to teach.

Cooper was an incomparable religious laywoman, activist, and educator. But she was not alone in this work at the beginning of the twentieth century: she was working alongside many other African American teachers to help improve the lives of Black people. In fact, Cooper's work was not widely read during her lifetime, and she had to work with many of her male counterparts (sometimes writing excoriating letters) to get her work published and out to a broader readership.[44] One such contemporary was W. E. B. DuBois, to whose work we turn now, beginning with his reflections on his early experiences as a rural teacher.

2

W. E. B. Du Bois

February 23, 1868–August 27, 1963

Hunting a School

William Edward Burghardt Du Bois grew up miles and worlds away from the poor rural communities where he started his teaching career. From his early life and early teaching experiences, it seemed unlikely that Du Bois would become one of the strongest advocates for Black people and their equal access to education—but he did. Du Bois described his early teaching experiences in rural Tennessee, while he was still a student at Fisk, as *hunting* for a country school. He saw firsthand the zeal that his young students had for learning despite not having teachers available to them consistently and despite the ways in which the mythos of "progress" harmed their lives more than helped. Du Bois described this school lovingly:

> There they sat, nearly thirty of them, on the rough benches, their faces shading from a pale cream to a deep brown, the little feet bare and swinging, the eyes full of expectation, with here and there a twinkle of mischief, and the hands grasping Webster's blue-back spelling-book. I loved my school, and the fine faith the children had in the wisdom of their teacher was truly marvelous. We read and spelled together, wrote a little, picked flowers, sang, and listened to stories of the world beyond the hill.[1]

It was also during his summers teaching in rural Tennessee that Du Bois first encountered different aspects of Black religious life and cultivated his love of the sorrow songs. He described the dual experiences of hearing "the sorrow songs sung with primitive beauty and grandeur" and of seeing "the hard, ugly drudgery of country life and the writhing of landless, ignorant peasants . . . [of seeing] the race problem at nearly its lowest terms."[2] The teaching experience at this first school and his love for the people there shaped Du Bois and helps us begin to situate him (and his subsequent teaching, writing,

Teaching to Live. Almeda M. Wright, Oxford University Press. © Oxford University Press 2024.
DOI: 10.1093/oso/9780197663424.003.0003

and advocacy) in a long line of Black activist-educators specifically, and more broadly of activist-educators who help us to understand better the complex roles of Black religion and spirituality in this work.

We know about Du Bois's country school not because of the public records or because of the physical building in which he taught, but because Du Bois wrote about it. His scholarship was part of his activism and of his project to improve the lives of Black people. Indeed, Du Bois placed his essay about this rural school teaching experience in his larger collection, *The Souls of Black Folk*. Given the array of Du Bois's writings and speeches on education, this essay is often overlooked in favor of some of his other works defining his educational philosophy or offering insights about the function of education. This essay includes discussions and critique of "progress" and describes the havoc wreaked in the lives of Black people in the name of progress as they attempted to pursue economic success, or as officials around them attempted to help move Black people forward without fully considering what that entailed for poor Black people barely twenty-five years out of slavery to survive, let alone achieve some sort of consistent "progress." Instead, many of Du Bois's other essays, such as "Of the Training of Black Men" or "The Talented Tenth,"[3] have been taught and referenced in schools of education and more broadly as exemplars of Du Bois's thought on how education should function in the lives of Black people in the early part of the twentieth century.[4] I, however, always come back to this telling of his hunt for this country school and the haunting story of Josie, who eagerly invited him to this community. Du Bois wrote of coming back years later to find that Josie has died, as a result of *progress*, of working too hard and trying to provide some sort of life for herself and her family. Instead of a joyful story of overcoming or a story of the amazing impact his little school had in the lives of this little community, Du Bois wrote of the realities with which this community wrestled, cut off from many of the resources of larger cities and from any efforts at fully enfranchising poor or Black people.

Du Bois's essay about his school and this larger community shows how deeply he loved them. To him, their stories were not mere field notes or sociological analysis. Rather, it was in places like this that his connection and commitment to "severely oppressed people" emerged. He wrote with respect and almost with reverence of the efforts that the farmers and students were making as they worked together. He took note also of the struggles they faced and overcame in their quest to learn. Du Bois attended both to the logistical struggles and to the fears of what "too much book learning" might do.

I also see in this essay an important part of what makes Du Bois critical to the work of religious scholars and educators at the same time. Here, we grasp his ability to see and genuinely love the people among whom he is laboring, a love so deep that he devoted his life to improving their world. This love is an essentially spiritual value and one that undergirded his activism (and that of other activist-educators, like Anna Julia Cooper and Septima Clark). Yet at the same time that he manifested love, he was also frankly elitist and sometimes paternalistic toward the masses of Black people.[5] Nonetheless, he contributed significantly to the fields of religion and education, even radical religious education, in part because of this underlying connection to his students and his genuine love for the people.[6]

Yet Du Bois's love of this community was not all that sparked my interest in him. Nor was it all that pushed me to consider his contributions to the larger connections between religion, education, and activism. His systematic study of African American life is also determinative. We can debate his initial motivations in wanting to study "Negro problems" and the efficacy of a project designed to produce incontrovertible evidence to help White people and the larger society better understand the effects of slavery and poverty on the efforts of Black people to live well. But his scholarship went beyond producing "better data." For in studying them Du Bois also tells Black people that their lives and specifically their religious lives are important and worthy of direct and significant attention. Du Bois asserts that Black people themselves can and should take the time to examine their lives and their institutions and to improve them.

Du Bois's writings defy classification in terms of genre. His writings attempted to capture the "soul" of a people. While early White audiences tried to diminish and dismiss his work—for example, writing in one review of the "overly flowery prose, that was typical of the Negro writer"[7]—they still had to recognize its ability to capture the experiences of so many people of color who often were not afforded opportunities to speak (or more to the point, to be heard) for themselves. And what was criticized as "flowery language" is now a gift, as Du Bois in the *Souls of Black Folks* writes in such a way that students (for example, those in my most recent seminar on this book) weep as he described his encounters with Black folks in rural Tennessee and feel enraged as he described how his inability to access proper healthcare resulted in the death of his son.

He wrote very personal essays on the one hand and rigorous ethnographic and empirical research findings on the other.[8] This combination of research and writings positioned him to have a significant impact on the work of religious scholars and religious educators, an impact that was felt far beyond any particular scholarly field.

Du Bois's Early Life

Du Bois's background and upbringing are almost at the opposite end of the spectrum to Cooper's in terms of gender, geography, religious orientation, and educational encouragement, among many other factors. Despite being born within a decade of each other, their early lives, I imagine, were worlds apart. Du Bois was born on February 23, 1868, in Great Barrington, Massachusetts just five years after the Emancipation Proclamation. He died on August 27, 1963, in Accra, Ghana, on the eve of the March on Washington. Like Anna Julia Cooper, Du Bois's life overlaps a unique span of crucial events in African American social, political, cultural, and religious history.

Du Bois grew up in a predominately White community, with "perhaps twenty-five, certainly not more than fifty, colored folks in a population of five thousand."[9] However, Du Bois also noted that his family had lived in the area longer than many of their neighbors' families and that they grew over the years by intermarrying cousins and other Black people, with what he described as "limited infiltration of white blood."[10]

Du Bois's immediate family included his grandfather, Othello Burghardt, a darker and good-natured man; his grandmother Sally, an energetic, "thin, tall, yellow and hawk-faced woman"; and his mother, Mary Sylvina (also born in Great Barrington, in 1831). Du Bois described his mother as being "rather silent but very determined and very patient." Beyond this description, we see her influence throughout Du Bois's life; she clearly played a crucial role in instilling in him his understanding of virtues and vices—including an admonition to abstain from alcohol—which he carried with him throughout his life. Du Bois's father, Alfred Du Bois, "a light mulatto," however, was more of a mystery to him. Alfred Du Bois died while Du Bois was still a baby, and therefore he was shaped predominately by his mother and her family.

Du Bois took pride in his family's long-standing connection to the Great Barrington community but also noted that no one in his family (or among the Black community) ever achieved wealth or even a higher economic status. For the most part, Du Bois's family supported themselves on small farms and as laborers and servants in town. He carefully noted the ways in which race and racism played out in this community. For example, his family never worked in the many mills in the community (these were most often populated by Irish and German workers), but his family did interact in the limited social life, primarily based in churches, with the other White residents.[11]

Du Bois paints a picture of the economic conditions of his family by describing the many places that he lived during his childhood:

I was born in a rather nice cottage which belonged to a black South Carolinian, whose own house stood next, at the lower end of one of the pleasant streets of the town. Then for a time I lived in the country at the house of my grandfather, Othello. . . . It was sturdy, small, and old-fashioned. Later we moved back to town in lived in quarters over the woodshed of one of the town's better mansions. After that we lived awhile over a store by the railway and during my high school years in a little four-room tenement house on the same street where I was born. . . . None of these homes had modern conveniences but they were weatherproof, fairly warm in winter and furnished with some comfort.[12]

This description also points to the ways in which his early life was shaped by the efforts of his widowed mother, who was doing her best to support them on the meager income of a part-time domestic laborer. Du Bois noted that she "boarded" an uncle, a barber, and relied on "unobtrusive charity" during his high school years. As he became more aware of the economic dimensions of his life (and as questions about his future arose), Du Bois took on several jobs to help his mother. These jobs included: "splitting kindling, mowing lawns, doing chores" and starting coal-burning stoves in one of the local businesses.[13]

His early childhood in Massachusetts, which he described as idyllic, was also shaped by interactions with White schoolmates and neighbors. While he grew up apart from a large African American community, Du Bois was never unaware of racism and racial discrimination. However, he was not fully connected to the larger concerns of the "masses" of African Americans during his early childhood. It was only as he continued his education, moved south, and even undertook several scholarly projects that he connected with and lived among more African Americans.

As many scholars have noted, this early distance and even his educational pursuits shaped Du Bois (and many other educated Black elites), and much of his research and even solutions for the "Negro problem" are colored by White, European American morals and standards. This is not to discount Du Bois as one of the fiercest advocates for Black people, simply a reminder that his social location of course shaped his scholarship and approach to education and religion among Black people during the early 1900s. In particular, Du Bois's early experiences of being near to but cut off from the "world beyond the veil," and his early attempts to "best" his White classmates academically as a means of wresting from them at least a few of the prizes of the White world can be seen as directly linked to his understanding of the role of education in preparing Black people for engaging the larger U.S. landscape and in ameliorating the "Negro problem." It also connected directly to his study of (and call for others also to study) the Negro and the contributions that the Negro has made since slavery. Celebrating the accomplishments of a people who previously were considered sub/nonhuman would have been essential if the idea was to "best" White people at their own game. To be certain, Du Bois's desire to study Black people goes beyond responding to the critique of the White gaze, but most of his *early* research is clearly undertaken with a desire to correct the erroneous assumptions and conclusions of those in power. Du Bois was a firm believer in the power of research and empirical data to advance the causes of Black people and to improve their lives.[14]

Du Bois graduated from Great Barrington High School in 1884, at the age of sixteen. It was there that he first experienced the power and world of academic success. He graduated as valedictorian of his class and, with the help of his principal who had put him in college preparatory classes, and his community, he attended college. The village Congregational church arranged for him to enter Fisk University after graduation. Although we can speculate about the racist tendencies of Du Bois's Great Barrington community—in that they could have raised money for him to go to Harvard (which was where Du Bois desired to go) or some other predominately White university—for Du Bois, journeying south to Fisk was a life-changing event.

Fisk was a completely new world for Du Bois, a world in which he began to forge very different (and new) connections to the Negro community, both on campus and in Tennessee more broadly. In fact, prior to Fisk, Du Bois recounts only having been in school with one other Black student, a young man with whom he did not get along particularly well because the young man was not at the top of their class and didn't seem to take pride in "besting" the White students as Du Bois did.[15] Thus, studying and engaging with other Black students at Fisk was eye-opening for him. Du Bois also described how his experience at Fisk taught him about racial violence in ways that he could not have imagined previously:

> The three years at Fisk were years of growth and development. I learned new things about the world. My knowledge of the race problem became more definite. I saw discrimination in ways of which I had never dreamed; the separation of passengers on the railways of the South was just beginning; the race separation in living quarters throughout the cities and towns was manifest; the public disdain and even insult in race contact on the street continually took my breath; I came in contact for the first time with a sort of violence that I had never realized in New England; I remember going down and looking wide-eyed at the door of a public building, filled with buck-shot, where the editor of the leading daily paper had been publicly murdered the day before.[16]

His summers teaching in the Tennessee hills likewise transformed him and gave new passion to his work for and among the severely oppressed, the poorest of the Negro population. Du Bois taught during the summers not out of economic necessity but because he had heard about "the country in the South as the real seat of slavery . . . [and he] wanted to know it."[17]

Du Bois's Complicated Religious Life

Alongside Du Bois's educational pursuits, his early religious life is essential to our understanding of his later research and activism. Du Bois recounts his early religious formation as part of his reflections on the social life and relationships in Great Barrington. This is in part because his early formal religious formation took place alongside of White people in his small community. Du Bois notes the influence of his Episcopalian grandmother and his Congregational mother.[18] He also wrote somewhat matter-of-factly that he "grew up in the Congregational Sunday school."[19] Yet other scholars, such as Herbert Aptheker, note that Du Bois never attended any church with regularity, either in his youth or in later life.[20] Aptheker nevertheless notes that Du Bois "was well aware of the enormous influence of the church upon the history and lives of Black people and upon his own life."[21] His lack of regular church attendance does not indicate a lack of religious formation or familiarity with the Bible or religious ideas. Indeed, he was well versed in scriptures and in a particular type of Christian morality (the influences of New England Congregationalism's puritanical carryovers are evident in much of his work). Religious themes are reflected in much of his written work, and his later critiques of religion are in fact deeply religious, pointing to his respect for the revolutionary and radical teachings of Jesus, and his high expectations of what Christianity should have been (in contrast to the justification of the status quo it had become).[22]

Du Bois arrived at Fisk with his childhood religious values and beliefs in place but noted Fisk's preoccupation with making sure that the students "did not lose or question our Christian orthodoxy."[23] Du Bois records being some-what confused about this preoccupation because up to that point it had never occurred to him to question his religious upbringing. He candidly wrote that "Its theory had presented no particular difficulties: God ruled the world, Christ loved it, and men did right, or tried to; otherwise they were rightly punished."[24] This basic theological understanding had served him well thus far. Only at the turn of the twentieth century did Du Bois begin to encounter aspects of Christianity that "affronted his logic." In his 1940s autobiography, Du Bois reflected that

> I became critical of religion and resentful of its practice for two reasons: first the heresy trials, particularly the one which expelled Briggs from the Presbyterian Church; and especially the insistence of the local church at Fisk University that dancing was a "sin." I was astonished to find that anybody could possibly think this; as a boy I had attended with my mother little parlor dances; as a youth at Fisk I danced gaily and happily. I was reminded by a smug old hypocrite of the horrible effects my example might have even if my own conscience was clear. I searched my soul with the Pauline text: "If meat maketh my brother to offend," etc. I have never had much respect for Paul since.[25]

Du Bois here is very clearly outlining the ways in which his relationship with institutional religion became strained when it became harder for him to hold together faith and his rational mind (and the ability for Christianity and modern thought and sciences to be held together). He also struggled when he could not hold religion together with his own experiences of what was right and good and beautiful, particularly his firsthand experiences of the beauty of Black life, experienced in dancing with his mother and in his youth. Of course, Du Bois's critiques parallel many of the ways that people begin to distance themselves from the religion of their origin as they grow and develop. However, for Du Bois, the Christianity of his upbringing and of his mother's morality was not the religion from which he was distancing himself. He instead developed a distaste for the ways that Christianity, in its battles over modernity, was evolving to be a more intolerant and rigid institution. As a result, as Du Bois continued through his life, his relationship with religion became strained. Yet he never rejected religion wholesale, or even of the idea of God. Instead, as a scholar we see him continuing to wrestle with the way that religion functions for Black life and continuing to admonish others to live into the moral teachings of his mother and his early Christian understanding of thrift, service, and sacrifice for a common good.

Du Bois did not ever hide his questions/discomfort about institutional religion or even public expressions of it. We learn a great deal about Du Bois's ideas on religion by how they intersected with his early teaching career. Upon returning from studying in Germany, Du Bois was hired to teach at Wilberforce (an African Methodist Episcopal college, where Anna Julia Cooper had also taught after she finished at Oberlin). He remained at Wilberforce for only two years, in part because of clashes with the expectation within Black religious institutions of higher education by both students and leadership that he should be able to lead public prayer extemporaneously. He described one such occasion:

> the student leader of a prayer meeting into which I had wandered casually to look local religion over, suddenly and without warning announced that "Professor Du Bois would lead us in prayer." I simply answered, "No, he won't," and as a result nearly lost my job. It took a great deal of explaining to the board of bishops why a professor in Wilberforce should not be able at all times and sundry to address God in extemporaneous prayer. I was saved only by the fact that my coming to Wilberforce had been widely advertised and I was so willing to do endless work when the work seemed to me worth doing.[26]

This issue did not end when Du Bois left Wilberforce. Instead, he encountered a similar set of expectations about leading public prayers when he began teaching at Atlanta University in 1898. Du Bois was excited to start his work on the Negro social problems at Atlanta (after a year of doing research in Philadelphia). And yet he also knew that he had to negotiate the expectations for shared religious life and worship that were part of the ethos of most African American colleges during this era. Du Bois noted that:

I eagerly accepted the invitation, although at the last moment there came a curious reminiscence of Wilberforce in a little hitch based on that old matter of extemporaneous public prayer. Dr. Bumstead and I compromised on my promise to use the Episcopal prayer book; later I used to add certain prayers of my own composing. I am not sure that they were orthodox or reached heaven, but they certainly reached my audience.[27]

Clearly Du Bois both knew enough about Black religious life and respected it enough to study it and to participate in ways that honored both who he was and the larger community. Du Bois noted not only that he was comfortable sharing prayers from the Episcopal Book of Common prayer, but also with adding his own written prayers—addressed if not to a Christian deity then at least to and for the students he was charged with teaching and leading. Du Bois's prayers for his students were only published after his death, but they were carefully collated and preserved, indicating that they had some significance to Du Bois, even as his own religious convictions continued to evolve.

The collection of *Prayers for Darker People* includes what Aptheker describes as not only prayers but also sermons and instructions by Du Bois for his young students. The prayers are coupled with instructions and Du Bois's vision of what is required by God and for flourishing in society. One prayer frankly begins, "Let us remember, O God, that our religion in life is expressed in our work . . . shown in the way we conquer our studies."[28] Du Bois here was admonishing his students not to waste "God's time" by squandering their opportunity to study and put forth their best effort. Some prayers included lessons about how failure was just as much a part of life as success and other life lessons, while others asked God to help "these young people to grow to despise false ideals of conquest and empire" and for them to see the God's vision of peace realized.[29] One particularly powerful prayer included an admonishment of his students, possibly on the occasion of their graduation. Du Bois prayed,

Give us grace, O God, to dare to do the deed which we well know cries to be done. . . . Mighty causes are calling us—the freeing of women, the training of children, the putting down of hate and murder and poverty. . . . But they call with voices that mean work and sacrifice and death. Mercifully grant us, O God, the spirit of Esther, that we say: I will go unto the King and if I perish, I perish—Amen. Esther 4:9–16[30]

This prayer demonstrates Du Bois's strong convictions regarding the call to work and serve for a greater purpose, and it reiterates his understanding of the powerful nature of biblical figures like Esther as an example of this type of sacrificial calling and work.

Herbert Aptheker helps us understand how these prayers fit into Du Bois's life while he was teaching at Atlanta University and into his larger corpus of work:

> These prayers show another facet of the complex totality of Du Bois—a facet rarely seen. . . . This is the private and young Du Bois, not in the act of agitating among peers or challenging an ignorant, racist foe. No, this is a Du Bois quietly talking to children and young people, as in a family group, and discussing how to care for oneself, the value of courtesy, the need for excellent work habits, of respect for elders and parents, the importance of inner preparation for the greater tasks, labors, and challenges . . . especially in a hostile world.[31]

Du Bois was writing these prayers and having these moments of inner reflection at the same time that he was completing one of the most ambitious studies of Negro life and launching radical social change organizations, namely, the Niagara Movement and the NAACP.

Sociological Research and Radical Education

Du Bois epitomizes the strand of radical education that sought not only to educate the Black masses, but also to educate White (and sometimes Black) elites about the "real" contours of life and the root causes of problems plaguing the Black community. Du Bois's particular brand of history and social criticism combined with his deep interest in empirical research opened him to this type of work and to his project of presenting a sociological account of the lives of African Americans. And while Du Bois's approach to educating Black people that were battling illiteracy and poverty was at times one or two levels removed from the actual masses of Black people (except during his time teaching at Black universities in the South and teaching in rural Tennessee during his summers at Fisk), he remained a staunch advocate for excellent education for African Americans and a fierce critic of it when he felt it was not being done well.[32]

In Du Bois's work (as well as other educational efforts during the early twentieth century), we see a shift from the initial Reconstruction and post-bellum project of sending missionaries (White and Black) south in hopes of educating newly freed slaves. While still pursuing a project of *racial uplift*, Du Bois and several of his contemporaries were also emphasizing that education and intellectual pursuits are part of a much broader project beyond providing basic education or information to survive. That project was one of expanding this basic educational work to include "making room" to tell "our own" stories. So, while many scholars with some justification attend to and critique what seems to be his focus on and obsession with the White gaze, Du Bois was in fact leading the charge in the work of writing and studying the *Negro* for himself and on his own terms.

Du Bois committed his life to the work of denouncing racism and White supremacy. But he did far more than that: he also devoted himself to intellectual projects that sought to provide concrete evidence and data to support his claims about the life, problems, successes, and potential of the American Negro. For example, in his classic text, *The Souls of Black Folks* (1903), he used the vehicles of poetry, autobiographical material, historical essays, and more to reflect on the diverse and multifaceted dimensions of the lives of Black people. Similarly, in his study of *The Philadelphia Negro* (1899), Du Bois undertook an ambitious research project contracted by the University of Pennsylvania in which he attempted to describe every aspect of Black life in Philadelphia's Seventh Ward. Even though his findings were commissioned by a White institution, he did not shy away from calling out the racism that created the atrocious living conditions of this densely populated African American community:

Du Bois describes the study's general aim as an inquiry that "sought to ascertain something of the geographical distribution of this race, their occupations and daily life, their homes, their organizations, and, above all, their relation to their million White fellow-citizens." Providing first a history of African Americans in the city of Philadelphia stretching as far back as the 1600s, Du Bois reserved the bulk of the more than 500-page volume to detailing every aspect of the Black community in the Seventh Ward from the size, age, and sex of the population to their level of education, health, income, and occupations. In particular, Du Bois addressed a number of problems the African American community faced, drawing attention to challenges imposed by current racism as well as those imposed by the lingering legacy of slavery.[33]

Du Bois undertook an even more ambitious study of the American Negro in his series of Atlanta University Studies and conferences. These studies, largely edited by Du Bois himself, took place primarily between 1896 and 1914, with other studies in the series continuing well into the twentieth century.[34] The topics in this series of more than twenty studies and conferences included death rates and social conditions of Negroes living in cities, the efforts toward social betterment, the college-educated Negro, the Negro church, and the Negro common school.[35]

Unquestionably, these studies show Du Bois's embrace of empiricism and his genuine belief in the need for good data. But we also find here a shift in Du Bois's almost blind faith in the ability of hard data and scientific methodologies to win over White communities. Particularly when he moved to Atlanta, Du Bois had to confront firsthand both the reality of lynching and other scientists' and scholars' equally insistent use of data to shore up their claims of superiority and White supremacy.[36] Indeed, Zuckerman writes that Du Bois was so shaken by many of the events happening around him in Atlanta that he began to reassess "the goals of his precious scientific investigations. Hence in subsequent studies . . . the goals were guided by the social activism of a man living at the epicenter of White brutality."[37] We recognize this difference in writing styles and goals when we compare Du Bois's earlier social scientific studies, like the *Philadelphia Negro* and the *Negro Church*, with the essays collected in *The Souls of Black Folks*. What changed was Du Bois's realization that supposedly neutral science and reasoning would not sway racists or stop violence against Black people. As he himself records,

> Two considerations thereafter broke in upon my work and disrupted it: first, one could not be a calm, cool, and detached scientist while Negroes were lynched, murdered and starved: and secondly, there was no such definite demand for scientific work of the sort that I was doing as I had confidently assumed would be easily forthcoming. I regarded it as axiomatic that the world wanted to learn the truth and if the truth were sought with even approximate accuracy and painstaking devotion, the world would gladly support the effort. This was, of course, but a young man's idealism.[38]

Thus moved by what he saw in Atlanta, he shifted toward social activism.

Du Bois's Contributions to Black Religion
(and Education about Religion)

With regard to religion *and* religious education, Du Bois's work is significant in this early era for its contributions to the study of Black religion and
religious life. In a comprehensive book-length study of African American
religion entitled *The Negro Church*, published in 1903, Du Bois employed
social scientific and historical methods to conduct and analyze hundreds of
questionnaires and denominational records. Lamenting the academy's lack
of engagement with Du Bois's *The Negro Church* as opposed to the critical ac-
claim that other works like *The Souls of Black Folks* received, sociologist Phil
Zuckerman begins to redress the imbalance by noting that *The Negro Church*
was "the first book-length sociological study of religion ever published in the
United States; it was the first in-depth analysis of Black religious life; and it
was the first sociological, historical, and empirical study of Black religious
life undertaken by Blacks themselves."[39] Zuckerman reminds us of the cut-
ting edge and radical nature of the project undertaken by Du Bois and his
team.[40]

In *The Negro Church*, Du Bois primarily explored the functionalist
dimensions of African American religion and churches. As a sociologist, he
focused on the roles that this institution plays in the life and communities of
African Americans. In his characteristically scathing way, he described both
the power and issues in churches; he wrote,

> The great engine of moral uplift is the Christian church. The Negro church
> is a mighty social power today; but it needs cleansing . . . once purged of
> its dross it will become as it ought to be, and as it is now to some extent,
> the most powerful agency in the moral development and social reform of
> 9,000,000 Americans of Negro blood.[41]

Indeed, here Du Bois described the church's primary role as that of racial uplift and had no patience for churches functioning in ways that were not in line
with his vision of the standards of morality and specifically purity that he felt
the Negro community needed in order to advance.

A particular set of survey questions to children (and youth) points to his
understanding of the functions of Black churches, as well as to some of the
blind spots of his approach. For example, Du Bois asked the children what it
meant to be a Christian, but instead of noting the array of answers, Du Bois

simply made a global assessment that Black churches were failing youth by not teaching them that an essential element of Christianity is to live a moral life. He reported,

> The children of twelve and under had the clearer and simpler idea of the direct connection of goodness and Christianity. The older children tended more toward phrases which sought to express the fact that religion had reference to some higher will. Indeed this was the more popular idea, and 70 percent of the children spoke of Christianity as "Love for God," "Belief in Christ," or some such phrase. Clear as such phrases may be to some minds, they undoubtedly point to a lack in the moral training of Negro children. [The children] evidently are not impressed to a sufficiently large extent with the fact that moral goodness is the first requirement of a Christian life.[42]

This data and its interpretation unsurprisingly reflect Du Bois's bias that religion is equivalent to morality. They also reflect in large part the Euro-American and New England Congregationalist focus on moral goodness and purity, which had shaped Du Bois in Massachusetts, and which he carried with him to the South. In this way, his religious location put him at odds with many of the masses of Black people he was researching and the more spiritual concerns of the Baptist and Methodist theologies and spiritualities that took hold among many African Americans of that era, particularly in the South. (This is not to say that the masses of Black people did not also have a functionalist view of religion. We can see from his study that they simply saw it functioning and producing different goods/ends than Du Bois did). While this myopic interpretation of the data is a definite problem in Du Bois's research (and so much other research), the actual collection of the data and the fact that he preserved it for future generations' interpretation and consideration remain significant.[43]

Yet through the content and structure of *The Negro Church*, Du Bois revolutionized the study of the religious lives of Black people. In particular he expanded the content of the conversation around African American Christianity and religion(s) by attending to Africa and the role of Africa in shaping the religious lives of Black people in the United States. Thus, he begins his study of the Negro church not with the emergence of established Christian churches or religious communities in the United States but with the process of transplanting African religions to the United States, attending to particular traditions that stood out, such as Obeah. Though his treatment of these topics leaves much to be desired for contemporary scholars and standards (at times his description is not only elitist but downright offensive), what remains groundbreaking and radical is the inclusion of these religious practices and his attention to the reality that African American religion was neither simply created out of thin air in the United States nor was the gift of enslavers to Black people.

Here Du Bois also hints at his later evolution and interest in Pan-Africanism. Later not only did he attend to the influences of past life in Africa on Black life in the United States, but he also continued to draw attention to the global conditions of racism and colonialism and attempted to create opportunities to address such issues confronting people of African descent all over the globe. This attention to the interconnected nature of Black people, religiously, culturally, and politically, was an instance of Du Bois's radical love and commitment to oppressed people all over the world. Du Bois bucked some of the norms of his times by telling the history of Black religion and Black peoples in ways that connected with a legacy far beyond and far broader than that of the transatlantic slave trade.

While I would never argue that Du Bois was a religious educator in the limited sense of focusing on intracommunal Christian nurture or formation, his sociological work undeniably had a significant impact on the education and even the religious development of generations of Black people. His work helped Black religious scholars (Christian and other) wrestle with questions about the purpose and function of Black religion and religious institutions, based on what it was historically, how it functions in contemporary society, and what it might become in the future.[44] Many of the current debates regarding Black churches' lack of impact on contemporary social ills are made possible because of scholars like Du Bois, who early on began to articulate an understanding of Black religion that is about much more than belief in a higher power.[45]

Du Bois's attention to the lived realities and practices of Black religious people of all ages was groundbreaking. It gave us snapshots of Black life that we now take for granted in sociological research, but that were not available before the practices and studies conducted by Du Bois and his team. Zuckerman helpfully reminds us to assess Du Bois's contributions based on this historical context, not contemporary standards. Zuckerman writes,

> By employing the methodologies of the social sciences within a less tangible—but equally important—moral framework, Du Bois sought

irrefutable evidence of Black humanity in an era obsessed with the relationship between numbers, measurements, and morality. This commingling of
facts and spiritual assessments was neither contradictory nor incidental;
on the contrary, *The Negro Church* was part of Du Bois' rational response
to the brutality of Jim Crowism, in a language and format familiar to the
era's finest minds. *The Negro Church* was emblematic of Du Bois' scholarly
attempt to compile vital statistics as they related to everyday Black existence, seek out the truth, and encourage social reform. Although the text
is fraught with ambivalence, the final "Resolutions" decidedly hone in on
the inequities of the South's social and political culture and offer a specific
course of action.[46]

Du Bois was clear in his high and often elitist expectations of what the
Black church and Black ministers and educators should do. He minced no
words in identifying how education and Black religious groups failed to contribute to the project of racial uplift. But he was also clear that the purpose
of his work was to expand the ways in which Black people contributed to
the wider society and to their own well-being. He created spaces for Black
people to tell their own stories[47] and to begin to shape the terms of their own
liberation.

Writing in the 1960s, toward the end of his career Du Bois reiterated the
rallying cries of many Black educators at the turn of the twentieth century
when he reflected on the moves toward racial progress. In his essay, "Whither
now and why," Du Bois clarified that he was never advocating for Black people
in the United States simply to have access to or become subsumed into White
American culture. Instead, his project was always about making room for
Black people to tell, know, and celebrate their own culture and stories—while
experiencing the freedoms afforded to those living in America. He wrote,

> I am not fighting to settle the question of racial equality in America by
> the process of getting rid of the Negro race; getting rid of Black folk, not
> producing Black children, forgetting the slave trade and slavery, and the
> struggle for emancipation; of forgetting abolition and especially of ignoring
> the whole cultural history of Africans to the world.
>
> No! What I have been fighting for and am still fighting for is the possi-
> bility of Black folk and their cultural patterns existing in America without
> discrimination; and on terms of equality.[48]

Through his various sociological projects and impassioned speeches and essays, Du Bois remained an advocate for Black people and insisted that they be treated with respect and be given credit for the unique and ongoing contributions that they made to the wider society and world.

Conclusion

The beginning of the twentieth century was an era in which newly freed Black persons were still trying to imagine what their lives could and should be after the thwarted hopes of Reconstruction and the rise of Jim/Jane Crow laws. It was a world in which Black people had to wrestle not only to provide for themselves, but against systems and structures that regarded and treated them as inferior and that had legal supports to uphold the dehumanization of an entire race. Part of my interest in the interconnected histories of education, religion, and social change (and the activist-educators who embody this history) derives from the reality that there are so many places rife with systemic and structural support for the *dis*enfranchisement of Black people in the United States. At the turn of the twentieth century, educators were on the front lines of the struggles to resist these dehumanizing forces and to advocate for ways in which others should see Black people as fully human, and the ways that Black people should begin to create and affirm their own roles as history makers and not just observers, passive recipients, or as *problems* to be fixed.

W. E. B. Du Bois and Anna Julia Cooper, and others like Carter G. Woodson, each in their unique ways exemplify the work of early twentieth-century educators and leaders who advanced an agenda for Black people that pushed back against those trying to thwart their positive sense of self or to allow others to speak on their behalf rather than letting them create or at least contribute to the narrative themselves. These educators were not doing the same thing as each other, and often what drove their actions were quite disparate motivations. But together they pointed to the ways that Black educators could create room for Black people to tell their own stories and to learn to value who they are.

In complementary but distinctive ways, Cooper and Du Bois also expand our understandings of religion and education as part of social change. Both were advocates for the emancipatory potential of scholarship, Du Bois through the systematic study of Black people and their religion, and Cooper through the systematic inclusion of women in all educational endeavors including theological ones. By attending to Cooper and Du Bois as both educators and scholars—two people with religious sensibilities and a genuine love of people—we are able to understand more fully the work of religious activist-educators at the beginning of the twentieth century. Their teaching and scholarship on behalf of Black people, as well as the care with which they attended to religious practices and ideals, paved the way for many generations of activist-educators and radical religious educators.

Building on the legacies of Du Bois and Cooper, in the next section we turn to the lives and work of two more exemplary religious activist educators: Ida B. Wells and Nannie Helen Burroughs. They expand this work beyond traditional educational arenas and the scholarly work of studying the religion and lives of Black people. In particular we explore the ways that Burroughs worked within denominational bodies to build institutions, including schools, and they ways that Wells expanded the way that the press worked as an educator and in activism—specifically for the education and uplift of Black people.

SECTION II
TEACHING TO LIVE

You have talked and sung and prayed about dying, and forgiving your enemies, and of feeling sure you are going to be received in the new Jerusalem. . . . But why don't you pray to live and ask to be freed? . . . Quit talking about dying; if you believe your God is all powerful, believe [God] is powerful enough to open these prison doors, and say so. . . . Pray to live and believe you are going to get out.[1]

The phrase "teaching to live" is an allusion to the words of Ida B. Wells, spoken as encouragement to a group of falsely imprisoned men to stop focusing on death and the afterlife. She instead admonished them to pray to live, to focus on God's ability to help them now, and to change the situation they were currently living through. Wells's admonition speaks to the way she lived her life and to how her work as a religiously inspired activist also taught so many others to *pray to live* and not simply concede to their lives being ameliorated only in the afterlife. Wells, like Burroughs and many other Black women educators, was focused on teaching and training the masses of Black people to live—to make a living and to act on their own behalf—in the here and now. In this section, I examine more deeply how religion, education, and social transformation intersect in the work of African American women educators and activists at the turn of the twentieth century.

In exploring the lives of Ida B. Wells and Nannie Helen Burroughs, I shift focus to activists and educators who were attentive to the masses (rather than only to an educated elite) as the place of racial uplift, and who were focused on knowledge that helps people live and live now. Granted, they were not involved in the limited debates over industrial education, nor did they focus only on the technical skills needed to be laborers. Nonetheless, women like these two hold in tension the need for people to be informed broadly about the world around them and by extension the need to be able to work for change in their own lives.

Contemporaries of Cooper, Du Bois, and Woodson, educators and activists Ida B. Wells and Nannie Helen Burroughs pursued related but drastically different projects. In part due to the ongoing patriarchy, sexism, and classism of religious and educational institutions in the United States, educators like Burroughs had to establish schools and curriculum for educating Black girls and women.[2] Others, like Wells, began teaching in segregated rural schools, only to be dismissed from teaching when they increased their activism and participation in protests. Both of these key figures also continued their religious and community engagement (in addition to their educational professions/work). For example, Wells and Burroughs were very active as writers and in creating women's clubs and conventions as conduits for their community work. While different from the establishment of academic disciplines, this work was equally influential and radical in its impact on the lives of their students and the organizing of Black women. Their legacy of Black women's education and activism continues to this day. Even though the contributions of women educators and religious leaders are prominent in each era, the next two chapters opts to attend particularly to the early twentieth-century radical activism and organizing of women.

Ida B. Wells and Nannie Helen Burroughs are also connected through their efforts at building institutions for the purpose of social transformation. They represent a somewhat different duo from the activist educators explored in the previous chapters; even though they were significant actors in effecting social change, they did so without the benefit of formal higher education. They became some of the fiercest proponents of education and training for women and the masses of Black people, but without having been able to complete formal or elite degrees themselves. At times this worked in their favor, possibly helping them to advocate for others in ways that may not have happened, if we take Woodson's critiques seriously about the chasm between the "educated Negro" and the masses. Yet more frequent are examples of these women being excluded from Black elite circles or of having to work "differently" within organizations (sometimes having to form their own) because of the expectations of who can or should be a leader in the Black community.

3

Ida B. Wells

July 16, 1862–March 25, 1931

I went to Grace Presbyterian Church and told them I was looking
for a church home . . . that I had been brought up in a Christian
home under the influence of the Sunday school and church and that
I wanted to bring my children up the same way. That I was not a
Presbyterian by doctrine, but since all Christian denominations
agreed on a standard of conduct and right living it seemed to me to
matter very little what name we bore.

I told them that if they would accept me with that confession of
faith I would like to come in. They did accept me, and I and my two
daughters united with that church. Shortly after I was asked to accept the position of teacher to the men's Bible class by the members
themselves.

I thus began that which to me was one of the most delightful
periods of my life in Chicago. I had a class of young men ranging
from eighteen to thirty years of age. The average attendance was
twenty-five to thirty a Sunday, and we had an enrollment of over
one hundred. Every Sunday we discussed the Bible lessons in a plain
common-sense way and tried to make application of their truths to
our daily lives. I taught this class for ten years.[1]

Here, Ida B. Wells gives an example of a religious, activist educator and of
Black *radical* religious education at its best. Yet the title of Sunday school
teacher or religious educator is usually the last in a series of titles ascribed to
Wells. She is best known for her pioneering work in the press and in launching
the antilynching campaign in the United States at the end of the nineteenth
century. However, a closer look at her early life and her personal diaries
reveals her inner spiritual strivings and her desire to serve God and Black
people better. Her faith, her passion for Black people (and for all people), and
her passion for standing up for justice cannot be separated. Many of Wells's

Teaching to Live. Almeda M. Wright, Oxford University Press. © Oxford University Press 2024.
DOI: 10.1093/oso/9780197663424.003.0004

critiques of contemporary women, activists, educators, and ministers are of their inconsistency in living up to her understanding of Christian values—which included a call to do what is right and fight against injustice. Again, Wells's outspoken nature and passion for justice are cut from the same cloth as her spiritual convictions. And while generations later we have often failed to hold both in equal esteem (we often strip her completely of her religious leanings or summarize them in a sentence or two), in this work I foreground not only her religious convictions but also the ways in which she connects these with her work as a religious laywoman and Sunday school teacher.

Ida B. Wells was a Sunday school teacher! I remember my initial surprise at reading this "fact"—and yet given the ways that she and many other African American women never separated their faith from their activism and education I should not have been surprised.[2] The realities of Wells's faith, and of her lifelong service as a Sunday school teacher alongside her legacy of activism and organizing, must not be easily dismissed or discounted. In considering Wells as an exemplar of the intersections of religion, education, and social change, for me it is her work as a Sunday school teacher that helps to solidify her contributions. Wells organized and developed classes for young men in particular, with the goal of helping them to grow in their faith and to apply this faith to their condition as Black people in America.

In her autobiography, Wells describes her experiences teaching Sunday school (and not her earlier work as a primary school teacher) as "one of the most delightful periods" of her life in Chicago. She wrote lovingly and with great pride about her class of young men, and of the ways that she attempted to teach and learn the lessons in a "common-sense manner."[3] Here we get a first glimpse of Wells's philosophy of religious education, teaching and learning that were easily understood and applicable to their daily lives.

Wells recounted several instances in which her passionate responses to injustices spilled into the Sunday school classroom and into her admonition of the young men in her classes. For example, in 1908 she described her outrage at three Black people being lynched in Springfield, Illinois. Alongside her outrage at the actual brutality and injustice, Wells could barely hide her dismay at the apathy of her fellow citizens:

> As I wended my way to Sunday school that bright Sabbath day, brooding over what was still going on at our state in the capital, I passed numbers of people out parading in their Sunday finery. None of them seemed to be

worried by the fact of this three days' riot going on less than two hundred miles away.[4]

Instead of continuing with the Sunday school lesson she had planned for the day, Wells spoke to her class about the injustices around them, of the responsibility of Christians to respond, and of their need to show their concern:

> I do not remember what the lesson was about that Sunday, but when I came to myself I found I had given vent to a passionate denunciation of the apathy of our people over this terrible thing. I told those young men that we should be stirring ourselves to see what could be done. When one of them asked, "What can we do about it?" I replied that they could at least get together and ask themselves that question. The fact that nobody seemed worried was as terrible a thing as the riot itself.[5]

In this moment, and in so many others in her life, Wells was clear that to see injustices and do nothing about them was reprehensible. Instead, she regarded it as her Christian duty to call out injustices and to help people organize and strategize as to how to respond to them. This event was also emblematic of Wells and a model of the type of integration of faith and social change, which I've come to describe as essential to radical religious education. Thus, out of this particular event and Sunday school class, Wells helped to establish the *Negro Fellowship League*.[6]

Of course, this was not the only organization she helped establish in response to myriad injustices, nor was it the only time she responded to the call to serve as a Sunday school teacher. Much earlier in her life, while still living in Memphis, Wells began teaching what we can presume to be her first Sunday school class, after reflecting on all that God had done for her. She desired to give back, to do more for the "one who had done so much for [her]."[7] Wells sought out opportunities to teach what she knew about faith and her understanding of what it meant to live fully for Christ. In this Wells reflects her mother's religious zeal and her embodied faith commitments to " 'do something' in the face of 'injustice or discrimination.' "[8] Womanist ethicist Emilie Townes reflects on Wells's decision to become a Sunday school teacher and her understanding of Christianity, writing,

> [Wells's] diary entries of January 1887 reveal a fully developed and unequivocal understanding of moral action and Christian duty. Wells decided to

teach." a Sunday School class to begin to work for God, who had done much for her. She found fault with the way the Bible was taught and preached and hoped to influence her charges "in a small degree to think of better things." She concluded her entry with a covenant plea and commitment to be a Christian in all her acts and a "master in the way of good works."[9]

Her diaries help us give her a fuller sense of the deep zeal Wells had for this work and the challenges she encountered in getting the young men to commit to attending each week. Scattered between her social reflections and her accounts of who visited, she includes sentences about her Sunday school in Memphis, such as the fluctuating attendance (from three to eleven students each week)[10] and her prayers to be able to teach them well, according to the will of God, and not simply by her own strength.[11]

For Wells, there was a particular urgency and commitment to teaching young men; Townes argues that Wells "understood the moral and vocational development of young men as crucial to the social uplift of the African American community."[12] Furthermore, Wells's concern for the faith and Christian development of young men was personal: she had struggled to find the patience to teach and share her faith with her own brother and to help him live fully for God. She wrote,

> But I seem to be a failure so far as my own brother is concerned, for I speak harshly or indifferently and repulsively to him . . . God help me be more careful. . . . Let not my own brother perish while I am laboring to save others![13]

Reflecting much of the evangelical theology of the late nineteenth century,[14] Wells's personal concern for the soul and faith of her brother and of other young people is tied to an understanding of an urgent need not only to confess a belief in God, but also to live fully and morally, to "work for the master."[15] However, we see in Wells not a primarily individualistic faith but a concern for how God calls her, as a Christian, and others to improve the lives and conditions of others. In particular, Wells's diaries contain frequent critiques of the ways in which preachers or ministers (who come to preach at the frequent religious services she attends, across churches in the city of Memphis, both White and Black) are approaching the Bible or teaching people to live according to it.

Wells's Early Life

Wells's lifelong political engagement, activism, and her service as a Sunday School teacher all reflect the powerful influences of her family and their commitment to education and freedom during her childhood. Wells was born in 1862 on a plantation near Holly Springs, Mississippi. Only with emancipation did Wells and her parents become free. Wells's childhood, like that of Cooper and Du Bois to a lesser extent, was dramatically shaped by Radical Reconstruction and the ways in which her parents, Elizabeth and Jim Wells, embraced their newfound freedom and attempted to take hold of all that this postbellum period offered them. Wells's parents fared better than many other newly freed Black people because they had trades. Her father had apprenticed as a carpenter, and her mother had worked as a cook; however, the intersection of her parents' fearless political engagement, their sense of Christian duty, and their commitment to education particularly influenced Wells.

Unlike some other newly freed Black families, her parents could make the space for their children to focus on education and to participate in the schools that had been newly established by Northern White missionaries for the education of Black people. Her autobiography shows she was well aware of her responsibility to become educated:

> Our job was to go to school and learn all we could. The Freedmen's Aid had established [in 1866] one of its schools in our town—it was called Shaw University then, but is now Rust College. My father was one of the trustees and my mother went along to school with us until she learned to read the Bible. After that she visited school regularly to see how we were getting along.[16]

Wells reflected on the way that both of her parents were involved in the education of their children and in supporting the education of members of their Holly Springs community. Wells described her mother not only as a religiously devout woman who valued Sunday school and church attendance for her entire family, but also as one who excelled at raising her children and training them to live, with attention to their education, faith formation, morality, and practical knowledge of how to take care of their home.[17] Wells writes with admiration of both her parents, but particularly of her mother, who modeled for Wells committed faith, education, and service. She described her as

A deeply religious woman, she won the prize for regular attendance at Sunday School, taking the whole brood of six to nine o'clock Sunday school the year before she died. She taught us how to do the work of the home—each had a regular task besides schoolwork, and I often compare her work in training her children to that of other women who had not her handicaps.[18] She was not forty when she died, but she had borne eight children and brought us up with a strict discipline that many mothers who have had educational advantages have not exceeded. She used to tell us how she had been beaten by slave owners and [about] the hard times she had as a slave.[19]

Due to the untimely death of her parents, Wells was only able to attend Rust College until she was sixteen years old. After this, according to historian Mia Bay, Wells's education consisted mostly of "reading the Bible cover to cover and imbibing all the most activist elements of the Judeo-Christian tradition."[20] Yet Wells's childhood was far from idyllic. Before she could even move beyond her "school girl" years, she was struck by tragedy: the devastating and simultaneous loss of both of her parents in the yellow fever epidemic of 1878, and the end of Reconstruction rights/freedoms for Black people. Bay describes this as a loss of "both her parents and the prospect of a brave new world" for Black people.[21] When Wells wrote her autobiography decades later, she returned frequently to this period of Reconstruction and mourning because its impact inspired her. For Wells, her parents represented all of the hopes and bravery of newly freed Black people. She admired their efforts to educate themselves and to prepare themselves to engage as citizens in a society that had gone out of its way to keep them out of politics and civic life. Bay asserts that above all else it was Wells's parents and her memories of the "political dramas" of her early childhood that shaped Wells's "enduring faith in the power of black people to educate themselves and to govern their own destiny."[22]

Teaching out of Necessity

Following the deaths of her parents, Wells began teaching at age sixteen, needing to provide for herself and her five remaining siblings, whom she refused to allow to be separated. Though she began teaching in a rural one-room school near Holly Springs, in 1882 or 1883 she moved to Memphis to teach in the city schools there; while preparing for the teacher exams, she worked in another rural Tennessee school to put bread on the table. It was a difficult task, notes Bay:

> [Teaching] was terrifyingly difficult in the beginning. She taught at the country schools, as she did not qualify to teach at a higher level. She taught mostly ex-slaves and their parents. She saw these people who needed all sorts of education . . . they needed to learn about life, living in a free society. And in the beginning she felt inadequate. But she also filled all of the educational needs and over time she began to feel more able to meet them, but she never felt that teaching was the way to do it.[23]

That Wells's own education had been cut short affected the types of teaching placements available to her and the ways that her teaching career could advance. Wells noted that in spite of her eventual success and hard-won reputation as a superb schoolteacher, she was unwilling to persist in a system and a profession that would not challenge her to work and effect change in more meaningful ways. Wells wrote in her autobiography,

> Although I had made a reputation in school for thoroughness and discipline in the primary grades, I was never promoted above the fourth grade in all my years as a teacher. The confinement and monotony of the primary work began to grow distasteful. The correspondence I had built up in newspaper work gave me an outlet through which to express the real "me" and I enjoyed [my newspaper] work to the utmost.[24]

In fact, wrote Wells, she "never cared for teaching" even though she attempted to be "very conscientious" in her work. But, as was also the case for many other Black women, "There was nothing else to do for a living except menial work, and I could not have made a living at that."[25]

Wells taught public school until 1891. This almost thirteen-year period of teaching was significant and one that helped shape the type of activist that Wells became later in life. It also aligned with her practical need to provide for her siblings while continuing her parents' legacy of valuing faith and education. This trajectory of starting as a teacher and then being dismissed parallels trajectories of later radical religious educators and activists, such as Septima Clark, who started working in public schools but were ousted from these positions (of respectability and Black middle-class life) because of their social and political stances.

Wells continued her activism and her teaching, but in different places. In particular, she continued her teaching as a Sunday school teacher, and her activism, while overlapping with her religious commitments there, expanded primarily to a writing career.[26]

Activist, Writer, and Educator: The Press as Educator

Wells recounts her beginnings as a writer very differently than her beginnings as a teacher. Wells found her way as a writer as part of her budding social life in Memphis. A major turning point was "joining a lyceum composed mainly of teachers of the public schools" in Memphis.[27] Their weekly recitations and conversations included readings from the *Evening Star*, which Wells described as a "spicy journal prepared and read by the editor."[28] After some time, Wells was elected to edit the *Evening Star*. Wells was a natural writer and storyteller and thus both enjoyed writing as a pastime and developed a devoted following of "people who came to hear the *Evening Star* read" at the Lyceum.[29]

Wells was serious about her writing. Many of the things that Wells found concerning about teaching also connected with her work as a writer. For example, she began using her platform in the press to offer many of the practical "things" she had noted while in the classroom that Black families needed, things that many pastors were not giving them in terms of advice and practical help. After editing the *Evening Star*, Wells was invited to contribute to a weekly Christian newspaper, *The Living Way*.[30] Despite her lack of formal training, she realized that she had a zeal for and calling to this work. From early on she had strong opinions about the role of the press and the needs of Black people. Wells noted that she "had an instinctive feeling that the people who had little or no school training should have something coming into their homes weekly which dealt with their problems in a simple, helpful way."[31]

For Wells, writing and producing newspapers were not simply pastimes or supplemental income, but ways to educate and uplift Black people in the United States. Supplemental, because Wells did not quit teaching to pursue writing full time but continued working as a teacher even after she started earning money for her writing and becoming part owner and editor of the Memphis *Free Speech and Headlight*.[32] Wells only stopped formal teaching when she was dismissed after writing an editorial critical of the Memphis Board of Education. She lambasted the conditions in separate (and clearly unequal) colored schools and the type of education and leadership offered to Black families and children.

In reflecting on Wells's transition from teaching in public schools to full-time journalism, we see her pushing the boundaries of what was expected of single women and teachers. In exploring Wells's life, we also begin to expand our understanding of how education functioned for Black people—including seeing the tools beyond formal schooling that were essential to improving the lives of and advocating for change within Black communities. Wells was pioneering and radical not in the ways that many of the other activist-educators included in this work were, but in establishing institutions and organizations to support the flourishing of Black people from all walks of life. Wells was an institution builder, not in the sense of building physical schools for Black people, but because of her work in creating and running Black newspapers.

Wells helps us to understand the educative role of the press, particularly in early African American communities. In part, Wells was able to build upon the early literacy education and to reach those who might not be able to continue going to formal schools. Wells generated access to the news and information that Black communities needed. Her writing also invited White communities to learn more about the conditions of African Americans in the United States.

The connection of the press and education is not unique to Wells. However, I highlight this as a continuation of the ways that she understood the role of teachers in Black communities at the turn of the century. Other early twentieth-century activists and educators also reflect on the ways that the press was significant in the lives and uplift of Black people. For example, Carter G. Woodson credits much of his early interest in Black history and Negro life to his experiences of reading newspapers to illiterate coal miners in West Virginia and engaging with these men in rigorous debates about events ranging from politics to economics.[33] Likewise, Nannie Helen Burroughs used written pamphlets and newsletters to reach the masses of Black Baptist women and saw this work as essential to improving their lives. Black people had been cut off from entire worlds. Black schools, churches, and newspapers often helped to expand their worlds and worldviews, and to provide the type of information and guidance that would help to ameliorate the concerns of these communities.[34]

Antilynching Campaign and Public Pedagogy

As Wells's reputation as an unflinching critic committed to "telling the truth freely" spread, she continued to develop her activist voice as a writer, investigative journalist, and educator. Of all these roles, Wells is most often remembered for her work as an antilynching crusader, particularly for launching one of the first national and international campaigns to shed light on the atrocities of lynching and vigilante justice in the United States. Of course, Wells's vehicles for reporting on this work and for raising awareness of the truth about lynching were the press and the many speaking invitations she received. In 1892, Wells published *Southern Horrors: Lynch Law in All Its Phases*. She continued writing about lynching and myriad other dehumanizing experiences of Black people in the United States, including the exclusion of African Americans from the World's Columbian Exposition hosted in Chicago in 1893. Her longest antilynching work—*A Red Record* (1895)—listed all the known lynchings that took place in the United States between 1892 and 1894.[35]

Wells's research and writing anticipated many of the justice causes of the twenty-first century. Her 1893 pamphlet included chapters on "The Convict Lease System" and "Lynch Law." She critiqued the myriad and layered injustices that are part of the criminal justice system and that further enslaved Black men during the Jim Crow era. Her vast knowledge of the interconnected systems of injustice (what we would now call intersectionality) impressively connected practices of leasing convicts and lynch law, for example, as well as those between so-called mob or vigilante violence and the legal criminal justice systems. She showed how such practices worked hand in hand to maintain White supremacy and disenfranchise Black people. Reading her words almost 130 years later pushes us to wrestle with what could have happened if the United States government had heeded Wells's warnings or if people had rallied around the injustices that she called out at the turn of the twentieth century. Would we still be seeing the harsh effects of the current prison industrial complex now? Would generations of Black people (men, women, and children) still be disproportionately incarcerated and disenfranchised in so many ways?

Wells was also participating in what other education theorists have come to refer to as a type of *public pedagogy* in her writings about lynching and in her earlier articles. Her first example of writing as a type of public pedagogy came when she documented her own experiences of racism and attempted to use the courts to ameliorate her ill treatment after being asked to ride in a segregated car on the train.[36] Public pedagogy has a long and complex definition among education scholars, ranging from the idea of education that takes place outside formal schools (in public), to the idea that education is often conducted with a goal of educating for a common *public* good, and to the connected focus on teaching and educating for public change, often related to social justice and activism.[37] Wells's writing and speeches were public pedagogy in the sense of focusing on education far beyond the formal classroom and in attempting to educate people for change and toward a better, common world. So, when she wrote about lynching, rather than merely recounting actual events she was shedding light on them to empower people to enact real change in response.

Other contemporary religious educators, like Mai Anh Le Tran, outline the contours of public pedagogy by pointing to the ways that both the witnessing of violence and the collective calling attention to this violence are public pedagogy. Tran's description helps us to identify as public pedagogy Wells's writing, investigative reporting, and her work of rallying others. Tran writes (reflecting on her experiences at protests in Ferguson, Missouri) that she "saw bodies employed as public pedagogy—mediums and instruments of instruction for a wide-eyed public."[38] In this light, we see Wells's writing and protesting as an equally powerful part of her contribution to educating Black people and the wider public. Wells's teaching and even her religious, activist education are not narrowly defined by or limited to a formal classroom or Sunday school: she used her larger national platform and journalism to educate as well.

Embodied Activism: Marriage, Motherhood, and Activism

Even in adulthood and after finding her calling to journalism, Wells's life was far from easy. The more that she engaged in public protest, the more endangered she became. Wells was never able to return to Memphis after writing her first exposé on lynching. Her life was threatened, her newspaper office was burned, and her reputation as an "agitator" was solidified. Wells spent time in Washington, DC, and New York before finally settling in Chicago. Chicago served both as a place where Wells continued writing and investigating lynching in the United States, and as one where she could begin to pursue other related causes, including organizing African American women in Chicago to demand the vote and to use it effectively. It was in Chicago that she met Ferdinand Barnett, "a man of similar militancy and complementary temperament, whom she married in 1895."[39]

Even in her personal, familial life, Wells was pathbreaking and radical. Wells continued to defy expectations of women (then and today)—by neither shunning the ideals of true womanhood as a wife and mother that she saw enacted by her mother, nor by fully embracing this role and in so doing departing from public life and her vigorous activism. Marriage and motherhood did not put an end to her activism and organizing. At most, it slowed them a little. Wells-Barnett (the name she chose after marrying) continued traveling and speaking, together with a nurse, after her first son was born. Only with the birth of her second son a year later did she decide to retreat from public life. Her two daughters were born soon after in 1901 and 1904. She gave up her newspaper, of which she was part owner, but she continued to work and spread her influence in local causes and organizations.[40]

In this era of her life, the Sunday school class described in this chapter's opening took place. Part of her rationale for joining Grace Presbyterian Church was the moral obligation she felt as a mother for her children, and particularly her daughters, to be involved in a church that fit her understanding of Christian morality and duty. Wells took seriously her role as a mother and chose to dedicate her energies to the moral and religious formation of her children. She wrote in her autobiography that she chose to

> emulate the "Catholic priest who declared that if he had the training of a child for the first seven years of his life, it would be a Catholic for the rest of his days."[41]

A firm believer in her own values and Protestant religious faith, Wells-Barnett stressed her desire to be there for the "training and control of her child[ren]'s early and most plastic years."[42] Her understanding of motherhood and her commitment to her family shaped the direction of her activism later in life, as she worked with other Black women in Chicago for access to better early childhood education and to continue to organize Black women to vote and to work for change locally and nationally. Wells-Barnett describes her efforts to help create a kindergarten for Black mothers, and the initial resistance she encountered from some of them. They feared that opening a kindergarten specifically for African American children might prevent them from being able to access schools opened and run by White leaders in the Chicago area. Wells-Barnett pushed forward and gained support for the kindergarten but frequently noted the ways in which fear and misinformation kept Black people from launching out and fighting for the things that were most needed in their own communities.

She continued writing about the educational opportunities and disenfranchisement among Black people in Chicago, noting that racism was as entrenched in the North as it was in the South. In an article on the Negro woman in the North, we get another sense of the chaos and difficulty of living both in the North and South during the early twentieth century. In 1910, Wells-Barnett wrote,

> The schoolroom seems to be the only American institution left in which the Negro woman of the North and her children may share equal opportunities; and as she reads the onslaughts being made on the mixed public schools of the North and observes the growing disposition of public school teachers and their White pupils to make it hard for her boy and girl to remain in school, the deliberate effort made to shut them out of the social enjoyment of school life—she wonders how long before the doors of even public schools of the North will be closed against them and they are told to flock by themselves.[43]

Uncompromising Commitment to Change

Wells struggled throughout her life to find a place and organizations in which she felt surrounded by kindred spirits. Bay describes how even after Wells returned from her second successful antilynching campaign in Europe, she was never embraced by White Americans (in the North or the South). Bay describes Wells as being "influential without ever being popular."[44] Others also describe Wells as being "uneasy" in organizations, in spite of the fact that she was part of establishing quite a few of them.[45] For example, Wells was part of the original Niagara Movement but was left out of the original leadership of the NAACP. Her work and national activism were also influential in the eventual merger of women's clubs to form the National Association of Colored Women (in 1896), and yet she was never considered for a national leadership role.[46] Her lack of ongoing leadership and participation in the many organizations she helped found was the result of various forces.

Those included her gender, her lack of formal higher education, which was becoming increasingly popular among the leading elite Black middle class (such as Du Bois and Mary Church Terrell), but most importantly her uncompromising religious and moral convictions.

Many of the critiques launched at Wells by her contemporaries, such as calling her difficult or "a bull in a china shop" because of her temper and passionate commitment to truth and change, cannot be separated from the sexism and expectations of women during her lifetime. Bay starts her biography of Wells by quoting her mentor, Black journalist T. Thomas Fortune: "If Iola [Wells's pen name] were a man, she would be a humming independent in politics. She has plenty of nerve, and is sharp as a steel trap."[47] Bay notes the tendency, even among Wells's admirers, never to compliment her leadership without noting that it did not suit her sex. Sexism undoubtedly circumscribed Wells's career. The critiques about her assertive personality are likewise intricately connected with the gender critiques—and characteristics that would not have been noted in a man. Bay summarizes:

> Whether Wells's career would have indeed taken a different path if she had been a man remains impossible to say . . . Wells had limitations above and beyond her sex when it came to sustaining a following. She often resisted the "restraints of organizations," as a later critic would note. Hardheaded to a fault, and possessed of a temper that she acknowledged to be a "besetting sin," Wells helped build a stunning variety of black organizations . . . only to find herself comfortable in none of them. More radical than most of her contemporaries, she also had no gift for compromise and often departed in a huff from the organizations that she helped to create, her famous temper flaring when negotiations did not go her way. As a result, her contemporaries considered her difficult.[48]

Little has been written about Wells in terms of the collective organizing tradition of Black church women, so I was hard pressed to find descriptions or analyses of Wells working among and with other Black women, as was traditional in Black Christian women's groups, even though we have abundant records of her activism, organizing, and church membership. Instead, most often we hear a recurring narrative about Wells being uneasy in these groups or only being in churches or organizations for a short time before she lost patience and left.

Yet rather than seeing Wells-Barnett as an outsider or outlier, I consider her to be a part of a larger tradition of independent, freethinking women activists and organizers who often did not conform to societal expectations. Instead, as we will see in many of the other women activist educators in this book and throughout the twentieth century, many did not conform to gendered expectations and were often labeled assertive or difficult. Wells and others like her, including Nannie Helen Burroughs, had an uncompromising sense of who they were in Christ and what they were called to do to help Black people. Reflecting on her activism later in life, Bay notes that Wells, as was her usual custom, relied on the "Scriptures and black America's long freedom struggle" to help guide her work. As noted in the opening vignette of this section, Wells-Barnett employed scripture and her understanding of the power of God to effect change in this world to encourage the falsely accused prisoners to pray for their liberation now. In effect, by admonishing them to "pray to live" Wells was teaching them (and us) to live and to connect our spiritual strivings with our current fights to transform society.

Wells-Barnett opened the last chapter of her autobiography with a reference to Isaiah 62:6–9, writing that "Eternal vigilance is the price of liberty."[49] There, she offers a scathing critique of the lack of such vigilance in the increasingly well-organized African American middle-class societies and groups. Even at the end of her life, Wells-Barnett was dissatisfied and uncertain about the ways that her work would continue, and whether those left in charge of advancing Black civil rights would remain vigilant. Wells-Barnett died in 1931 of kidney disease. While her long-standing profile as an uncompromising and vigilant advocate for change was never paralleled, her life and work inspired many other women activists and educators who came alongside and after her.[50] Instead of continuing the narratives about Wells as difficult or even uncomfortable in organizations, I place Wells's work and legacy in conversation with other strong-willed women like Nannie Helen Burroughs, who were similarly criticized for attempting to live fully into their understanding of the call of Christ and their Christian duty as Black women.

4

Nannie Helen Burroughs

May 2, 1879–May 20, 1961

Nannie Helen Burroughs was a visionary leader and a fierce proponent of Christian virtues and education, particularly education that empowered women and girls to live and make a living. Opal Easter's biography gives us a snapshot of Burroughs's teaching and of her commanding presence. Easter includes in her book interviews with a few of the young women who attended Burroughs's *National Training School*. One of her students, later known as Mrs. Carnegia Gordon, recounts the lasting impact of Burroughs on her life, even though she spent only one year (1928–1929) at the school. Gordon noted,

> Burroughs mingled with the students and knew all of them by name. She would talk to them, asking about parents, or ill relatives or their grades. She usually joined them for breakfast and lunch if she was in town. She attended their assemblies . . . Burroughs also gave each student a small gift at Christmas.
>
> . . . Burroughs always smiled . . . [was] tall and very erect. She had a "presence." She wore beautiful blouses with puffy sleeves and high collars, and long dark skirts. She was a stickler for cleanliness.[1]

Gordon's description of Burrows notes the ways in which everyday interactions with Burroughs became a lasting legacy. Easter also documented the invaluable lessons Gordon learned by attending this all-Black women's enclave shaped by Burroughs:

> She learned comradeship, working together, and sharing. She learned Black history and Black pride. She also learned how to walk with her head up and to be proud of her name. Burroughs told students to walk with their heads up as though "they were the Queen of Ethiopia." She would not allow the

Teaching to Live. Almeda M. Wright, Oxford University Press. © Oxford University Press 2024.
DOI: 10.1093/oso/9780197663424.003.0005

girls to use nick-names; she did not believe in them. She said that they must be proud of their names.[2]

Why would Burroughs tell students studying domestic science to walk as if they were the Queen of Ethiopia? What does this teach us about Burroughs and her legacy as a religious leader and educator? Clearly Burroughs was instilling in Black women and girls a sense of pride and self-respect, as well as practical skills that would empower them to work and live in ways that never left them beholden to anyone. Easter's description helps to capture the ways in which Burroughs's school and work went far beyond providing *industrial* training or skills to Black domestics. She demanded that her students know who they are and take pride in knowing their own name and where they had come from, both in a cultural and religious sense. Even if the school was ostensibly about learning the ins and outs of domestic science and labor, it also trained women to take pride in their race and heritage. Burroughs did not necessarily set out to "dignify" domestic work, but her calling was a pragmatic calling: she understood that if a great deal of Black women and girls were going to have to labor as domestics, they should do so with pride and the best training possible.

Though Burroughs is probably best known for her work as a school founder, she was much more than this. Years before she realized her dream of opening a school for women and girls, Burroughs's skills as an orator and writer made a way for her and launched her into national debates and social justice campaigns. One of Burroughs's first national speeches was a call to allow Black Baptist women to organize their work and expand their efforts in local congregations, as part of their Christian service and duty. Burroughs boldly proclaimed,

> We come not to usurp thrones nor to sow discord, but to so organize and systematize the work that each church may help through a Woman's Missionary Society and not be made poorer thereby. . . . We realize that to allow these gems to lie unpolished longer means a loss to the denomination.
>
> For a number of years there has been a righteous discontent, a burning zeal to go forward in his name among the Baptist women of our churches . . . the work is too great and laborers too few for us to stand by while like Trojans the brethren at the head of the work under the convention toil unceasingly.

. . . We unfurl our banner upon which is inscribed this motto, "The World for Christ. Woman, Arise, He calleth for Thee." Will you as a pastor and friend of missions help by not hindering these women when they come among you to speak and to enlist the women of your church? . . . Surely, women somehow have had a very important part in the work of saving this redeemed earth.[3]

Like Wells, from a young age Burroughs was a force to be reckoned with. Burroughs addressed the National Baptist Convention in 1900, at the age of twenty-one, and in no uncertain terms told the male leadership that women were just as capable and just as called to the service of God as anyone else. Historian Kelisha Graves argues that it was this early speech entitled " 'How the Women are Hindered from Helping' that defined what would become Burroughs's major life agenda: the uplift and education of Black women and girls."[4] Essential to Burroughs's project was her understanding of the call of Christ to service and her unflinching ability to stand up to anyone or anything that attempted to thwart the mission of Christ. Like Anna Julia Cooper,[5] Burroughs had to entreat Black men to "get out of the way" of Black women and the work that they were called to do. At the same time and in parallel denominations, we see Cooper and Burroughs appealing to the religious zeal of male clergy to support (or at least not hinder) the work of Black women. Historian Evelyn Brooks Higginbotham writes that "Black Baptist women encouraged an aggressive womanhood that felt personal responsibility to labor, no less than men, for the salvation of the world."[6] Burroughs felt this responsibility deeply and was a leading example of this type of *aggressive womanhood* that took seriously the urgent need for women to work for God. An overwhelming passion and missionary zeal fueled these pioneering women activists and religious leaders.

Burroughs stands out among the other activist-educators we have explored thus far in part for her commitment to working for change within Black Baptist circles and for empowering women for leadership and service through their local churches and denominations. Even in this speech, Burroughs never denounced her Baptist roots or the work of male ministers and pastors. Instead, she was urging the men to help women to become better equipped and trained to lead and teach—to be allowed to do their part in and for their churches, denomination, and by extension their race and the world. So it is already in her early life that we see the intersection of Christian faith, pride in oneself, and the domestic work of Black women that shaped the direction of Burroughs's life, activism, and eventually the vision for the school she founded.

Early Education and Activism

Nannie Helen Burroughs was born just seventeen years after Ida B. Wells. However, she was born after Emancipation, after Reconstruction gains had been overturned, and thus into a very different world. Attending to the family history of each educator helps us to recognize the particular path by which they came to activist education and were nurtured in their faith. As we have already noted, parents, either absent or present, are important in the narratives of each of these religious activist-educators. Just as the Reconstruction era politics and civic engagement of Wells's parents shaped Wells's life, so too was Burroughs's life shaped by her parents but in more complicated and sometimes indirect ways. Burroughs was the daughter of formerly enslaved parents. John Burroughs was a country farmer and itinerant Baptist preacher, and following Emancipation his family worked to become landowners. Though this gave her father's family some advantages, Burroughs's early life was nonetheless marked by financial instability.

Higginbotham describes Burroughs's reflections on her early childhood and her parents, noting both her respect for her mother's hardworking, independent, sweet, and proud nature and her disdain for her father's shortcomings as a "breadwinner," for he worked only sporadically and did not earn a steady income.[7] Even though John Burroughs had attended what became Virginia Union University in Richmond, he never was able to secure a full-time pastoral appointment and had to rely on his parents and sister to supplement his income.[8] Higginbotham includes Nannie's description of her father's family thinking "he was 'too smart' for ordinary work" and that her father evidently "concurred in their opinion."[9]

When Nannie was barely five years old, her only sibling, Maggie, died.[10] Soon after, in 1883 her mother Jennie (Poindexter) Burroughs, decided to leave rural Virginia for Washington, DC, in hopes of giving her remaining daughter better opportunities. Little information survives about Burroughs's father after she left rural Virginia, not even a mention of why her father did not move with them.[11] What is clear is that Burroughs's mother had a dream for their lives and knew that education was essential to it. And so, she made sacrifices, including moving in with her sister in DC and finding work as a domestic to provide for Nannie.

By moving to Washington, DC, Burroughs entered the world of educated Black elites, an enclave of private and public schools that were led by and produced Black leaders. Burroughs attended M Street School,[12] from which she graduated with honors in 1896. Though that was a few years before Anna Julia Cooper served as the school's principal, Nannie became connected with Cooper and named her as one of her role models for Black women educators.[13] M Street School, as we noted in chapter 1, was unique in offering its students both classical and technical education and for support them in pursuing the vocation of their choosing.

While at M Street, Burroughs studied domestic science and business. She also started the Harriet Beecher Stowe Society, a club in which students worked on their literary and public speaking skills.[14] In her early education we thus find many of the seeds of her later work—of her writing of plays and her long career in public speaking, as well as her desire to cultivate these skills and opportunities for the students at her school, even for those who considered this outside the realm of what was required or necessary for industrial or domestic sciences education.

Her choice to combine domestic science and business in high school is perhaps surprising at first blush. But it is important to recognize the ways in which Burroughs was attempting to defy classification and expectations of Black women even in her high school career. Higginbotham has written about the ways that Burroughs had to counter the advice even of her mother (and her mother's White employer) to take the safer route of domestic service, and to give up any ideas that there might be a career path for Black women in accounting or secretarial work.[15]

Burroughs's desire after graduation was to work as a domestic science teacher in the Washington, DC, schools. That dream was thwarted by the intracommunal politics and colorism that plagued the area's Black elite circles.[16] In reflecting later on this early rejection, Burroughs noted that it became part of the catalyst for creating her own school and spending her life providing opportunities for those Black women who were not well connected and might otherwise not be able to get an education or find meaningful wage-earning work. Burroughs wrote,

> It broke me up at first. I had my life all planned out, to settle down in Washington with my mother, do that pleasant work, draw a good salary

and be comfortable for the rest of my life. . . . An idea stuck out from the suffering of that disappointment that I would someday have a school here in Washington that school politics had nothing to do with, and that would give all sorts of girls a fair chance, without political pull, to help them over-come whatever handicaps they might have. It came to me like a flash of light, and I knew I was to do that thing (establish a school) when the time came. But I couldn't do it yet, so I just put the idea away in the back of my head and left it there.[17]

Burroughs was resourceful and knew that she did not have the option of wallowing in her disappointment or even of not finding alternative work. Burroughs was able to find work in Philadelphia as an associate editor at the *Christian Banner*. While it is not clear exactly how Burroughs gained this job, a family member suggested that it was most likely through her pastor, Rev. Walter Brooks at the Nineteenth Street Baptist Church.[18] The *Christian Banner* was a Baptist newspaper, and here Burroughs was able to expand her early Christian work in and for her denomination. In spite of her desire to teach, this "alternative job" also defied the limited expectations of the type of work that Black women could do at that time. Most often, Black women were limited to teaching in Black schools or working in domestic service. The position at the *Christian Banner* employed her clerical skills and her love of writing, both of which she had been cultivating at M Street School. Her work at the *Christian Banner* also expanded her connections within the larger Baptist world.

Yet Burroughs certainly did not move seamlessly from high school to ed-itorial and clerical work, denominational leadership, and school founding. Burroughs's early work history had several more twists and turns, each im-portant in shaping her commitment to provide education and training for Black women of all backgrounds. For example, while working for the *Christian Banner*, Burroughs also studied for a civil service exam, and, having scored well on the exam, she returned to Washington with the hopes of be-coming a clerk. Again racism thwarted her dreams when the city informed her that it was not hiring "colored clerks."[19] Again Burroughs had to find a different way and she worked cleaning an office building before finding work as a "bookkeeper and editorial secretary for Rev. L. G. Jordan . . . the cor-responding secretary to the National Baptist Convention's Foreign Mission Board."[20]

Educator and historian Kelisha Graves notes that "The four years fol-lowing her graduation seemed to have been filled with dashed hopes and odd jobs. Nevertheless, she maintained a steadfast desire to one day start an institution where she could provide the kind of opportunities that seemed to consistently elude her."[21] The odd series of jobs she held reminds us not only that Burroughs never had the luxury of not working or earning a wage, but also that her experiences of watching her mother, aunt, and grandmother having to work to provide for themselves shaped her work ethic, too. Instead of viewing these jobs as odd or simply noting the variety in her early résumé, I see each of these positions and her struggle to find work she desired as what helped to shape Burroughs, what drove her to create her school, and what motivated her advocacy of women who were not well connected *and* who didn't have the luxury of not working. Burroughs, like Cooper and Wells and many other activist-educators, was called to and driven to the work they did because of the harsh realities of their lives. They had to build institutions and advocate for themselves and so many others like them—who were caught in systems and structures of oppression—simply by nature of their birth.

Burroughs's resourcefulness and work ethic helped to connect with and expand her field of influence as she worked for Jordan. So too did her continued work in Baptist churches, work fueled by her understanding of the importance of having Black women do Christian missionary work. Around 1900, Burroughs moved to Louisville, as the headquarters for the National Baptist Convention (NBC) Foreign Mission Board had moved there. Education scholar Shante Jackson notes that this move to Louisville was fortuitous, affording Burroughs the opportunity to connect with Black Baptist denominational leaders and to work in Black elite circles that would have shunned her back in Washington, DC.[22]

While working in Louisville, Burroughs began to test out her vision of opening a school to train Black women and girls. It was also there that she created the Women's Industrial Club, an organization that attended to the interests and needs of working women in Kentucky. Easter notes that it "provided day and evening classes for the women in bookkeeping, shorthand, typing, sewing, cooking, child-care, hygiene, sanitation, cleaning, and handicrafts."[23] To finance the activities and to help the women raise enough money to buy a house to host all of the club's classes and activities, Burroughs also designed strategies like selling lunches to Black workers in the area and requiring a modest membership fee (of 10 cents).[24]

It was this same ingenuity and organizing skill set that Burroughs drew upon in Louisville to rally support both for a national school for women and girls, and for the work of women in the National Baptist Convention. In 1900, Burroughs delivered her rousing address to the "parent body" of the NBC in support of a separate women's convention.[25] She succeeded where many of her predecessors had been faced with rigid opposition or retracted promises and was elected as the corresponding secretary of the newly formed Woman's Convention (WC)—a position that wielded considerable power to address and represent the ideas of the Woman's Convention to the denomination's growing membership.

It was also through the Woman's Convention that she began to share publicly her vision for a National Training School for Women and Girls. She first raised the issue in 1901 and continued to raise it annually while working as the corresponding secretary. Eventually, thanks to her now familiar persistence, Burroughs garnered support for the school. The Woman's Convention established a committee in 1904 to work out the plans for the school and to start fundraising efforts (including a charge to all of the WC officers to raise $100 each before the next annual meeting).[26] The NBC came on board a few years later, and the National Training School Committee was formed in 1906. Burroughs's vision was beginning to become a reality. Yet the forming of this committee represented only nominal and sometimes inconsistent support for the National Training School for Women and Girls from the NBC, with NBC presidents in subsequent years vacillating, and often trying to take control of the school and the funds of the Woman's Convention.

None of this deterred Burroughs. She pressed forward, finding a location for her school and raising the money for the down payment and the remaining cost of the land, so that the school could open debt-free in 1909.[27] Burroughs described her experiences of having to raise money for the school and of overcoming many obstacles to open it by noting the ways that God provided at every turn:

> I went out and raised it [the money]. From my own people . . . I'd prayed about this thing for a long time. I wanted to be sure God was leading me. I felt God wanted me to go ahead, and I knew if I did what I could and trusted Him, He would see it through. And He did . . .
>
> And of course, we had nothing to open it [the school] with. So, I continued to work in Louisville for two years until I was able to raise and pay the rest of the $6000 and the $500 to the lawyer. More than once failure peeped in on me but God always slammed the door in his face.[28]

The National Training School for Women and Girls stands out because it was started by a Black woman and supported primarily by Black people. This was in contrast to many other schools for Black people during the late nineteenth and early twentieth century, which were either started by White missionaries or significantly indebted to White financial contributions for their success. This of course was only possible because Burroughs was a strategic fundraiser and was able to use her networks of Black Baptist women to raise funds to pay off the initial loan for the school land and building before beginning to enroll students.[29]

Burroughs wanted the school not to be exclusively for one denomination or class of women, but to be open to all women. While there was an egalitarian vision for the founding of the school, Burroughs maintained strict standards about acceptance to and attendance at the school; she only accepted students of the highest character and Christian morals. Burroughs intentionally located the school in Washington, DC. She wanted it to be a national school, and she knew that it would greatly benefit the numerous Black women who were already flocking to DC as domestic laborers each year. Beyond these pragmatic reasons for locating the school in Washington, no doubt she also located it in the place whose layers of racism and internalized oppression had prevented her and so many other Black women from getting the education that would have helped them chart their own courses.

It takes a special kind of person to start an institution, but it was particularly arduous as a woman—and a Black woman at that—to build a school that would have a lasting impact on her community. The difficulty of the task did not sway Burroughs. Instead, as Audrey Thomas McCluskey wrote, Burroughs (and other pioneering women school founders) "place[d] faith in God and themselves and [brought] about change by building institutions of learning."[30] McCluskey notes that there were several Black women who took up this task, including those featured in this text, and others who are less well known or celebrated. She points toward these women as exemplars of the "great importance attached to education for race uplift as well as the fact that women assumed leadership in providing it."[31]

Burroughs's Educational Philosophy and Curriculum

Burroughs did not stop organizing once her school was open. She was equally (if not more) intentional about the curriculum of the school—an interweaving of a Christian missionary vision and a curriculum that was decidedly pragmatic in its approach to education and the training of Black women and girls. Her earliest articulation of the mission of the school thus included the training of women missionaries, the preparation of women "as teachers of the Word of God in our Sunday Schools," and training women to become more capable homemakers and domestic workers.[32]

While many people, including some elite Black intellectuals, eschewed domestic labor, Burroughs knew intimately that Black women needed to earn money and realized that work in the domestic sector was a way to Black women's financial survival and independence. Therefore, the focus of her National Training School for Women and Girls was on equipping women and girls with these practical skills. Her commitment to educating Black women for actual jobs and wage earning was founded on a much broader philosophy and sense of urgency about this domestic problem, as she called it. As early as 1902 (seven years before she founded the school), Burroughs was writing about the importance of training Black women in the domestic sciences and the need to eradicate the contempt that many Black people themselves felt toward domestic labor. She described the

> peculiar condition under which women are living and laboring without the knowledge of the secrets of thrift, or of true scientific methods in which the mind has been awakened, and hands made capable thereby to give the most efficient services. It is a condition of indifference on the part of our working women as to their needs to how we may so dignify labor that our services may become indispensable on the one hand and Negro sentiment will cease to array itself against the "working girls" on the other hand. It is a question as to how we may receive for our services compensation commensurate with the work done. The solution of this problem will be the prime factor in the salvation of Negro womanhood, whose salvation must be attained before the so-called race problem can be solved. The training of Negro women is absolutely necessary, not only for their own salvation and the salvation of the race, but because the hour in which we live demands it.[33]

In this early speech, Burroughs carefully outlined the need to dignify the domestic work of Black women so that they would actually be employable,[34] be able to earn a fair wage, and be respected among their own people for their hard work. However, here Burroughs is further outlining her conviction that addressing the practical needs and training of Black women was essential to any program or project geared toward ameliorating the "problems" of the "Negro race." Recognizing the situation through what might today be called an intersectional womanist analysis, Burroughs knew that racial uplift could not occur by attending to Black men only nor by discounting the centuries of domestic labor that Black women had provided in the United States.

Burroughs had no sympathy for the educated Black elite who felt that they were too good or "too educated" for domestic work. In a scathing critique of the hypocrisy of shunning service work, she wrote,

> Our intelligent Negroes, even though they may not have bread to eat, in many cases shun service work. . . . The race whose women have not learned that industry and self-respect are the only guarantees of a true character will find itself bound by ignorance and violence or fettered with chains of poverty. There is a growing tendency among us to almost abhor women who work at service for a living. If we hold in contempt women who are too honest, industrious and independent, women whose sense of pride is too exalted to be debased by idleness, we will find our women becoming more and more slothful in this matter of supporting themselves. Our "high-toned" notions as to the kind of positions educated people ought to fill have caused many women who cannot get anything to do after they come out of school to loaf rather than work for an honest living, declaring to themselves and acting it before others, that they were not educated to live among pots and pans.

She ends with a flourish:

> None of us may have been educated for that purpose, but educated women without work and the wherewithal to support themselves and who have declared in their souls that they will not stoop to toil are not worth an ounce more to the race than ignorant women who have made the same declarations.[35]

More than Trade Education

Burroughs's understanding of the importance of dignifying service work and offering training so that Black women could be successful at this work are a distinguishing focus of her radical and transformative curriculum. However,

Burroughs's understanding of what was required for the education of domestic laborers was never narrowly conceived. The National Training School for Women and Girls, from its opening in 1909 forward, centered on a philosophy of "the Three Bs—The Holy Bible, The Bathtub, and The Broom."[36] According to Opal Easter, "The Bible was a guide to everyday Christian living (Clean Lives). The Bathtub symbolized personal cleanliness (Clean Bodies) and the Broom symbolized cleanliness of the environment (Clean Homes)."[37] Burroughs's emphasis on "cleanliness" was not simply or primarily for appearances or even respectability (though she emphasized that). Her combination of Victorian era values was coupled with her understanding of upright, moral, Christian living—both in the service of communal uplift. In a later essay, Burroughs eloquently expounds on the importance of these:

> The Negro can actually use the bathtub, the Bible, and the broom—weapons and emblems of health, righteousness, and industry, and make of himself and his environment things of loveliness and beauty. It is within him—within his grasp—within his power—within his group. If he uses them religiously, the race will "rise and shine."[38]

A school brochure (from 1956) reiterates this interconnection in the focus of the school and adds the 3Cs of Culture, Character, and Christian Education, noting the need to focus on these in support of the work of the three Bs.[39] Feminist scholar and educator Victoria Wolcott observes that

> By incorporating industrial education with training in morality, religion, and cleanliness, school founder Nannie Helen Burroughs and her staff attempted to resolve a conflict central to the lives of African-American women: their role as wage laborers in ghettoized service occupations, and their role as guardians of the community and models for "the race."[40]

This need to attend to the reality that innumerable Black women were working as domestic laborers and Burroughs's understanding that regardless of one's occupation, all Black women were called to work for Christ *and* called to participate in "uplifting the race" meant that the range of subjects offered at her school was vast. Indeed, so was her mission.

Wolcott suggests that part of what was taking place at the National Training School was a shifting and expansion of the "respectable" roles of women to include the home as well as "the community and the work place."[41] However, even this expansion does not fully capture the ways in which Burroughs's vision and expectations also included expanding the spheres of women's work globally and spiritually—to be missionaries and Christian leaders at home and abroad. Burroughs's self-understanding and starting place could never separate her sense of calling to serve Christ from her work as an educator training Black women. Even her discussions of racial uplift are intricately connected with advancing the cause of Christ and empowering Black people to live fully into who God created them to be.

For Burroughs, domestic labor and trade education were not simply about providing manual skills. Social education researcher Sarah Bair helpfully frames the complexity of Burroughs's curriculum when she writes,

> Given Burroughs's emphasis on practical education, the curriculum at her school reflected a surprisingly classical flavor. In addition to their trade preparation, all girls took academic courses in English, history, mathematics, health and physical education, economics, language (French or Latin), psychology, science, civics, and public speaking. Students completing the junior college course also took sociology, law (business), and art. Undated lesson plans and samples of student work show that students studied writers such as Shakespeare, Wordsworth, Browning, and Austin, as well as the Greek and Roman civilizations. . . . The NTS received praise from advocates of both trade and classical schools.[42]

Many might wonder about Burroughs's inclusion of "classical" subjects in addition to trade education. However, given Burroughs's own education at M Street high school, which offered both domestic sciences and college preparatory education, and her decision to take a domestic science and business track, she knew the value of this more expansive curriculum. Also, in minutes from a 1942 faculty meeting, we find that Burroughs outlined and justified this expansive nature of the curriculum to her teachers, saying, "This is a trade school, but we can't teach a trade without academic background . . . therefore, for that purpose only, do we offer the literary subjects that we have in order to round out the necessary qualifications for useful citizenship."[43] While Burroughs was clear that hers was not a "college preparatory" school, she was equally clear that any girl attending her school should leave with a stronger sense of pride in herself and in her ability to work and be a leader in her community.

Black History and Racial Pride

Burroughs's school was pioneering, even among Black schools, in its early inclusion of courses on Black history. As with all things, Burroughs's commitment to teaching Black history was also intricately connected to her understanding of what God wanted for Black people and how they could participate in their own betterment. For example, in a 1927 article Burroughs outlined the ways in which God was calling Black people to work *with* God to improve their lives. With her characteristic assurance in God's ability to work on her behalf and on behalf of her community, she wrote,

> God wants to help the Negro work out his own salvation. The Negro need not be skeptical as to the outcome, because the Almighty is at His best when He is working with an individual or race to prove that the weapons of His warfare are not carnal, but spiritual. . . . Preachers, teachers, leaders, welfare workers ought to address themselves to the supreme task of teaching the entire race to glorify what it has—its face (its color); its place (its homes and communities); its grace (its spiritual endowment). If the Negro does it, there is no earthly force that can stay him.[44]

This speech demonstrates not only Burroughs's commitment to teaching and learning Black history; it also helps paint a picture of how glorifying and taking pride in what Black people had done undergirded her understanding of how true and lasting transformation would take hold among Black people.

In her endeavors, Burroughs supported and connected with other Black educators, including Carter G. Woodson, later using his Black history textbooks in her school. In turn, Woodson often wrote editorials in support of her and the type of women who graduated from her school.[45] Theirs was a friendship of mutual support, one that pushed both of them to go beyond a simplistic understanding of the type of education that should be available for Black people, and Black women and girls in particular.

Yet Burroughs's (and Woodson's) work in teaching Black history did not go unchallenged. In the early twentieth century (and in some ways still today) their efforts to teach the history of Black people in the United States and around the globe aroused suspicions and even put Burroughs and the National Training School under government surveillance. Sarah Bair described how, during World War I, Burroughs's and Woodson's interest in Black history and their anti-segregation activism caused them both to be targets of the federal surveillance program that also plagued anti-lynching activist and war critic Ida B. Wells-Barnett. . . . [T]he Military Intelligence Division (MID)—a branch of the U.S. Army and the precursor to the Central Intelligence Agency—first began monitoring Burroughs's activities and opening her mail in 1917 because she had been critical of President Wilson. That same year the MID, which considered the study of Black history potentially anti-American, began monitoring Woodson's Association for the Study of Negro Life and History (ASNLH) and its Journal of Negro History.[46]

Burroughs did not change her school's curriculum, she did not temper the values that she taught her students, nor did she slow her activism in the wider community in response to such surveillance. Burroughs was modeling the type of leadership that she expected of her students and for which she trained them. Therefore, her curriculum included and required students to develop wage-earning skills as well as leadership skills, including religious studies, Black history, public speaking, and current events as part of their focus on social education.[47]

The Ballot, the Dollar, and the Bible: Political Change

Much has been written about Burroughs's emphasis on respectability and attempting to work for change by addressing the Black community internally (often through harsh criticism).[48] Her emphasis was typically on the need for individual Black people to "better themselves" and to attempt to refute the racism. Higginbotham writes of the prevalent "respectability politics" of this era and of the ways that the emphasis on cleanliness, thrift, proper conduct, and so forth "often blamed Blacks for their victimization."[49] Burroughs was a fierce proponent of respectability politics and of helping Black women learn how to offer the best home life for Black children, writing about the importance of what is taught at home for countering the effects of racism:

Men and women are not made on trains and on streetcars. If in our homes there is implanted in the hearts of our children, of our young men and of our young women, the thought that they are what they are, not by environment, but of themselves, this effort [of racist] to teach a lesson of inferiority will be futile.[50]

We must, however, look beyond respectability to see more fully the complexity of what is taking place through the activism of African American women in the early twentieth century. Burroughs's long activist career included but went far beyond advocating for respectable homes and personas. She consistently made intersectional analyses and suggested multilayered approaches to engaging in the wider community and to responding to injustices. Her efforts in forming the Woman's Convention helped to create "the largest collectivity of Black women in America" at that time.[51] Through the Woman's Convention, as Higginbotham notes, Burroughs and the other women had created a discursive space where women of all classes gathered and where their voices were "neither silent nor subordinate to men."[52] Therefore, forming the Woman's Convention also helped Burroughs and the women address the "need for collective self-criticism, in order to eradicate inequalities and exclusions within the Black community itself."[53] In other words, Burroughs's activism was directed at the racism perpetuated by White people, as well as at the sexism, classism, and colorism that was rampant within the Black community.

Burroughs did not fit neatly into one category, nor could her activism. For example, the Woman's Convention created a complex platform in 1913, which outlined "the pressing needs of Black Americans" for

1. Well-built, sanitary dwellings . . .
2. Equal accommodation on common carriers [meaning trains, buses, etc.].
3. [The f]ranchise for every [adult] Negro—North, South, East, and West—who is an intelligent and industrious citizen.
4. Equal treatment in the courts.
5. Equal division of school funds.
6. Lynching stopped.
7. Convict lease system broken up and . . . humane treatment of Negro prisoners.[54]

The list includes matters pertaining to personal health and well-being as well as to political engagement and equal treatment under the law. It also reflects the work of Burroughs and the Woman's Convention in supporting antilynching legislation proposed by the NAACP and advocating for campaigns to increase voter education.[55] Again, Burroughs did not separate her political work from her Christian service—and the Woman's Convention called for similar change. Among the latter was a 1919 call for a national Sunday of fasting and prayer to protest the "undemocratic and un-Christian spirit of the United States as shown by its discriminating and barbarous treatment of its colored people."[56]

Burroughs's efforts to effect change spread from and much further than the Baptist Woman's Convention and her school. She was involved in a dizzying array of clubs and organizations. Her activism on behalf of women was both political and intersectional; witness her involvement in creating the National Association of Wage Earners in 1921, work not only to dignify domestic labor, but also to push the boundaries of what was expected by organizing "a historic labor union for African American domestic workers."[57]

Similarly, Burroughs worked tirelessly to organize women voters, first as part of the long battle for women's suffrage and, once ratified, to encourage women to make effective use of the ballot. Like most African Americans during the early 1900s, she was a member of the Republican party and in 1924 organized the *National League of Republican Colored Women* (NLRCW) to unify the efforts of Black women voters.[58] The league reminded women voters that

> Since Negro women have the ballot, they must not under-value it. They must study municipal problems—men and measures, parties and principles. The Race is doomed unless Negro women take an active part in local, state, and national politics. They must oppose parties and candidates opposed to equal citizenship. They must organize to fight discrimination and class legislation. The must not sell their votes. They must use them to elect the right brand of Americans to office.[59]

Burroughs was elected inaugural president of the NLRCW, along with Mary Church Terrell (treasurer), Maggie Walker, Ida B. Wells Barnett (as head of the publicity committee), and Charlotte Hawkins Brown (member of the Executive Committee).[60]

Burroughs wrote frequent editorials in her role as corresponding secretary and for other Black periodicals, urging the Black community to engage the political process and by extension to transform their lives. One of Burroughs's most popular editorials was entitled "Ballot and Dollar Needed to Make Progress, Not Pity."[61] In it, Burroughs argued for the strategic employment of the "Dollar and the Ballot" in protesting racism and advancing Black people. She recognized both the economic and political power of Black people and was advocating strategies of boycotts of racist businesses and collective strategizing that would be used for generations to come, including during the civil rights movement.

Burroughs responded to what she described as a "self-pitying, sychophantic, poetic, prattle," which asked the question of what would become of the "Negro Race." Burroughs's response left no doubt that a way forward and through oppressive structures would never be won by attempting to win the empathy or pity of the broader community. Her vision for social change was decidedly a program of self-help; as she wrote, "Mr., Mrs., or Miss Hazel asks poetically, 'Shall no one lend a hand?' NO! The Negro has his two hands and from now on he will get what he wants."[62] Burroughs's editorial compared the Bible narrative of the liberation of the children of Israel and the way that God asked Moses, "What is in your hand?" Burroughs argued that Moses did not yet understand the significance and power of the rod that was in his hand, and that it was only in using the overlooked thing in his hand that he was able to liberate the children of Israel. Likewise, she admonished her community in 1934 to use what was in their hands to take hold of what they needed. Burroughs wrote,

> The Negro has enough ballots in his hands and enough spending change in his jeans to get what he needs and to get him where he should go. The ballot and the dollar are the shield and the sword for any people in a democracy. . . . When the Negro has the ballot, he has the one thing that the white man fears. When he has the dollar he has the only earthly thing that the white man worships. The ballot is the Negro's sacred, blood bought heritage; the dollar is his economic sweat bought possession. Instead of whining about what the white man is doing to him, the Negro can take his ballot and do or undo him at the ballot box. Instead of fussing about what the white man is not doing for him, he can spend his dollar where he can be employed to do something for himself. It isn't what white people are doing to the Negro that counts against him half as much as what he is not doing for himself with what he has.[63]

Through her powerful skills as a writer and speaker with her organizing skills, Burroughs created a fierce toolkit for her activism and to call Black people through their own agency to live fully into who they could be.

The Worker: Educational Curriculum for Black Christian Women

Even before she was able to fulfill her vision of starting a school, Burroughs's attention to the training and uplift of Black women always included a parallel emphasis on making sure that women had access to resources to organize and educate on the local church level. Burroughs understood the importance of having empowering, well-crafted, and suitable instructional materials and resources in Black churches and of local Black women supporting their churches' missionary and educational work. As early as 1902 in her role as corresponding secretary to the Woman's Convention, Burroughs was taking steps for "Black Christian women to have access to literature and teaching materials in order to prepare themselves to be leaders in the churches and organizations."[64] Burroughs responded to convention members' requests by providing materials on a wide range of topics. Those materials she either curated from trade presses or wrote herself. Among the latter was *The Worker* magazine; she began sending out subscriptions to it in 1912.[65]

The Worker was relaunched in 1934 with the help of a White missionary named Una Roberts Lawrence and the Women's Missionary Union of the Southern Baptist Convention, now transformed into a quarterly "missionary magazine and teaching tool."[66] It sold for 50 cents a year and noted clearly that it was "issued quarterly for the Woman's Convention, Auxiliary to the National Baptist Convention."[67] The first quarterly volume, produced in the midst of the Great Depression, included articles ranging from "The American Standard" to "The Bible, a Cure for Depression," as well as prayers and an outline of topics and devotionals for weekly missionary meeting throughout the quarter. For example, the first week's devotion was on "Evidence of True Religion" and included songs such as *Yield Not to Temptation* and *God Will Take Care of You*, as well as prayers for deliverance from evil. The mission of the magazine, said Burroughs's editorial, was to help women become "more efficient in their work in the churches."[68] Convinced about its merits, she also admonished the women actually to read and apply what they learned from the magazine, noting,

If our leaders will only co-operate with us, read the magazine, use the material, study the lessons carefully, secure subscriptions, it will not be long before the local societies will take on new life and the local leadership will do better work, know more about God's work, win more souls and work more earnestly for the salvation of a lost world.[69]

Burroughs continued editing *The Worker* until her death in 1961. Its format evolved over the years, with the content becoming more systematized, but the focus on missionary work and training for Christian women leaders remained consistent. For example, a 1950 issue began with a similar outline for weekly missionary meetings, providing structure and uniformity across the local women's societies. This more formal structure also evolved to include a "Christian Woman's pledge":

I am persuaded by the teaching of the blessed Bible—by daily reading—meditation and communion with my Lord and Saviour Jesus Christ—to live an upright Christian Life, to practice his teachings in my dealings with my fellowman—to dedicate my talent and give of my time, influence and means to teaching or spreading the Christian Religion at home and abroad—to win souls through personal service for Christ—to encourage and help in the enlistment of young people in Christian work—and make my home a center of Christian life and love.

　　To these ends—I pledge—to devote myself and seek divine aid and guidance daily—that I may become a living witness and a bright and shining light for my Lord.[70]

The pledge reflects the missionary zeal of both Burroughs and the Women's Convention to evangelize at home and abroad, as well as her firm belief in the centrality of the home (and women's work) in carrying out the work of Christ. The pledge captures other changes expressed in later issues of the magazine.

　　In this later magazine we also see evidence of the newer Young People's Department of the National Baptist Convention, and a shift from Burroughs's role in the Woman's Convention from corresponding secretary to president. The expanded content and topics are also striking. For example, the weekly topics focus on mothers and children growing together, how to teach God's word, and even a lesson asking, "what do the young people of your church think about their future responsibility in the world?" Her editorials likewise went beyond offering an overview of the purpose of the magazine and the need for training materials for local leaders and missionary boards. Instead, her editorial, entitled "What Profit Is It to Negroes to Disappear into a Ready-Made Race?" (for example) drops us into what feels like a larger national discussion of the validity of assimilation into White culture and even interracial marriage, perhaps for the sake of improving the Negro race. Burroughs calls for Black people to have self-respect and to know their self-worth, instead of attempting to be like another race or to value that race over their own.[71]

Burroughs's correspondence also included innumerable readers' letters affirming the significance of *The Worker* and its impact on local missionary societies. For example, a 1957 letter requesting fifty copies of *The Worker* also expressed gratitude for the "practical sense it affords and the splendid help we receive in planning our programs."[72] More poignantly, a 1957 letter from a Mrs. G. S. Casey in Kansas not only requested twelve copies of the magazine but also conveyed the publication's transformative power in her area:

> We have realized more real spiritual growth in our Mission group since we have used the Worker. May God bless you for your wonderful courage, to speak the Truth to us as you do in the Worker. That is just what we need so much.[73]

Mrs. Casey's letter, and many others, points to the ways that *The Worker* was received and the impact of Burroughs's plain and courageous speaking in helping women learn and feel empowered to grow in both "protest and Christian service."[74] As we saw in Ida B. Wells's work, Burroughs understood the powerful role of written publications (her editorials and curriculum) in educating Black people and particularly in empowering Black women from all class strata to learn and have access to training materials. Burroughs's work as the editor of *The Worker*, from its founding until her death in 1961, leaves a lasting legacy and a reminder of her commitment to Black women across the nation and of their ability to serve God and uplift their homes and communities.

Contributions to Radical Black Religious Education

Each activist–religious educator in this book expands our understanding of the ways in which religion, education, and social change intersect. They embody the nuances and complexities of living at the intersections of so many communities and commitments. Burroughs stands out, even among this group, because of her firm commitment to working-class Black women and to the cultivation of their leadership within local churches and on national and international missionary and political stages. She also stands out because of her commitment to working for change within and through her denomination. Burroughs embodied a seamless life of protest and Christian service. In her many efforts, she sought to reform the Black Baptist church as well as to empower lay Baptist women to be leaders in the cause of racial uplift and transformation. Like others, her vision expanded who had access to education. Unlike others, Burroughs's commitment was particularly to working and poor Black women. She radicalized our understandings of the sacredness of ordinary and even menial work. Her vision was to "dignify" domestic work—and she succeeded not only by instilling in Black women pride for the work they did, but also by clarifying for them the interconnections between this work, their commitments to Christ, and their service to the wider Black community. Burroughs believed in the power of the masses of Black people, and of Black women in particular, and she wanted them to be fully equipped to wield their power.

Burroughs expands what we define as radical education, in part because often (following the Du Bois and Booker T. Washington debates) industrial education was not considered radical education. However, for Burroughs and for many women leaders after her, there was no disconnection between dignifying Black women's domestic work and protesting for full access and rights of citizenship. Likewise, Burroughs expands how we understand Christian social witness and change. Burroughs supported and trained women as national and foreign Christian missionaries. And she was an early suffragist and political organizer. Driving all of this was her understanding that Christ was calling Black people to participate in and bring about their own salvation.

To describe Burroughs's work as pragmatic radicalism does not quite get at the heart of the matter. But it was both pragmatic and radical for her to want to empower Black women to be wage earners. She was cultivating leaders, not merely servants. And she helps us to see the powerful ways in which Black domestic workers were already leading and could be trained to lead their communities by virtue of having steady paychecks, wisdom, and independence.

SECTION III
RADICAL LOVE, CITIZENSHIP, AND EDUCATION

The U.S. civil rights movement . . . and education? It's this uncommon inter-section of topics that not only are explored in this book but also are the topics that prompted it. For while Martin L. King Jr. has long been celebrated for his charismatic leadership and for the sermons that inspired and expressed the religious and moral grounding of the civil rights movement, here I focus instead on the educators and organizers who made King's work possible. Among those who worked before, alongside, and long after King are Septima Clark and her work in the Citizen Schools, and James Lawson, teacher and adviser first to students in Nashville and later to national student nonviolent campaigns.[1] Each of these leaders exemplified the radical vision and tactics of nonviolent social change, as well as the power of religious ethics to call for mass social reform. This third section foregrounds the ways that nonviolence and a love ethic, student-centered learning, and improvisational teaching were all part of a radical religious social change program. Clark and Lawson embodied different transformative ways of educating in order to bring about change steeped in a radical, Christian ethic of love. They introduced me to the ideal of religiously inspired, activist-education, and it is to their lives and pedagogy we now turn.

5

Septima Poinsette Clark

May 3, 1898–December 15, 1987

Historian Katherine Charron, in her exploration of Septima Clark's life, urges us to consider not only the Black church but also the schoolhouse as equally important institutional bases of the civil rights movement.[1] She pushes us to rethink the ways in which education functioned to support the Black freedom struggle and also to explore how the work of activist-educators like Septima Clark and others expands our understandings of this movement. Clark is an example of someone who transcended oppressive structures, creatively taught literacy for citizenship, and consequently enhanced the self-esteem of myriad children and adults.

That Clark at the height of the civil rights movement was already a senior citizen gave her the *respectability* to create change, in part because no one would ever suspect this "grandmother" of "agitating." She consequently traveled across the South, training teachers and raising funds for the Citizenship Education Program. Her influence was so widespread that some leaders, like Andrew Young, have credited Clark and the Citizenship Schools with "training" an entire generation of leaders across the Southern United States.[2]

This chapter starts by mining the published and unpublished writings of Clark, as well as secondary sources from her over sixty-five years of work as an activist-educator. These sources help us to understand the intersection of her teaching, activism, nascent feminist critiques, and her faith. They also offer a better picture of her radical, pragmatic, and improvisational pedagogy.

Clark's Early Teaching Career

In 1916, when she was only eighteen years old, Septima Poinsette Clark started teaching at a school on the southern tip of John's Island, a rural island off the coast of Charleston.[3] Even the segregated schools of Charleston (where Clark was born and lived) did not hire African American teachers at that

Teaching to Live. Almeda M. Wright, Oxford University Press. © Oxford University Press 2024.
DOI: 10.1093/oso/9780197663424.003.0006

time. And though called *Promised Land School*, the conditions under which she was teaching were a far cry from any vision of a "promised land." Yet like the community after which it was named, Clark's little school represented for many of the local families an opportunity to approximate something of their visions and dreams for freedom.

Clark, like so many Black teachers in South Carolina during this time, had to work under daunting conditions. Her school was a two-room building, with two teachers and 132 children. Her colleague taught first through third grade, and Clark taught the fourth through eighth graders. Lacking even a chalk board, Clark started teaching using her skills of improvisation, writing on paper dry-cleaning bags that she brought with her from the city. Likewise, she created stories and vocabulary lists from the things the students were encountering around them every day, "the trees, the foliage, the animals," words and spellings from the *Gullah* language used by many of the descendants of the enslaved people living in that area that had evolved from the mixing of French, German, English, and different African languages:[4]

> When I taught reading, I put down "de" for "the" because that's the way they said "the." Then I told them, "Now when you look in a book, you're going to see "the." You say "de," but in the books it's printed "the." . . . to teach reading I wrote their stories on the dry cleaner bags, stories of their country right around them, where they walked to come to school, the things that grew around them, what they could see in the skies. They told them to me, and I wrote them on dry cleaner's bags and tacked them to the wall . . . [5]

Clark created these stories out of necessity, as she never was able to get enough textbooks for each student to have one, and because she knew the importance of helping students learn from and about their immediate realities. She described the ways in which she (and teachers like her) had to use her creativity to break down lessons and to introduce students to learning (even in the upper grades) because most were not yet able to read basic words.

> That's the way I taught all the time. It's a task that teachers have to learn to do. You can't say, "Get a book and open it." You have to do all of that introduction. You have to say, "Look at this picture . . . " This is the way you build up your story; that's the way I do.[6]

Even when she had textbooks, she candidly described the reality that she had to teach those stories as "vicarious experiences"; her students had never heard of most of the things in the stories from the West and the Midwest, such as great cornfields or farms that made thousands of dollars. Even without knowledge of these worlds beyond their island, Clark saw in and elicited from these students amazing capacities, such as their ability to memorize (even before they could read). And she spoke with great pride of the accomplishments of the students she taught there.[7]

Clark's reflections on her early years as a teacher on John's Island and the strategies she employed exemplify how she approached her teaching vocation. Her commitment to helping young students learn regardless of their location or ability directly influenced her ability to develop successful strategies for teaching literacy and citizenship to so many adults across the South.

Clark's educational philosophy was built upon a profound trust or belief in all persons' capacity to learn and change, and to participate fully in their own lives:

> I've seen growth like most people don't think is possible. I can even work with my enemies because I know from experience that they might have a change of heart any minute. Sometimes my own growth embarrasses me. I don't like to admit, even to myself, that I was once ill at ease with White people or so middle-class in my attitudes that I had a hard time teaching poor people. But I overcame those things . . . it took 40 years.[8]

Clark applied this perspective on growth to her students (children and later adults), to leaders (political and community leaders), and to herself. Whether naive or not, for Clark this faith in people is what enabled her to work with so many people. She never presumed that people were unworthy of education or too uninformed or rigid or racist to work on improving the world around them. This faith in people and in their capacity to grow and change was part and parcel of her Christian faith, her understanding of the transformative power of love, and her sense of being called by God to work for change in spite of potential backlash.

An Activist Forty Years in the Making: The Roots of Clark's Activism

Septima Clark's unwavering faith in people and commitment to working for change throughout the South grew out of her childhood and early experiences in Charleston, South Carolina. Clark was born in 1898, years after the Reconstruction era and after many of the gains made by Black people in the South after the Civil War had been rolled back. However, Septima Clark's family and early childhood life were shaped by growing up in Charleston with a formerly enslaved father, and a mother who though born free was never able to achieve middle-class status and worked as a laundry woman. Clark described the rigid and almost haughty ways of her mother as deriving in part from her caste and color consciousness. This contrasted with her father's generally generous nature and willingness to engage with and help out anyone, Black or White.[9]

The colorism and class-based caste systems that operated particularly within the African American community added a layer of complexity to Clark's life in Charleston. They determined with whom she could socialize, where she could go to school, and even which churches her family attended. Clark admitted that she internalized some of her mother's uneasiness engaging with folks not of her ilk, but she also learned her father's values of care and concern for all, regardless of their background. Only when Clark moved to teach in other parts of South Carolina, such as Columbia, did she begin to socialize and organize with broader coalitions, specifically with White people and among the more middle-class African American community. The color caste system in Charleston impinged somewhat upon Clark's ability to organize among the Black community there. Yet Clark's marginal position prepared her to work with rural farmers and the poor within Black communities.[10]

Clark's Early Education

Both of Clark's parents emphasized the importance of education and wanted her to have better opportunities than they had. Clark started elementary school at one of the segregated public schools in Charleston, one beset not only by problems of extreme overcrowding but also by an absence of Black teachers, who were not allowed to teach in the city's schools. Clark's mother decided to move her to a private house school in Charleston led by a Black woman who had learned to read during Reconstruction:

> I went to what they called Mary Street School, and at that school they had what they called at that time an ABC gallery where the children of six years were placed. There must have been a hundred children on that gallery; it was

like a baseball stadium with the bleachers. You sat up on those bleachers. And the only thing I could see the teachers could do was to take you to the bathroom and back. By the time she got us all to the bathroom and back, it was about time to go home. We didn't learn too much, and my mother was aware of that so she took me out of that public school, and there were numbers of elderly women in Charleston who kept little schools in their homes. And so I went to one on Logan Street, . . . run by a Mrs. Nuckels, [there] I learned to read and write.[11]

While Clark was critical of having to "learn the hard way"—she described her teacher as "whipping" each letter into a student's hand if they misspelled a word—she remembered these teachers at private home schools as good teachers, and as instilling pride in children like her. Those early experiences of learning had a lasting impact on Clark's later choice to teach.

Clark returned to public schools in fourth grade but also continued her education at Avery Normal School, which provided her with a secondary school education and the requisite teacher training for her to begin teaching at the age of eighteen. Clark was able to attend Avery because she looked after the children of a local seamstress and the seamstress paid her monthly tuition of $1.50. At Avery, the majority of Clark's teachers were White women from New England; the American Missionary Association had started the school and did not hire Black teachers until 1914. Clark describes these White teachers as treating her well and being committed to providing access to education for Black children. She even describes the ways in which a few White teachers attempted to be allies with their Black students by refusing to go to the White churches in Charleston and instead worshiping with the Black students and their families. (In part this was also likely due to the White teachers not being welcomed among the White Charlestonians either.)

Clark desired more education but had to deal with the reality that college was not an option for her in 1916. She had to start teaching to earn money and to send money back to her mother.[12] Clark, like others in this book, such as Cooper, never gave up on her dreams of getting an education and took courses during the summers at Columbia University (New York City) and Atlanta University, where she studied with Du Bois. Her goal was to find ways to improve the reading and writing outcomes of her students and to get a better sense of how to work with rural students. In 1942 she finally completed her BA at Benedict College (in Columbia, South Carolina) and later completed her MA at Hampton University (1947).[13]

Faithful Christian

Thanks to her family, and particularly her mother, Clark's early life, education, teaching, and her activism were pervaded by her faith. Her mother took seriously the idea of honoring the Sabbath, and thus no work (including no cooking and no punishing of children) was allowed on Sundays. And even though her father was often working and seldom attended church, Clark remarks how she learned from him how to live as a Christian—in particular how to treat others and "strengthen their weaknesses and . . . how you could improve yourself towards them."[14]

Clark's faith was also cultivated by attending church and Sunday school with her family and by taking advantage of the church's ability to address both spiritual and social needs within the Black community. A typical Sunday would find Clark and her sisters attending Old Bethel United Methodist Church with their mother, while their father was a member and sometime attendee of Centenary United Methodist Church.[15] Clark also participated in an array of religious services and classes on Sundays: she went to Zion Presbyterian for Sunday School first, then regular morning services at Old Bethel. She had afternoon religious education at Old Bethel as well and attended evening services at Emanuel African Methodist Episcopal Church with her family.[16]

In those church communities, Clark learned how to lead and from an early age also learned more about community organizing:

> I've been working in the church all my life. In the Sunday School when I got big enough I became chairman of the youth group. A little bit later on our church bought an organ . . . and raising money for that organ fell on me. I went from house to house raising over $4000 . . . [at] eighteen years of age.[17]

Even as Clark wrote of her church activities and the social role of the church, she also had a strong sense of the spiritual significance of her faith. For example, she described being "christened" in her mother's church when she was a baby, but also of having a conversion experience as a young teen. She recounted her experience of going to revival on Good Friday at her brother's church, where she "felt the difference" and at thirteen became "born again." From that point on, she took special classes to "be trained up into the workings of [the] church . . . [and] was confirmed on an Easter Sunday."[18] Yet these few details about her religious life are best understood as laying the foundation of the rich theology and Christian ethics that undergird Clark's approach to teaching and to her activism.

A Born Activist

Clark's work for social change and activism was likewise a part of her identity from a very young age, emerging long before the height of the civil rights movement. In some ways, the seeds of her activism were sown by her parents. Her father's willingness to work with anyone no doubt shaped Clark. And she watched her mother (as haughty as she was) unflinchingly stand up for herself and her children, for example, when, as historian Katherine Charron writes, Clark's mother went toe to toe with a racist neighbor who wouldn't let Clark or her siblings skate on the street in front of his house, and how rather than back down from White police officers, her mother accused the officers of trespassing on her property.[19]

Clark's activism overlaps and intersects with her religious life and educational endeavors. She joined the NAACP when she was twenty years old and still teaching on John's Island. An NAACP representative had come to speak at one of the local Presbyterian church conferences. Clark considered the work they were doing—trying to "help people who were treated unjustly"— and joined the organization.[20] Clark noted that others around her, including other teachers and her siblings, did not have this same connection to or zeal for organizing and action. However, Clark's sense of justice and concern for her neighbors and students motivated her. While Clark typically identified her NAACP membership as central in her narrative and legacy of activism and community organizing, she actually participated in numerous civic and religious organizations, taking on leadership roles in almost all of those organizations.[21]

Clark was part of the larger national Black women's club movement through her participation in the South Carolina Federation of Colored Women's Clubs. There, Clark was able to broaden her experiences of working for change and to get a sense of the types of processes that were effective against Jim Crow laws and in pushing for full citizenship for Black people.[22] Charron writes,

> Clark's [early] activism expressed itself in woman-centered professional and civic organizations whose collective impact proved potent fertilizer for some of the most important germinations of this period . . . Clark gained access to this network of women for the first time in the 1930s and they significantly shaped her vision of leadership . . . she also acquired political lessons that sharpened her understanding of how educational outreach informed successful community organizing.[23]

Through the women's club movement and her work at the YWCA, Clark forged alliances both with middle-class Black women and with White allies.[24]

Clark was a member of the Palmetto State Teacher's Association (PSTA), a Black teacher's union that helped Black teachers have some say in the type of education that Black students received and that advocated for better wages and conditions for Black school teachers. It was through her participation in the PSTA while teaching in Columbia, South Carolina, that Clark began to reimagine and share strategies for what citizenship education could look like for Black children. The ideas shared in the local PSTA meetings and at national Black teacher conferences reaffirmed the efforts of Black teachers like Clark by advising them to "create 'school activities which will bring the child into immediate relationship and knowledge of governmental functions,' especially by providing practical instruction in the duties of various state and local officials as well as tax collecting and public spending."[25]

Clark, however, was often an outspoken member of the PSTA, at times bumping heads with the male leadership and pushing for more radical reforms than the other teachers thought necessary. While Clark valued her membership in the PSTA and the ways that it helped her see firsthand the power of collective action and Black educators coming together, she also stayed true to her instincts and supported more direct action or legal confrontation when it was necessary. For example, Clark supported the NAACP's efforts in the 1940s for pay equality for Black educators in South Carolina through lawsuits and court battles, instead of the PSTA's more gradual approach. It was her participation in this campaign that transformed Clark and propelled her to take on more leadership roles in the NAACP.

Her ongoing connection to the NAACP is significant because it was her refusal to hide or give up her membership that led to her later activism and her crucial role in the civil rights movement. Once the NAACP garnered larger legal successes, such as in the 1954 *Brown v. Board of Education* case that set the precedent to end legal school segregation in the United States, Southern states and governments attempted to limit the reach of the NAACP, asking first for its membership rolls to be made public and later barring city or state employees from being members. South Carolina enacted such a law, and thus in 1956 Clark was dismissed from teaching in the city of Charleston.[26] Clark credits her dismissal from public school teaching as ultimately opening the way for her to begin her work at the Tennessee Highlander School and to her role in creating the *Citizenship Education Program.*

Clark had already been attending workshops at the Tennessee Highlander Folk School before 1956. She was inspired by Highlander's models of inter-racial dialogue and efforts at grassroots leadership development and voter rights education. Myles Horton, the director of Highland, was equally impressed with Clark and, after hearing about her bold stance and subse-quent dismissal, invited her to head Highlander's Citizenship Education pro-gram. The program was initially designed to get more Black people across the South registered to vote, but Clark saw immediately that the first step was to help people learn to read and to extend these basic skills to other areas from which they had been disenfranchised.

Clark appreciated the work of the Tennessee Highlander Folk school be-cause she saw the urgent needs of many Southern Black people to be trained to face the challenges in their communities. Highlander brought people to-gether to air their problems and to develop practical strategies to amelio-rate them, but Clark knew that this process was not easy and not something that people would do without help. Instead, she reiterated a statement at the core of her educational philosophy: "They had to be trained." In part she was reiterating that when people looked at their current reality and thought it impossible to change it or challenge it, they simply needed to be *trained.* She did not berate parents for putting up with poor and unjust conditions for years but instead recognized that it was her work to help train them and find confidence that they were capable of transforming their communities and advocating for their children. As in so many other arenas, she had faith in the ability of society and the world to become better and in the everyday people with whom she was working.

Education for Citizenship: Clark's Radical, Improvisational, and Pragmatic Pedagogy

In exploring her commitment to training the people and her larger contributions to our discussions of the intersection between religion, ed-ucation, and social change, Clark's pedagogy is central. In her methods of teaching and engaging with students we see more fully her embodied faith and activism. Clark expanded upon her work of teaching her students on John's Island by empowering people not only to read but also to become full citizens. Clark characterized this work of hers in a short poem for children:

> I'm a Negro.
> Born black in a white man's land.
> My name is Septima Clark
> I am a teacher.
> I have spent nearly all my adult life teaching citizenship
> to children who really aren't citizens.[27]

Her words are a helpful synopsis of the tension and struggles of her work and that of many African American activist-educators. More pointedly, they help us to see that Clark's focus in her teaching was never simply or only about teaching literacy. Instead, she had a vision of helping Black people gain access to the entire world from which illiteracy excluded them. She understood this work as being about forming citizens. Clark's words also demonstrate the realities of the extremely slow process of working for change. Her words are a reminder of the effort needed to keep working even when she knew that the basic skills and rights for which she was advocating were in direct opposition to what the dominant society desired for her and her children, students, family, and community.

With that vision and those goals in mind, Clark's pedagogy was improvisational, communal, and infused with a deep faith in God and love of the people. To describe it as improvisational pedagogy is meant neither as a pejorative nor a superficial description:[28] Clark used this description herself. For example, in a lecture at Howard University in 1974, Clark offered a comparative study of education among Whites and Blacks in South Carolina. Prior to that 1954 decision, Black teachers had to *improvise*, she wrote.[29] Clark outlined how Black schools and teachers had "limited materials and no equipment," and that even when there was a "book rental" program, the parents could not afford it. White teachers, by contrast, had "workbooks, [a] variety of books, and a library."[30]

Describing Clark's pedagogy as improvisational, furthermore, does not indicate any lack of training, preparation, or experience. On the contrary, improvising requires considerable skill, resourcefulness, care, wisdom, and courage to try something that one has not done before; to see if it will work;

and to be brave enough to go with it if it does or shift approaches if it does not. Unlike most top-down educational reform or generic philosophies of transformation, improvisational pedagogy is flexible. It is open to risks.[31]

Clark's improvising included the willingness and ability to create by using whatever was available. Indeed, such improvising, such creating and transforming the limited things on hand into something that both works and often is beautiful, is a learned skill and legacy of African Americans in general; recall the quilts, cuisine, music, and much more. Clark constantly had to figure out how to educate adult learners and to develop resources specific to their contexts, needs, *and* dreams. But to capitalize on what was readily available also meant taking the time to cultivate the human resources, or the people power. Clark quite deliberately cultivated leadership among the "common folk," employing them first as teachers and then as a cadre of organic local leaders and change agents.

Communal Pedagogy: Learner-Centered, Organic Leadership

Connected with the attentiveness required for improvisational pedagogy is the necessity and joy of connecting with the actual people. Clark and her fellow teachers were credited with having higher success rates in rural South Carolina than literacy programs with proven national track records because they valued the dignity of the people. For example, Clark championed participatory pedagogy by designing lessons that took seriously the desires of the students and what they wanted to learn. As a rule, she selected teachers who did not consider themselves superior to their fellow learners.[32] Before student-centered pedagogies were the norm, before movements toward adaptive, personalized learning goals/outcomes were common, Clark was employing them. But Clark also was embodying the skills on which later educators reflect. bell hooks describes the social transformation and empowerment that her teachers were undertaking in their efforts to educate young African Americans (preintegration) as participating in education as a practice of freedom.[33]

Despite much initial resistance, and despite their differences in teaching philosophies, Septima Clark worked to win over male leaders like Esau Jenkins on John's Island in South Carolina to the harder but much more effective methods of cultivating leadership among the people.[34] Male leaders like Jenkins often did not fully acknowledge the resources that were around them. For example, when asked about organizing in a particular neighborhood, Jenkins initially hastily concluded that "there are no leaders there."[35] Clark immediately called him out for this assumption. Likewise, Clark called out key male organizers for not coming "together and work[ing] for the common good."[36] She shared reports of younger organizers going into communities and taking over rather than involving the people in their own futures, a practice she found offensive.[37] Clark wrote that she believed "unconditionally in the ability of people to respond when they are told the truth. We need to be taught to study rather than believe, to inquire rather than to affirm."[38] In this statement, from one of her many greeting cards, Clark points to her unwavering faith in people. Working with people and training them to work for themselves was the longer, harder, and more thankless work, but she knew it was the way to foster true engagement and lasting change.

Faith in People, Faith in God: Clark's Radical Love Ethic and Theology

Deeply connected with her improvisational pedagogy and her genuine love and valuing of the people was Clark's faith in God and in the people. While many previous scholars have described Clark's work and life, they have paid limited attention to her spirituality and faith convictions.[39] I find it impossible to read Clark's actual written reflections without noting the centrality of her faith. Beyond her autobiographies, Clark's other published articles and speeches include several essays that explicitly outline how she understood the connection between the Gospel of Jesus and working for equality. For example, in "Citizenship and Gospel," Clark drew a direct connection between Christianity and democratic values. She connected the work she undertook in the 1950s with "the first words of Jesus' public ministry" where he announces that

> The Spirit of the Lord is upon me, because he hath anointed me to preach the gospel to the poor; he hath sent me to heal the brokenhearted, to preach deliverance to the captives, and recovering the sight to the blind, so set at liberty them that are oppressed. [Luke 4:18][40]

She pointedly argued that "Where there is obedience to the gospel, there will be concern for the less fortunate."[41] For Clark there was no separating her self-understanding as Christian from justice work. In this essay and elsewhere, Clark was quick to critique pastors or leaders who did not recognize this connection. She wrote: "missionaries could not be content preaching the gospel to hungry folk."[42] Nor did she stop at people's physical needs: she emphasized that Jesus's own ministry addressed reforming corrupt governments and systems: "If we really are to contribute to the 'deliverance of the captives' it is necessary to do something to redeem the system which keeps them in captivity."[43] Clark espoused what we might now call a theology of liberation that was deeply rooted in her own faith and experience, and in her work for societal change.

However, Clark's faith was neither naive nor did it require a love ethic blindly or without recognizing the cost of such a faith commitment.[44] While she often deferred to the male clergy leadership, Clark never shied away from critiquing clergy for inaction or from pushing her Southern Christian Leadership Conference (SCLC) colleagues to make sure that they attended to the complex emotions and struggles that some of the participants in the Citizenship School trainings were experiencing. In particular, during a summer training in Georgia, Clark encountered a young woman who was crying profusely and struggling to participate in the sessions, which included singing religious music and prayer. Clark recounted having to tell Andrew Young and Dorothy Cotton literally to open their eyes so that they could see what was taking place among the participants so they could better address some of the traumas people were working through as they practiced loving their neighbor:

> I saw a young woman who was really crying, and her face was so distorted, and I wondered what was wrong with her. And she had come from that part of Georgia where [Koinonia Farm] is, and a policeman had arrested her at [Koinonia], and when they arrested her they put her on the square. They called her a mulatto, and they wanted to make her ashamed . . . they put the cattle prods to her heels to see her jump up and down. And so she couldn't sing "I love everybody." She said, "I just can't sing it." So, I called [this to the] attention [of] Andy and Dorothy. I said, "You've got to open your eyes and see what's happening to this young woman. She can't sing that song. She can't love everybody when the people treated her so mean. And she came from there into this workshop." . . . Andy and I really had some words about that. . . . [laughter] And he told me that I must have been a saint. I said, "Well, there are all kinds of saints. I don't know who you're talking about,

but I want you to keep your eyes about you and see what's happening, because don't expect this young woman to sing that until she can feel more
comfortable."[45]

On a different occasion, Clark struggled to be patient with some younger
attendees whom she characterized as having more "Black Nationalists'
leanings." After she had talked with them for hours and they had discussed
"how divided the Negroes are . . . and how hatred is building up against [the]
SCLC," she attempted to let Andrew Young talk with them, deferring to his
theological training. However, Clark was unable to contain herself. Instead of
her typical ways of teaching, she "blurted out [her] feelings before the class
while Rev. Young was teaching. We really silenced the more radical of the
two"—but not without causing her to wonder later about the "smoldering
hate" and the ways that the strategy of love and nonviolence was not easily
undertaken.[46] She, however, found a connection to Christ for help in wrestling with the task of loving one's enemy:

> I am certain Jesus understood the difficulty inherent in the act of loving
> one's enemy. He never joined ranks of those who talk glibly about the eas-
> iness of the moral life. He realized that every genuine expression of love
> grows out of a consistent and total surrender to God. Our responsibility as
> Christians is to discover the meaning of this command and seek passion-
> ately to live it out in our daily lives.[47]

When scholars explore Clark's faith and faith during the civil rights movement, it is easy to focus on the pragmatic value of belonging to a church, such
as for its collective organizing power and its centrality as one of the few places
where African Americans could meet and organize at that time. I recognize
the importance of this dimension of religious life for social change. But in
Clark we find much more than a functionalist understanding of religion. In
her statement of the philosophy of the movement she shows her religious
convictions and her understanding of her sense of calling and responsibility
to do the work of justice:

> Peter said I must obey God—This is the philosophical basis of the move-
> ment. No obedience without representation. Wherever there are people
> who have no right to make the laws, why should they obey them? When

we petty law-makers are gone, God lives on. The world is marveling at the courage of black people who have nothing in their hands but the law of God as they face the dogs and the water hoses. When you come to the end of your journey of life, you won't have to answer to any city judge, any board of education or any Supreme Court. You will answer only to God; and God is going to say, well done, well done. Have faith in God, the sun will shine. Have faith in God.[48]

The context of these comments is not clear. Stylistic markers point to the possibility of an oral presentation, testimony, or sermon that crescendoes to celebration at the end. However, what is evident in the comments is her understanding about God as the ultimate authority, higher and more significant than human authority.[49]

Clark also makes an interesting connection between God being the highest judge and authority and her affirmation that there should be no obedience without representation. In that historical moment, the most pressing issue (or solution to racism and systemic oppression) appeared to be to help people become empowered to govern themselves and to participate fully in democracy. Alongside her tremendous faith in God was Clark's genuine faith in representative democracy—not as it had been practiced historically, but in how democracy could function when all people were fully included.[50] However, her faith in democracy cannot be separated from her overarching faith in God, in part because though she had not yet seen democracy work for the oppressed, she nonetheless affirmed that God was still ultimately in control. Therefore, she walked in the tension of pushing for full participation in social change movements and the belief that God is pushing and calling her and other Black people to fight on.

Clark was embodying that for which so many before and after her have longed: a genuine and unapologetic conviction that God was on her side and that obedience to this God was all that mattered—in the final judgment. In her philosophy statement, Clark was pushing for and naming the genuine within herself and in others. She modeled Howard Thurman's call to listen for the *sound of the genuine* in all of us.[51] In listening for the sound of the genuine, Clark worked with an amazing assurance that this was the work that must happen and that the work would sustain people. Her short statement of her philosophy underscored much of what drove her long career of public service.

Contributions to Radical, Black Religion, and Education

Like Anna Julia Cooper, Clark put her love of people and her students front and center in her work, even when it cost her personally. Clark, however, offers us something that many of the other previously studied educators do not: her close connection to regular people. One might say she was crafting a type of "folk education" with and for regular folk. While Clark definitely held onto visions of Black middle-class success and even remained committed to her belief in American ideals of participatory democracy, she moved far beyond classical or elite models of education and even industrial education, expanding those visions of education to include the masses of Black people who could not access even basic reading and writing skills, let alone anything more advanced.

Clark embodied commitment to faith and to work for social change. Her work, like that of Burroughs and others, reminds us of the power of women's organizations and churches as training grounds for educating people to participate in larger-scale social change movements. However, Clark also stands out from many of the other activist-educators because of the model of leadership development that she created that was based on her faith in God and her equally strong faith in people. Even if we are able to point to particular theologies or schools of biblical interpretation connected to social change, in the end those do not make sense and cannot be executed without the even more foundational commitments to the full humanity and abilities of regular people that Clark embodied.

6

James Lawson

September 22, 1928–

Alongside the basic literacy skill building and training for full citizenship, another type of radical education was taking place and undergirding the civil rights movement. Studying James Lawson moves us from examining the life-long educational work of a "retired grandmother," to the life and teachings of a young minister and his even younger cadre of college students and leaders. Lawson also stands apart from the other activist educators we have explored so far in this book thanks to his primary training and identity as a minister. Because of this distinction, most accounts of Lawson's work pay sustained attention to his religious formation and beliefs. By most accounts Lawson was a religiously motivated activist and chief strategist of nonviolent resistance during the civil rights movement. What is less celebrated and acknowledged about Lawson is his role as an educator. Here I explore both the ways in which his faith informed his activism and the ways in which his teaching shaped and was at the heart of his activism. Lawson points to the ways in which training (or education) is central to the work of religiously motivated activism and activists.

Indeed, "before there were marches, there was education." Such a statement reflects the behind-the-scenes work of teaching and literacy training done by Clark and her cadre of citizenship schoolteachers. But it also points to the planning, training, and education that were part of the direct actions and protest of the civil rights movement. James Lawson was and is much more than an activist. At his core he is also a religious educator.[1] He has been "a teacher of nonviolence for more than six decades"—starting in the mid-twentieth century civil rights movement, but continuing as a pastor, university professor, and teacher in local community organizations.[2]

His many students' descriptions and experiences of his teaching allow us a fuller vision of Lawson the teacher. Students often describe Lawson as being different from what they expected, both in style and delivery, and in how he taught and lived nonviolence. In particular, for many of the students it was

Teaching to Live. Almeda M. Wright, Oxford University Press. © Oxford University Press 2024.
DOI: 10.1093/oso/9780197663424.003.0007

not just what they experienced in the classroom that solidified Lawson as their teacher of nonviolence, but the way that he enacted it as well. One such student, Bernard Lafayette, was not alone in having doubts and misgivings about nonviolence both as a strategy and as something that he could practice for himself. He struggled with whether he was truly ready for nonviolent action, ready to act (or not react) out of Christian love, or whether he was only pretending to love his enemy while secretly raging.[3]

However, Lafayette recalls an exchange between Lawson and a group of White racists who had attacked one of the students on the way to a sit-in at the lunch counters. Lawson, in the midst of what could have been an extremely violent mob scene, calmly walked over to where the first student had been beaten and where Bernard had dropped to cover that student with his own body to protect him from further blows, as he had been trained. As Lawson stood there, one of the White men spat on him. Instead of reacting violently, Lawson asked the man for a handkerchief. Lawson's response took the man off guard. Without thinking, the White man gave Lawson the handkerchief. As Lawson wiped off the spit, he noticed the young man's motorcycle jacket and asked if he owned a motorcycle or a hot rod car. And the two continued talking for a few minutes more.

Lafayette observed this exchange, disoriented and in awe. He recognized that in that moment Lawson was attempting to find common ground and was talking with this White racist man about horsepower and engines. For Lafayette that was a transformative moment—both because of how much he respected Lawson's coolness and seeming ease in that situation and because Lafayette realized that the work Lawson was doing and teaching them to do had very little to do with what his so-called enemy was doing or what they thought of him. Rather than just as a strategy, Lawson was teaching them nonviolence as a way of life grounded in their love of God, self, and neighbor.

But how did Lawson get to this way of being and teaching, both inside his workshops and in his day-to-day exchanges with racist people and structures? Below we explore Lawson's reflections on training students in nonviolence, the many inspirations for his own conversion to nonviolence as a way of life, and the essential elements of his pedagogy.

Early Background and Conversion to Nonviolence

James Lawson was born miles and generations away from the childhood world of Septima Clark—in 1928 in Uniontown, Pennsylvania, to Philane

Mae Cover and Rev. James Morris Lawson Sr.—and raised in Massillon, Ohio. He is the son of immigrants, his mother having immigrated from Jamaica and his father from Canada (to where his great-grandfather had fled during slavery).[4] He is also the son and grandson of pastors and in many ways continued in the "family business," becoming licensed to preach in 1947 while he was still in high school. They were the consummate pastor's family, trying to live into the faith that their father preached and that his mother taught James and his eleven siblings. He describes growing "up in a climate, an environment of love and truth-telling, music and talk and education,"[5] and being "quite comfortable in [his] skin from a very early age."[6] This sense of self-worth and love did not, however, shield Lawson from experiencing racism and violence from an early age.

As a young boy, Lawson, like many other Black children, experienced racism firsthand and had to navigate a world in which people hurled racial slurs at him on a regular basis. He recounts being sent on an errand for his parents in downtown Massillon. On the way a little White boy called him a racial epithet. Without thinking, Lawson walked over to the little boy and smacked him.[7] Lawson noted that up to this point, fighting in response to such a situation was a pretty regular occurrence for him.

Things changed that day. When he had finished his errand, he ran home and told his mother of the exchange. Without so much as turning to look at him, she asked him, "Jimmy, what good did that do?" His mother continued talking to him (not really expecting a response; in fact, Lawson calls her words a soliloquy), explaining to him how his behavior did not align with the family's lives, their congregation, or their commitment to the love of God and love of Jesus. Lawson remembers her ending by telling him, "Jimmy, there has to be a better way."[8] That sparked in Lawson a search for that better way.

Lawson notes that even as a child, from that day forth, instead of fighting every time a kid called him a racial slur, he would talk to them and try to engage them. (He admitted that he often wanted to talk to younger kids long enough for their parents to show up, so that he could tell them what their child had done.)[9] That moment in his mother's kitchen is what Lawson notes as his numinous experience, the pivotal moment in his life at which he felt called to live and work "that better way." Thus, whenever one asks Lawson about the most significant point in his journey toward nonviolence, he does not mention his many degrees, his experience studying at Baldwin College, or even joining with long-time Christian pacifist A. J. Muste and the Fellowship of Reconciliation.[10] Nor does he point to his time in India, serving as a United Methodist missionary, teaching, and studying the teachings of

Gandhi. Instead, Lawson always points back to the conversation he had with his mother in their Massillon, Ohio, kitchen when he was eight years old.[11]

Like Clark, Lawson's early activism had both spiritual *and* practical roots in his faith and in churches and religious organizations. A committed Methodist, Lawson attended the Methodist Youth Fellowship, which was a "training program in addition to their schools."[12] In reflecting on this organization later in life, he noted that "Youth ministry at its best then was a ministry that said to young people, 'you are human beings, you are people of faith. You should be following Jesus, and you have to do the work of ministry.'"[13] We see in his early experiences of faith with his mother and in this para-church organization that Lawson was laying the spiritual and practical foundations for his long life of religiously motivated activist education.

The Religious Foundation of Lawson's Activism and Teaching

Lawson's Faith in Action: Love as a Force for Change

The journey from Lawson's early consciousness raising with his mother and his lifelong commitment to educating people for nonviolent social change is full of other spiritual and numinous encounters. In particular, as a young student and budding religious thinker, Lawson was deeply influenced by the teachings of religious leaders and writers including Gandhi, A. J. Muste, Howard Thurman, Harry Emerson Fosdick, as well as his contemporaries and fellow activists like Bayard Rustin and Martin L. King Jr. Lawson was not simply reading and researching the best religious ideals: he was thinking about how these ideals could be lived out in real life.

Gandhi scholar and political scientist Veena Howard offers one of the most recent treatments of the religious ideas and convictions at the heart of Lawson's understanding and practice of nonviolent social change.[14] Her interviews with Lawson help us trace his commitment to nonviolence and even his trust in nonviolent struggle to the "Gospel of Jesus, which [for Lawson] is [the] gospel of compassion, love and justice."[15] Like Howard, historian Dennis Dickerson helps both to clarify the broad and expansive influences on Lawson's theology and religious understanding and to ground them in his Christian, and particularly his Methodist, faith. Dickerson reflects on the writings of a young James Lawson, who at age twenty-three wrote of how he wanted to "emulate 'the life of Jesus, St. Francis, George Fox, Gandhi, Gautama (Buddha) . . . and other great religious persons.'"[16] Dickerson notes that while other scholars mischaracterized Lawson's religious background, overlooking the wide array of religious influences in Lawson's life, Lawson read all of these religious figures through the lens of how "one lived out humane values." For him, this was more important than adhering to any one structure or doctrine.[17]

Lawson characterized himself as a "Jesus Follower," pointing to his understanding of how Christianity had been tainted by connections to political ideologies and structures and to how Howard Thurman had influenced his worldview. For example, Lawson identifies the work of Howard Thurman as truly speaking to him and helping to give him a language for how he understood the connection between the life of Jesus and Lawson's commitments to find that "better way." In an interview, Lawson stated:

> One of the people who helped me a . . . good deal in the 1950s was Howard Thurman who wrote a little book called *Jesus and the Disinherited* in about 1949, 1950 . . . and he told me in that book what I had learned through my practice of the ethics of Jesus. He said the gospel of Jesus is a survival kit . . . not the gospel about Jesus but the gospel of Jesus is a survival kit for those who have their backs up against the wall. Those who are the people who are being repressed and oppressed and vilified. That was a great revelation to me when I saw that it confirmed what I thought about Jesus.[18]

In Thurman, Lawson found an African American Protestant pastor and theologian who helped him connect the dots between his desires to live as a Christian and to know that his faith had something to say to the oppressed people around him, at home and abroad.

Lawson began reading Gandhi at Baldwin Wallace College, first on his own and later in conversation with others. It was also in college that he became engaged with the work of Christian pacifism in the person of A. J. Muste and the Fellowship of Reconciliation. Here Lawson found a vision of religious and Christian alternatives to violence. Lawson later summarized Muste's vision of nonviolence and the call to practice the love of Christ personally and in public action, by saying, "You will love the Lord, you will work actively for Him, and thereby because His belief is love and His life is love, you will end up seeking a concept of greater social justice and a more just (and peaceful) country and planet."[19]

By reading and studying so many thinkers, Lawson began to develop his own language and practices for living nonviolently and for putting the love of Jesus into action. Lawson felt a deep calling not only to study religious ideas, but also to live them out and help others to put them into action. For example, Lawson enacted his understanding of Christian nonviolence by rejecting and not participating in the United States' involvement in the Korean War. He refused to concede to these violent practices by being drafted and instead used his time in prison to continue studying pacifism and nonviolence. He was placed first at a minimum-security facility with other conscientious objectors and thus had company in his studies. He was eventually moved to a maximum-security prison and work camp when the public's views toward conscientious objectors shifted. There, Lawson had to wrestle with his own fears and the strength of his commitment to nonviolence as a way of life, even when it cost. Dickerson argues that it was precisely in this prison, primarily in isolation and solitary study, that Lawson began to connect his commitment to pacifism as an ideal with the praxis of nonviolence:

> For Lawson, nonviolence activated and energized pacifism and provided it with both interreligious and philosophical depth. . . . When Lawson entered prison, he was a Christian pacifist. Before his release, he advanced to Gandhian nonviolence. . . . An embrace of Gandhian nonviolence became the synthesizing factor for Lawson's religious thinking. The social holiness of his father's Methodism fit . . . the Christian pacifism that he drew from his mother. He mobilized these ethical influences from within his family in the broad context of war in Korea and the rise of atomic armaments. This background created in Lawson opposition to all violence, whether in warfare or in the social suppression of subject peoples either in India or in the American South. Determining how to fight for world peace and social justice and how to blend seemingly disparate ideas became Lawson's intellectual challenge.[20]

Thus, even before entering seminary, Lawson was beginning to try to make theological and practical sense of his commitment to nonviolence and to fighting oppression and structures around him. Once released from prison, Lawson's return to Baldwin Wallace College to complete his studies was difficult because of his views, his time in jail, and his interactions with White students through his praxis of resisting segregation even in social settings.[21] However, Lawson's focus was not on college, for even when he was in prison he strove to expand his understanding and experiences by learning about the religious and social systems of Africa and Asia and by beginning to study how other cultures (under Gandhi's influence) had begun to dismantle and resist oppressive structures. Lawson decided then to become a short-term missionary, serving as a teacher and sports coach in Nagpur, India. His understanding of nonviolence grew thanks to studying with followers of Gandhi in India and to being able to observe the events in the United States from a more critical distance.

Through these experiences Lawson's understanding of nonviolence was enriched and enlivened, such that his later understandings of nonviolence can be summarized as combining Gandhi's work with that of Christianity and adapting them to the North American context. In the intervening years, when Lawson reflects on his early influences and religious sources of nonviolence, he often calls to mind Gandhi's idea of soul or love force: "Love is power, it is the greatest force available to humankind and humanity needs to learn how to use it."[22] Lawson's work is therefore grounded in his deep respect for the worth and dignity of humanity—individually and collectively.[23] In his speeches and writings, he therefore defines nonviolence as "trying to use the power that life gives you in ways that solves problems and heals you, and transforms you, and changes and transforms others."[24]

Upon returning to the United States, he continued his studies at Oberlin College, where he met Martin L. King, Jr., and found in King a kindred spirit trying to live out and create massive social change nonviolently. That recognition prompted Lawson to accept King's invitation to come to the South quickly, even before he completed the advanced theological education that he had envisioned for himself.

Training for the Revolution: Lawson's Radical Pedagogy of Nonviolence

In order to grasp Lawson's contributions to our understanding of religious activist educators, it is important to go beyond his theology and explore his strategies of teaching and training students in nonviolent[25] resistance. Veena Howard notes that while Lawson was a preacher, his approach to teaching and training the students was through workshops or the classroom and not through the pulpit or sermons. Some might note the necessity, as I did with Clark, for more clandestine places of learning and training for direct confrontation with corrupt government systems.[26] However, I argue that Lawson's workshops (and even the choice to use workshops and teaching) was more deliberate and reflects the strategic nature of the calling in which he was inviting his students to participate. Lawson was not inviting them to a lighthearted or impulsive experience, but to count the cost of that to which they were committing themselves.

Lawson described his early workshops as experiments.[27] Like Clark and so many other activist-educators during this period, much of what they were trying to accomplish in the United States during the civil rights movement had not been attempted before. And even though Lawson had studied Gandhi's practices and experiences with nonviolence, and he had great hope for how they could translate those to the United States context, this work had not been systematically implemented before. Lawson therefore had to teach people the strategies of nonviolence and more importantly to convince them that nonviolence could indeed work. He had to teach them that there was power in love and in their collective, disciplined resistance. But more than that, he had to teach them how to implement these ideals in real life. He saw his early workshops as having "the same purpose as boot camp in the army. You bring people together and you help them to begin to discipline themselves, to work together as a unit using nonviolence instead of violence."[28]

Lawson's radical pedagogy and teaching strategies actually began with whom he chose to recruit and saw as essential to the workshops: young idealistic and energetic people. Rather radically for his time, he included the student leaders in every event and in the leadership of the Nashville movement:

> We did some radical things such as we had no mass meeting where we didn't have at least the students speak and a community person, maybe a clergy person. We organized the Central Committee to provide the structure . . . we said, we will have students always chair it so that we would be training persons to give leadership in those two categories speaking and chairing. Some students had reservations. But my insistence was, "you're engaged in a struggle, you have to learn these skills" and this is a part of how you run a movement for social change.[29]

Lawson's insistence on having students in these roles is an example not merely of teaching people to protest but, akin to Septima Clark, of teaching and cultivating leadership skills among the people he recruited, and as such creating much longer-lasting change by developing generations and communities of leaders committed to resisting oppressive structures. Lawson knew that his work was about much more than desegregating lunch counters. He therefore taught his students to think beyond these immediate goals or direct actions.[30] He taught them to develop a bigger vision and to commit themselves to a way of life—of fighting injustice more broadly, and of doing so nonviolently.

Teaching for Conviction and Conversion

Journalist David Halberstam in his incisive book on the Nashville contribution to the civil rights movement noted that when students gathered to work with Lawson in the fall of 1959, many "were disappointed at first."[31] The students came expecting to study with this young passionate minister who, like many of the preachers around them, would inspire crowds through impassioned preaching. While the students recognized his brilliance and intelligence, initially Lawson did not seem as passionate or as charismatic as they had hoped. Lawson was soft-spoken and often addressed them in a somewhat detached manner. Instead of becoming louder and more emotive, when he wanted to emphasize his point, he became "cooler and more careful," so much so that at times students had to strain to hear him.[32]

Halberstam writes that

> Lawson deliberately did not want to touch the powerful emotional chords within [the students]. He was wary of the power of emotion . . . [;] what he wanted . . . was to let them find within themselves the things he had already discovered within himself.[33]

I imagine Lawson was wary of fleeting emotions in part because of the dangerous work in which he was inviting the students to participate. This was not something that one could simply be excited or mad about. Passions might spark someone's interest in working for change, but they could not be the only driving force. Thus, Lawson dissuaded the college students from basing their responses and work purely on emotion. Lawson knew that these emotions could pass, fade, or be replaced by other equally powerful emotions like fear or self-preservation. Lawson knew he had to teach in a way that tapped into something more foundational—something that would sustain them.

Therefore, Lawson's approach to teaching and training the students in nonviolent social change started with the longer and messier work of getting students to tell their own stories and to share their experiences of injustice with others around them, *and* of beginning to wrestle with how they were going to respond—violently or nonviolently. Lawson was essentially teaching the students and inviting them *to convert to nonviolence as a way of life*.

In some ways the idea of teaching for conversion, or for a change of mind, heart, and action, may sound odd in relation to social justice movements. However, elsewhere I have argued that conversion can be both a religious experience (including encounters with the divine) and a reorientation and re-visioning of how to respond to dehumanizing structures.[34] In particular, Lawson was inviting students to search within themselves and their myriad experiences of injustices for that *better way* for which Lawson likewise had been searching since his youth.

In his early workshops, Lawson outlined four aspects of "training for nonviolence." These included:

1. Meditation and Prayer
2. Study—scriptures
3. Begin with personal relations in home, church, and community
   a. Restrain from violence in any form
   b. Speak the truth
   c. Seek to forgive and love
   d. Develop healthy habits of understanding others
4. Experiment with the non-violent resistance to certain customs of discrimination and segregation
   a. Bus travel, waiting rooms, drinking fountains, and restrooms
   b. Develop habits of respect to all persons
   c. Do this quietly without announcement; as one begins to practice this, courage will increase for bigger efforts[35]

Lawson started by noting the importance of prayer and meditation for each of those involved in this work. He knew that the work had to be grounded in something much larger than themselves. For him that was a divine and spiritual practice and calling. He therefore invited the students to read the scriptures and texts from religious visionaries that he had read, not simply to convey facts about philosophies of nonviolence, but to invite them into living into and trying out these ideals.

Teaching for conversion or transformation is much more difficult than teaching to memorize. Lawson knew that he had to help teach students both the ideals of nonviolence and how to try them out and to live into these ideals. Thus, prayer and meditation were quickly followed by putting these ideas into practice.

During the early training sessions, Lawson did not attract large numbers of students. Instead, the basement of Clark Memorial Methodist Church held a smattering of students who were at first dubious about Lawson's approach and his content.[36] Many of the students had to wrestle with their own doubts about nonviolence. For example, Diane Nash recalls that "I thought nonviolence would not work. . . . But I stayed for one reason and that was because it was the only game in town."[37] Lawson recounts seeing the doubt on the students' faces and their uncertainty about ideas like "love your enemy" and the task ahead of them. Lawson, like Clark, was trying to inspire and convince people who had not experienced a different way of being in the world that first and foremost change was possible and that they were the ones who could bring about this change. Beyond this first step of pushing them to imagine or dream beyond what the current structures and conditions permitted, Lawson was also attempting to teach them that the best tools to bring about this change were "their faith and their willpower . . . by offering themselves up as a witness against [the] degrading system [of segregation]."[38] From the beginning of their training sessions he therefore set out to convince students that while systems might seem large and impenetrable, they could be changed. Reports Halberstam of Lawson,

> the most important thing he had to do was change their mind-set, and to prove to them that though their numbers were small, and forces aligned against them seemingly mighty, they could do it, that the great power was in the righteousness of their idea.[39]

Lawson was essentially teaching them and training them in Gandhi's philosophy of nonviolence, which he translated into Christian nonviolence. It centered on strategic reminders that they were emboldened and empowered by the power of their idea, and by their collective people power. Halberstam writes that Lawson's primary and most basic lesson was to remind the students: "Your idea is not too small . . . and because your idea is not small, your numbers will not be small either."[40]

Lawson encouraged the students by telling them that if they persisted and strategized, then when local authorities responded to their campaigns of civil disobedience, they would no longer be unknown, and their actions would inspire others to participate likewise. Their vulnerability, risk-taking, and the righteousness of their idea would be a catalyst for a movement, he insisted: *"Ordinary people who acted on conscience and took terrible risk were no longer ordinary people. They were by their actions transformed."*[41] Lawson admitted that strategic civil disobedience would inevitably create tension and confrontation with unjust forces and local law enforcement. And these confrontations would also help in their cause, in their recruiting. After all, he was modeling these strategies on the work of both Jesus and Gandhi in fighting corrupt systems, a fight based primarily on the righteousness and power of their cause.

Pedagogy of Community and Radical Listening

Often when we think of conversion or even of reimagining a way forward, we focus on individual conversion and changing individual minds, sometimes believing those things might eventually have a larger effect on the collective. Yet such individual conversion was not the only or primary mode of transforming the minds and lives of the students in Lawson's workshops. Closely related to Lawson's pedagogy of conversion is his pedagogy of community or communal transformation. Lawson's workshops created an alternative community for the students. It was in the communal exchange and community formation that the ideas began to take hold and to be grounded. Granted, the doubts of the students were not fully overcome simply by Lawson's teaching of new ideas and philosophies. Instead, as the students worked through their doubts they committed more fully and converted to a broader understanding of the community or the collective good of the community that they were building in the workshops and beyond.

Lawson realized early on in this community work the power of listening to the stories of the workshop participants, particularly the women students and the clergy wives who spoke about the humiliating and degrading experiences they had trying to do the most basic of things, such as shopping downtown.[42] They each had stories of the humiliation of having to tell their child that they could not eat lunch at a store restaurant, sit on a bar-stool to drink juice, or even use the bathroom at any of the stores they visited. The women had stories of their young children wetting their clothes because there was no bathroom they could use. Others had stories of never being able to try on clothes. However, all of these stores happily accepted their money. By listening, Lawson immediately recognized that the target of their nonviolent protest would be the downtown Nashville department stores and lunch counters.[43] Just as Lawson was radical in his insistence on including student leaders in all aspects of the Nashville movement, Lawson was also pushing the boundaries of the entrenched patriarchy operating in Black communities and even in civil rights organizations by both honoring the experiences of women and by recognizing early on that their experiences and participation (as leaders and advisors) were essential.

Besides the practice of listening as part of Lawson's communal pedagogy, Lawson's workshops began to create a radical, intra-, and interracial community that bridged lines of difference that never would have been bridged elsewhere. As we noted in the lives of other Black activist-educators, class and color caste systems persisted within the African American community, in part because of the corrupt systems of oppression that often pit members of oppressed groups against one another instead of working together for a common goal. Similarly, when Lawson arrived in the 1950s, Nashville was still rigidly divided along class and color lines for both Black and White people.[44] These differences were seen prominently in the expectations of who could/would attend the various Black colleges in Nashville. Fisk University was considered an elite college for Black middle-class students and families from all over the United States. At the other end of the spectrum was the struggling American Baptist Seminary, which typically attracted poorer Black male students from rural areas who were training for the ministry. Lawson's workshops were a different space. There, students from all of these universities, students who would not typically interact with each other, were working together, sharing their experiences of racism and oppression, and strategizing how to change them—together.

For example, the core team of Lawson's class included Diane Nash, an upper-middle-class Black Fisk student from Chicago. She emerged as an outspoken leader in the group, in so doing overturning the gendered expectations of who could or should be leaders and who should be part of working for change. Other students from American Baptist Seminary, mostly from poor, Southern rural families, among them John Lewis (from a poor, rural

Alabama farming family), Bernard Lafayette (from a poor Tampa, Florida, family), and James Bevel, became part of this core group of students. Lawson's group also attracted a few of the White transfer students, such as Paul LaPrad, who was studying at Fisk. These students were demonstrating the possibility for this interracial and intraracial collaboration that never would have been imagined outside of the basement of Central Memorial Methodist Church. Whether an intentional goal at the beginning of the workshops or one of the myriad byproducts of this type of transformative pedagogy, Lawson's workshops and teaching relied on the sense of community that was forged among the student activists. Many of the core leaders noted that even when they had doubts or fears, they pressed forward because they knew that they could not let down the other members of this community. This same sense of community also expanded what type of learning and actions could take place from Lawson's workshops. Veena Howard writes,

> In Lawson's workshops, the young men and women found courage by being with one another, united by the common interest creating communitas (intense community spirit and cohesive bond). . . . The common bond for confronting the unjust laws transcended any differences of distinctive personalities and backgrounds. The bond of friendship, built on the foundation of Jesus's love and shared mission, was strong and continued among many of them.[45]

Concrete Goals: Practicing, Rehearsing, Preparing, and Mental Fortitude

Lawson's workshops (and by extension his pedagogy) included more than the theology of Jesus or the teachings of Gandhi that emphasized love-force or soul-force. Alongside the process of inviting students to convert to nonviolence as a way of life and in the process of forming a radical community (across difference), Lawson knew that he had to offer practical strategies and *rehearsals* for the revolutionary tasks ahead of them.[46] It was one thing to say (or try to say) that you wanted to participate in nonviolent resistance, and another to know how you would react in the heat of the moment when someone was hurling condiments or hot coffee at you along with racial epithets and curse words.

Lawson's pedagogy had to be experiential and practical. He developed unique role-playing activities as a key method of training the students.[47]

Lawson "would ask two people to stand at the front of the room. One person would be tasked with verbally assaulting or even slapping the other person to determine how the first person would respond."[48] Lawson wanted the role playing to be as realistic as possible, so he included getting students used to hearing the N-word, so that they would know the emotional and physical harm that was possible and would learn how to stay focused during the conflicts. In short, Lawson got students to rehearse hearing these words and tactics and in so doing helped to shield them from harm without further endangering them by appearing to "fight back" or "resist."[49]

Training for nonviolent resistance also required considerable mental (and spiritual) fortitude. Lawson trained students to resist their ingrained and internal sense of rage at being insulted and violated. The stories of the physical and verbal abuse endured by the student leaders during the sit-ins and later freedom rides are harrowing. But at the center of these stories are Lawson's teaching and strategies of nonviolent resistance. Lawson knew that the workshops needed to help discipline the students and offer clear, well-thought-out, and executable strategies of nonviolent resistance. Thus, the students rehearsed likely interactions and became physically, spiritually, and mentally prepared for these attacks on their humanity. They developed strategies for what to do when (not if) a student was beaten or pulled off a stool, strategies for what to do when students were arrested or had to engage with police officers, and systems of lookouts and leaders who were able to call for help and to alert others to come—while not directly engaging in the action or the protest.

Lawson was strategic in how he taught the students to anticipate the reactions and to respond in ways that would "overwhelm" the system. For example:

> Lawson prescribed a tactic to confound the opposition. As one group would sit at the counter only to be arrested, another set of activists would move in, take their seats and get hauled off to jail, followed by the next group. The ongoing waves of demonstrators exhausted and overwhelmed authorities and their resources. Moreover, it signaled that the activists were organized, unbowed by fear, immovably determined—and could overwhelm the opposition's endurance and capacity.[50]

Lawson "had learned the tactic from Mahatma Gandhi's historic march on the Dharasana Salt Works in 1930, whereby rows of volunteers would step forth and approach armed guards, who beat them mercilessly."[51] Not only learning the strategies but also becoming disciplined (teaching and practicing and rehearsing as part of this disciplining process) were key to Lawson's approach and success. Lawson states,

> We had a specific strategy. We knew the techniques we were going to use, sit in, poster walks, economic boycott, marches, and parades if necessary . . . we had a target. We had a set strategy. We had the techniques and the methodologies we were gonna use. So, I was able to train folk in the workshop about these different techniques that we were going to use.
>
> Well, that's basically at the heart of the success the training the strategizing and then the carrying out of the program from a plan, we didn't write the plan down formally as far as I remember. But we talked the plan out and we thought it out and then we carried it out . . . we became a highly disciplined movement and we had a tremendous blend of community and students engaged.[52]

While there are myriad insights that can be learned from Lawson's philosophy and teaching of nonviolence; I have outlined three essential elements of his pedagogy: that he was teaching for both conviction and *conversion* to a way of life; that he was teaching in, from, and for *community*; and that he was preparing students for *concrete* disciplined application and implementation. Lawson was teaching students both for the current campaign in Nashville and more importantly developing in them the vision and skills to commit to lives guided by attitudes of nonviolent change.

Lawson's core message is that "nonviolence is the only way." In speeches he often reflects on the ways that the United States is addicted to a culture of violence. Thus, in his teaching, preaching, and activism he demonstrates that there is another way to be—that we can fight against injustices and transform systems nonviolently. Lawson affirms that "across the years, [he has] seen all kinds of people change as a consequence of his witness [to the power of nonviolence and the love of Jesus] and to the church's witness."[53]

Conclusion

Reflecting on the lives, Christian faith, and pedagogy of Septima Clark and Jim Lawson helps to shift our focus on the driving force of the civil rights movement. But it does much more: their lives also demonstrate the continued integration of religion, education, and social change in the mid-twentieth century. Some might argue that this was the pinnacle of such integration of these at times disparate fields/forces. However, we have focused throughout this book on many different ways that religion, education, and social change intersect for good in the lives of religious activist-educators. In this section we see in particular the ways that a radical ethic of love (centered in Christian and non-Christian examples) took shape in the lives of so many teachers. Clark and Lawson were both operating from this radical love ethic—of not only loving their students but seeing love as the most powerful force available to transform all of society.

Clark and Lawson were working to bring about a vision of a beloved community that grew directly from their Christian (and specifically Methodist) faith. They both embraced a vision of a beloved community that was intentionally interracial and predicated on cooperation with those beyond the African American community and across class and color lines within the African American community—such that they built organizations and strategies of training and leading that empowered students and community members to not only see the rightness of their own cause, but to also aspire to transform the hearts and minds of those who might be considered enemies.

In Clark and Lawson, we also see a shift from earlier focuses on educational curriculum or even education that took place primarily in schools and among children. We saw how Clark created a type of folk pedagogy for her adult learners that not only met their immediate needs of learning to read but also emboldened them to participate more fully in society throughout their lives. Both Clark and Lawson taught and led in ways that model the best of communal pedagogy, as well as their commitments to working for larger and longer educational strategies. Even as they created strategies that would be employed in various cities across the Southern United States, both Clark and Lawson recognized the importance of centering the experiences and context of the particular communities in which they found themselves. This too connected with their religious practices and beliefs of respecting the dignity, worth, and even wisdom of the communities and people with whom they were working.

At times Clark and Lawson's efforts and strategies during the civil rights movements might seem impossible to bridge. I am noting the ways that Lawson and younger activists sometimes resisted the more gradual and behind-the-scenes work of literacy education and the ways that Clark similarly criticized the seeming disinterest of some activists in the longer work in favor of being on the front lines and participating in direct-action strategies.[54] In spite of these seeming differences in their strategies and focuses, both Clark and Lawson embody a commitment to work for change that is grounded in their deep and abiding Christian faith and in their commitment to educate and train people in the strategies and tools they needed to resist oppressive structures. In fact, I see their work as essentially connected and supporting (not opposing) the work of the other. Clark's work focused on literacy and empowering people to act/live fully. Lawson's work focused on teaching the strategies of nonviolence—but also with the goal of helping people to live fully, as God had called and created them.

In Clark and Lawson, we see models of religious activist-educators who could never disconnect their religious convictions from the social transformations they were seeking. However, theirs was never an individualistic or private faith. Like other educators and activists explored in this book, both Clark and Lawson continue to expand our understanding of how religion functions as a public faith or helps to offer a public theological witness for what is taking place in society and communities around them.

My initial exploration of questions about how religion, education, and social change intersect started with the civil rights movement of the 1950s and 1960s. I wrestled primarily with the question of how people could be educated or trained to participate in social change movements, but what I unearthed was much more than what strategies were used to help people become organizers. Instead, I encountered the rich and complex narratives of educators who were doing the hard work of teaching for communal conversion and social transformation. Their pedagogy could never be reduced to mere techniques for enacting direct actions or literacy. Taken in its fullness, we see that the efficacy and power of their teaching rests in their total commitment to live the ideals of their faith and callings.

Lawson and Clark, as they reflected on their lives work and commitment, offer continuing insights for the work of religious, activist educators, as they both note not the immediate success of their efforts or their feelings that everything that they tried was correct (or even enough). Instead, Lawson and Clark both worked throughout their lives (long after the civil rights movement) because of their sense of "integrity with truth and mystery and beauty."[55] And it is that integrity that has kept Lawson to this day waking up and pressing forward to continue educating and advocating for freedom.

SECTION IV
RADICAL BLACK RELIGIOUS EDUCATION: POST–CIVIL RIGHTS MOVEMENT

Historian Barbara Savage describes the mutually affirming intersection of religion and social change as a "miracle." And indeed, the civil rights movement brought to the fore unprecedented models of religious activism, such that it was an extraordinary experience witnessed by only a few.[1] As miracles go, Savage reminds us, the aftereffects and remembrances of them are often expanded and generate a host of retellings. The awe-inspiring intersecting of religion and social change, particularly among a few Black Christians during the civil rights movement, indeed led to and advanced many conversations that had not taken hold (in mainstream America or formally sanctioned theological and educational spaces) prior to the mid-twentieth century.

Of course, radical and liberationist theological voices had been part of the Black religious experience throughout Black life in the United States,[2] but during the civil rights movement and as it evolved to an even more radical Black Power movement, African American religion and education also evolved. In fact, an entire book could usefully be written to capture the significance of the innovations that emerged in theological education during the mid-twentieth century. The emergence of Black liberation theology (as a theological discourse taught, articulated, and written about in White theological spaces) was also nothing short of a miracle. The parallel emergence of womanist theology and theological reflections emerged from and in a similar set of examples of the audacious self-expression of Black people, and Black women who dared not only transgress but also name themselves and name their God.[3]

Similar to earlier radical assertions of the humanity and dignity of Black people, which resulted in the creation of systematic projects to study Black life, the emergence of Black liberation and womanist theologies represented a radical move at the intersection of religion, education, and social transformation. This work was best embodied by religious activist-educators like James Cone, Katie Cannon, Delores Williams, Grant Shockley, and—the focus of the next two chapters—Olivia Pearl Stokes and Albert Cleage. Though lesser-known figures in religious and theological education, their groundbreaking life and work helped all Christians—but specifically Black churches—to reimagine what their educational mission could entail.

7

Olivia Pearl Stokes

January 11, 1916–May 24, 2002

In the past the central function of the Black Church School was to acquire knowledge of the Bible on the assumption that one would therefore be a good Christian. Previously, the central purpose of the Black Church was to meet the spiritual needs of persons and secondly to nurture the oppressed. Today, to these concerns must be added the formal education for liberation in the face of pandemic struggles for full freedom and justice as defined by Christian faith and as seen from the Black religious perspective. To address these new concerns and needs, the ethnic church school is now emerging as a promising pattern for Black religious education in the future.[1]

—Olivia Pearl Stokes

Olivia Pearl Stokes is the only radical educator depicted in this book who self-identified as a professional religious educator. As such, Stokes's life and work both continue the legacy of other religiously inspired, activist-educators throughout the twentieth century and offer a somewhat different example of the interconnections of religion, education, and social change. Stokes charted a different path even before the mid-twentieth-century landscape of religious and theological education was beginning to transform in response to the gains of several intersecting movements for civil and human rights. In fact, Stokes was breaking barriers long before she became the first African American woman to earn a doctoral degree in religious education in 1952.[2]

The Making of a Young Christian Leader: "God Made Us Significant"

In the words of writer Cole Arthur Riley, "some people are born knowing their worth."[3] Olivia Pearl Stokes was one of those people. Stokes's accounts

Teaching to Live. Almeda M. Wright, Oxford University Press. © Oxford University Press 2024.
DOI: 10.1093/oso/9780197663424.003.0008

of her early life and family help us to understand her accomplishments and her general way of living boldly and freely in the face of myriad systems of oppression. From those accounts, it appears that Stokes always knew that she should be a leader and speak truth to power. Stokes was born on January 11, 1916, in Middlesex, North Carolina, and grew up on what she fondly referred to as the *Stokes Place*. The Stokes Place was a collection of farms that had been in the Stokes family for generations. Her father, William Harmon Stokes, was a "gentleman farmer," and her mother, Bessie Thomas Stokes, worked as a schoolteacher in her early years and before starting her family.[4] Olivia Pearl Stokes was proud of her family heritage, of the fact that she was "born into property," and that both of her grandfathers owned land.

> My grandfather, T. O. Stokes . . . gave the land for Stokes Chapel to the community. . . . It's the historical or heritage family church. My grandfather had . . . eight or nine children. And they were all significant—they were clergy, teachers, and gentlemen farmers. And he had, all the years that I knew him, over two thousand acres of farm and timber land. So we were land wealthy.[5]

She was also proud of the ways in which her family contributed to the civic, economic, and religious life of the community around them and by extension of how the family gifted Olivia with an unwavering sense of worth. In particular, she recounted the ways that she was never "taught as a child to behave myself." Her mother instead simply instructed her to "Remember, you are a Stokes."[6] This simple admonition carried the weight of her identity and responsibility to live into that birthright. Stokes reiterated the significance of embracing early on this sense of self and the gift of being taught that she was truly and fully *somebody* as she reflected on her lack of connection to some of the forms of self-assertion she encountered later in life:

> So when all these children and young people in the sixties went through this business of "I am somebody," or "I am a man," . . . that was strange to me because I have known, I think I've known even before I was born, who I was.[7]

And while her statements might be interpreted not as self-confident but as arrogant or even as a disconnection between the Stokeses and younger generations, she was clear about the importance of self-knowledge and dignity for her and for all Black people. In fact, she reflected on the gift her parents gave her and her siblings by teaching them that "God made us significant persons, and that every other person in the world was significant, and that you had a right to go and approach them no matter what your age level."[8]

Stokes's strong and early sense of self persisted and carried her through many transitions of her life. One such transition happened early in her childhood. Her father died when she was only seven. One can imagine how important it became for Olivia to have strong self-confidence when her mother then decided to move Olivia and her three siblings from the family enclave to Harlem in New York, in part for the educational and cultural opportunities there.

Upon arriving in Harlem, Stokes's mother quickly connected the family with the Abyssinian Baptist Church, where Stokes became and remained a member for the rest of her life. Abyssinian was significant for Stokes. It was there that she encountered her first professional director of religious education in the person of Dr. Horatio Hill. Stokes recounts her mother taking her and her siblings to Dr. Hill and telling him, "These are my children. Educate them."[9] Stokes recalled her mother wanting the experience of Abyssinian, with its beautiful edifice and professional staff, to be a central part of her children's religious experience and education.[10]

It was also in New York and often in her Abyssinian community that Stokes was introduced to many other exemplary African American leaders, including Mary McLeod Bethune, Nannie Helen Burroughs, and Benjamin E. Mays, and that she worshiped under the leadership of Adam Clayton Powell Sr. Besides, she was coming of age during the prime of the Great Migration era for African Americans in the United States. Like many other African American families, Stokes's family migrated from North Carolina to New York in search of work and better educational opportunities for their children. Her early religious life thus also reflects many of the nuances of urban migration trends. As members of Abyssinian Baptist Church in Harlem, the family in the mid-1920s and '30s participated in or benefited from many of the social programs of the church, as well as the religious life.[11] Stokes later recalled that the religious educator there developed "after-school programs for us in Bible Study, in music and art, in drama, in education—everything we wanted was at that church."[12] These early church experiences at Stokes Chapel in North Carolina and at Abyssinian in New York had a tremendous effect on Stokes's early life and her later pedagogy. The impact of her experience at Abyssinian is especially clear in her later emphasis on

African cultural heritage and the interconnection of Christianity with African culture.

Stokes's participation in several networks of youth-serving religious organization likewise shaped her. Along with her family and church, she credits the Young Women's Christian Association (YWCA) with linking her to the world, and with giving her space to exercise her leadership skills. She recounts participating in a dizzying array of parachurch and civic organizations in her teenage years, organizations that afforded her opportunities to travel around the United States and Europe:

> The Y was linked to the world, our church was affiliated with the Protestant Council of the City of New York . . . I became active in the youth movement in all the Protestant churches in New York, and finally in 1941, became the secretary of the United Christian Youth Movement of North America . . . I became president of the New York State Christian Youth Conference. . . . In Harlem, we [Dorothy I. Height and I] founded the Harlem Christian Youth Council, and led that.[13]

And while the list of her church-related leadership activities is impressive on its own, it also points to the ways in which, from a very early age, Stokes was envisioning what and how young people and churches could interconnect for the transformation of the world. Her involvement also continues the long line of Black women's involvement in clubs and social organizations and even the earlier work of activist-educators including Nannie Helen Burroughs in organizing Black Baptist women to be trained as Christian educators and leaders.

It was also during her volunteer and paid work at the YWCA that Stokes learned more fully about the ways that being connected to organizations can strengthen and amplify the ways in which one can prompt change and transformation. For example, she recounted an incident from her young adult years while she working as the director of the information desk at the YWCA:

> I'd never forget. I was civic minded and curious person. Once day I went down to Radio City, just as a citizen, to enjoy entertainment, and saw a minstrel show. I came back that evening to work . . . and sat down to in the quiet of the evening and wrote a letter to the manager of Radio City protesting White folks being made black—just out of my youth, curiosity, and resentment. And I wrote on YWCA stationery out of my innocence. The next

day the manager was on the line of the YWCA asking what he could do to correct the race problem. That day [her boss and mentor] Mrs. Saunders invited me in and showed me the power—that was my introduction to the impact of power—that the Y had in the world, and what I had done, and how I had unconsciously, and without authority, used this instrument.[14]

Stokes was eighteen years old when she wrote this letter and learned a valuable lesson. It was a lesson that she never forgot and one that prepared her to work from within organizations, often interracial and ecumenical Christian organizations and networks, to effect change.

Stokes's Early Education

Stokes's early life not only focused on the interconnected worlds of family, church, and ecumenical youth organizations; it also had a strong emphasis on education (religious and secular). Stokes recalls that "education for the Stokes was a very important thing . . . every child was expected to go to school, go to elementary school, go to high school, go to college."[15] This was true of her mother's family, the Thomases, too. Stokes took pride in that fact that her family was well educated; even those members who were farmers went to Hampton (and other schools) to learn to become better farmers.

This educational legacy continued from her early experiences in a rural school in North Carolina and through her move to New York City after third grade. Stokes fondly recounted her first elementary school principal in Harlem, Mrs. Gertrude Ayers.[16] Stokes remembered her as the first Black woman principal at P.S. 89. And despite some reports of this elementary school having a "bad" reputation, Stokes and her family were excited to be part of it and to be inspired by the work and leadership of Principal Ayers.

So we had this first black woman principal, and I loved that woman, until she died at eighty-six . . . she must have been in her thirties when we met her. We followed her for fifty-some years. She was an inspiration to us.[17]

Her reflections on Mrs. Ayers point to the significant work of Black teachers in inspiring the excellence of future generations of educators and leaders— and for how Black teachers and principals played a role in the lives of their students well beyond their school years. Mrs. Ayers was the type of teacher Stokes strove to become.

Mrs. Ayers prepared the way for many of Stokes's other education endeavors, including being recommended to attend Hunter College's special high school for gifted students. However, Stokes could not take advantage of the full experience of Hunter College High School, for toward the end of her tenth-grade year, her stepfather (to whom her mother had only been married for about eight years) died. And while her mother never indicated that Olivia needed to switch schools, on her own Stokes determined that "going to college was going to be more of a problem because of his death."[18] Without informing her mother, she transferred to Wadleigh High School in order to take a commercial secretarial course and develop employable skills. Because of the differences in the curriculum (and the number of credits that Stokes carried over from Hunter College High), she was able to finish her high school education in three years and start working full-time.

However, though she was pragmatic about the need to work given the loss of her stepfather's support in her family, Stokes did not entirely give up on going to college. Instead, while working full-time, she decided to enroll in City College, taking classes at night—for twelve years. She persisted, transferred to New York University, and completed her undergraduate degree in pre–social work and education in 1947. Once she had settled on this academic discipline, she quickly completed the course work for her master's degree; she graduated only a year later in 1948.

That Stokes spoke jokingly about getting her "doctorate by accident" was an indication not of a haphazard approach to her education but, rather, of not having intended to pursue doctoral education. Instead, she recounted not being stimulated by the minds of those with whom she was working and for that reason being drawn back to academic communities.[19] She won a fellowship to pursue her doctorate in religious education at Columbia University's Teachers College. Stokes was at Teachers College during the height of many of the advancements in progressive religious education and while the college was forging a partnership with Union Theological Seminary to advance the work of theological and religious education. She was mentored by Dr. Harrison Elliot, a pioneer in the development of a social theory of religious education.

Stokes was also drawn to doctoral studies because of the work that she was already doing in New York at the Baptist Educational Center as the associate director, and training leaders in and for the church.[20] The Baptist Education

Center was sponsored by the American Baptist Churches and worked with churches from both Westchester and Harlem; though these included both White and Black congregations, the majority of participants were Black. Stokes recalls that it trained "over 500 church people, in 157 churches every week."[21]

In her dissertation, she analyzed the leadership education being offered by Protestant churches and made recommendations to improve how this work should be done. Stokes noted that for her there was never a disconnection between her educational pursuits and her work and her church life. She was always actively working in churches and teaching leadership while she was researching. It was this integration of work and study that empowered Stokes to understand church leadership and how to work creatively to implement new ideas for helping form and transform people in and for the life of faith.

Stokes defended her dissertation in May 1952 and took her place as the first African American woman to earn an Ed.D. in religious education. Stokes noted that there were several other African American men who were already working in religious education and doing doctoral studies (including Grant Shockley, who also earned his Ed.D. from Columbia University's Teachers College / Union Theological Seminary in 1952).[22] However, Stokes was charting a path not only for Black people but specifically for Black women in this work.

Pioneering Work: The World of Professional Religious Educators

Part of Stokes's legacy and unique contribution to our understanding of the ways that religion, education, and social transformation intersect among Black activist-educators is in her pioneering work as a professional religious educator. After Stokes completed her doctorate, she became the Director of Religious Education for the Massachusetts Council of Churches (MCC). Stokes's first task, even as she was interviewing for the position, entailed having to educate most of her board and other denominational leaders to stop underestimating Black women. Stokes candidly recounts that the hiring committee did not know that she was Black when she was called to interview. And while her race did not hinder the board from hiring her, she was clear about the ways that racism was at play in many of her interactions long before she attempted to implement any type of educational program for the million and a half Protestants who were under the purview of the MCC at that point in the twentieth century. Stokes dealt with the ongoing incredulity that a "black woman could have a doctorate and thirteen years professional experience."[23]

Of course, Stokes was not new to ecumenical and interracial church networks and work. She had been serving in leadership roles since her teens and was recommended to the MCC through the National Council of Churches. Stokes did, however, have to deal with racism in new ways with the move from Harlem to Massachusetts—including having "a whale of a time trying to get an apartment where [she] wanted to live."[24] She also had to deal with the ongoing racism in churches and had to confront supervisors and board members who attempted to censure her commentary and dictate what was in the purview of her position as director of religious education. Stokes recounted a particularly heated exchange with one executive director of the MCCs:

> Oh, I had to deal with racism, always everywhere . . . I delivered an address, and I pointed out that one of the issues, for me, in this society and the work of the church, was to deal with the whole question of race relations—we didn't call it racism then. And I said, "At supper tonight, we sang that song about little darkies" . . . black darkies or something . . . I pointed out that people of good will innocently were not analyzing what this did to those of us who were minorities. The next day, fifteen people called my director or sent letters in about the fact that I referred to their being . . . unchristian because of this . . . and he told me that I wasn't supposed to be dealing with race relations, they had a social action person who was supposed to deal with race relations.[25]

She responded in such a way that clarified for the director who she was and how she approached her work:

> I said to him, "Dr. K. . . . as a religious educator, I was born black, I was born a woman, and I now have acquired a doctorate, and I can never erase any of those things until the day I die. Further, as a black person, I've experienced bad race relations and good . . . but that wasn't good." . . . And I said, "You have the privilege as executive of this Massachusetts Council of Churches to hire whom you want, but as long as I am director of the Department of Religious Education, I will always talk about the issue of human relations and race relations. So you can fire me if you wish, but I told the board before you came . . . I would stay if I found out the executive was somebody I could work with in terms of philosophy."[26]

For, Stokes being the director of religious education included helping to educate churches about racism and the ways in which this played out in Christianity and society. She also made clear that her embodied knowledge and experiences as an educated Black woman could never be separated from any ideals/notions of religious education. Therefore, Stokes never shied away from directly calling out racism, sexism, or any other affronts she encountered to her humanity—even (or possibly more so) in her role as director of religious education at the MCC. The unconcealed racism of Massachusetts, in the both the churches and the society, did not surprise Stokes; she took it in stride as part of the pathbreaking work that she had to do in order to effect change in churches and society.

Stokes worked for the MCC for almost fourteen years (from 1953 to 1966) and contributed to expanding the vision of what and how religious education could take place in Massachusetts. She recounted the ways in which she implemented seemingly minor transformations, such as setting up religious education programs at resort center churches (at nighttime) to address the needs of the many seasonal workers and the astonishing impact of these interventions for persons who otherwise would have had to give up many of their core religious practices in order to work during the summers. Stokes, however, came with a very ambitious agenda for the MCC, and she was proud of the ways that under her tenure

> [e]ducators had deepened their theological studies, because education was thought of as methodology, and in the church, for me, it was theology and the story of Jesus . . . We started with theology. We brought in the Greek Orthodox Church. . . . We had a lot of opportunities to learn. The Greeks, the fundamentalist Christians, the Pentecostals, the liberal Christians—all together came out with great strength. . . . [And w]e produced books in education for use in the churches.[27]

Stokes also knew the ways that her work was pioneering—simply because she was embodying Black excellence and showing many White leaders (for the first time) of what Black leaders were capable. Stokes stated that her contribution to the MCC was simply being "a capable educator, administrator." Her work at the MCC opened opportunities for her to lead prayer at the state senate, to teach and work in consultation with several institutions of higher education, including Andover Newton, Boston University, Harvard Divinity School, and at Tufts in the early childhood programs.

In her role as director of religious education, Stokes had access to congregations and pulpits that would otherwise have been barred to her because of her race, gender, or denomination. Even as Stokes noted the significance of the ways that she was breaking down misconceptions and prejudices of White Christians and leaders, there was also a way in which her work at the MCC was equally important for how it was pushing back against limits and barriers within Black congregations. For example, Stokes knew that her early childhood experiences with a professional director of religious education at Abyssinia was a rarity. In fact, Stokes described the ways that most often African Americans (women or men) who wanted to work as religious educators often had to pursue positions in church-affiliated organizations, like the YMCA and the council of churches networks. And while there were likely innumerable reasons for the lack of official or paid professional religious education positions within African American churches (from financial resources to differing understandings of what was required for a robust Christian education and faith development, and even some possible anti-intellectualism or lack of consistent educational requirements for pastors in/across Black denominations—particularly among the Black Baptists), Stokes was also caught at the intersections of race, class, and gender.

Stokes actively resisted ordination initially because "in the black church in America, particularly in the National Baptist Convention, Inc., there was just no place for women clergymen [sic]."[28] Churches often attempted to use women who expressed interest in ministry "as secretaries and not educators and not pastors and not associate pastors," because of the prevalence of sexism in the Black Baptist churches.[29] Stokes further asserted that

> As educator, I could enter places I could have never entered as a minister. I could enter the same pulpit as Bishop Stokes [a White Episcopal Bishop], but if I had gone in as a clergyman, I'd have been second and third and down the ladder.[30]

Education and Black Theology: A Vision for Education in Black Churches

Even as Olivia Pearl Stokes spent much of her professional career working in interracial or predominately White spaces, she was particularly committed to the Black Church and to improving religious education with and among African Americans. My own introduction to Stokes's work came through her writings about how to reimagine religious education in Black congregations such that they took seriously the teachings of Black liberation theologies and the liberation of Black people. Stokes was committed to this work, in part because she argued that the "greatest missionary field . . . is to the black educated persons of the last twenty years [1959–1979]."[31] Even prior to the civil rights movement and Black Power struggles, she understood the many ways in which middle-class and educated African Americans had a complicated relationship with the Black church. She knew that they, like many previous generations, wondered whether being in the Black church was compatible with participating in political struggles and movements. Stokes was particularly disheartened by the shift in levels of social responsibility among Black Christians toward the church and their religious development. She argued,

> Most have just moved out of any responsibility in the Christian church and community. They haven't left the faith, they still believe in Christ, but they don't do anything about exercising responsibility or educating themselves in theology.[32]

Stokes reflected on the ways that upper- and middle-class Black people had moved out of or lost faith in the institutional church. In part she decided to pursue positions in religious education (and not simply higher education) because she saw the (relative) proliferation of other educated Black people in those fields. But in part she was aware of the absence of Black people in religious education and of the ways in which (in her assessment) Black Protestantism was more "affective than cognitive" and that most Black churches were not hiring religious education directors (then or now).[33]

Stokes's understanding of the flight of Black professionals from churches remains helpful today. When asked how we could imagine attracting Black professionals to churches once more, she was clear that she didn't "think they should have ever left."[34] For Stokes, the emphasis was less on how institutional churches should change to meet the growing needs of Black professionals, and more on how educated Black people should have devoted their knowledge and skills to transforming the church. She stated boldly,

> I think you get education and training in order to get in, and serve your people, or any people . . . black educated people have to get back in the church and make the church the strongest force we've ever owned. They must do lay theological study, and come to a strong set of beliefs and dialogue with each other. And just take over the church for the race, cause

I think that's our only salvation—the making of the church the kind of strong institution that serves our people, politically, socially, and spiritually . . . that's a heritage we haven't yet grasped.[35]

Although she gave a biting critique of the individualism and materialism that she saw among Black elites, she saw a glimmer of hope in the emergence and articulation of Black theologies of liberation during the 1960s and 1970s. These conversations she perceived as offering opportunities for educated Black people to integrate/understand their struggles for freedom and their faith commitments. However, even here Stokes's vision of religious education and Black theology were exacting. For example, she told the story of leading a session for Black clergy in Cambridge and Boston, Massachusetts, on James Cone's first book, *Black Theology and Black Power*. Her assessment of the book was that

It is an accurate analysis of existing theologians, what they have focused on, and what they have omitted from their theology. Their omissions represent an absence of sensitivity and awareness to the black perspective, the black heritage . . . but what Dr. Cone has written is not theology, it's sociology. It is an analysis of the omission of white theologians in their theology. This is not theology. Theology is when you write what God has revealed to you, not an analysis of somebody else's omissions.[36]

For Stokes, theology, and especially theology from and for Black people, had to be more than a discussion of what others had not done. Stokes felt justified in her opinion and in sharing it with Cone and others. In truth hers was not a critique of the Black theological project, but of this early work that centered mainly on a critique of White theologians rather than on what was at stake for Black people. She was calling for people to take seriously African American perspectives and experiences as sources of theology and of reflections on the revelation of God to Black people.[37] Stokes noted that her audience did not initially appreciate her assessment of Cone's early work and only later came to understand the fullness of what she was envisioning and demanding:

Well, I was almost murdered. But ten years later, these clergy realized I was right. I went to Jim [James Cone], whom I respect, love and adore, and who has developed in his own theology through the years, and told him the same thing. . . . Jim and a half dozen other people have written through the years. We now have a significant body of theological insights. The need now is to take black theology and translate it into the educational implications for use in the educational program of the black church.[38]

And indeed, Stokes did just that. She translated Black theology into a program for Black religious education. We see this in the extensive and detailed model of education from the African American perspective she presented in her 1974 article "Education in the Black Church: Design for Change."[39] Here Stokes both surveyed the historical role of education within Black churches and noted the pressing need for change, including the fallout of what she called the "social-racial revolution" of the 1960s.

These intersecting movements that were paving the way for change within Black churches and their educational efforts included "Black persons having a reversal of feelings about themselves—from little self-esteem to feelings of genuine self-pride . . . to value their life experiences as 'expert' knowledge."[40] Stokes understood Black pride and agency as essential for honoring the African and Black American religious experience and for helping Black churches reimagine their educational efforts.

Stokes started from a baseline assertion that

> The Black Church, holding Christian values and standards, sees itself as a servant of social change—by which education functions to help build an informed and critical citizenry that is able to function politically, economically, socially, educationally in the institutions that are the fabric of the society.[41]

Yet she did not limit understandings of religious education to being primarily or only concerned with religious matters and doctrine. Instead, for her such religious education included a charge to help prepare people to be engaged citizens. This charge hearkens back to many of the exemplary activist-educators in this book, such as Septima Clark and others, who were attempting to teach literacy and other subjects in service of a larger goal of full citizenship. Their shared understanding of citizenship or citizenry points to a larger mid-twentieth-century ideal in the United States of a citizen, with all their rights and privileges, as being both a social and religious ideal. Similarly, as noted in the epigraph to this chapter, Stokes understood religious education in the Black church as making a shift to include education for liberation—which builds upon Christian faith and struggles for freedom and justice.[42]

Stokes was not building her vision of religious education in Black churches in a vacuum. Instead, she was also building upon generations of Black religious leadership and from conversations hosted through her ecumenical work at the National Council of Churches. For example, a statement on "The Mission of the Church from the Black Perspective," created in 1969 during a conference hosted by the Department of Educational Development of the NCC,[43] included many ideals found in articulations of justice-oriented Christian theology and theologies of Black liberation. However, it also provided a theological grounding for the educational ministry of Black churches:

If [God's] mission prevails, men [sic] should be fully liberated and would then be free to worship his Creator and serve the needs of his fellows. Only the man who has experienced the psychological and spiritual freedom can stand for sociological, political, economic and educational freedom. A Christian man becomes responsible for justice among men because he believes in a just and righteous God, who wills the abundant life for all of His creatures. Therefore, anything that dehumanizes a person, in any way, is contrary to the will of God. . . . Thus it is the educational task of the Black Church to join theological reflection with those processes which expose the structures to those values of the Black experience for building community for God's people.[44]

From this shared mission statement, Stokes outlined seven theological affirmations to guide Black church religious education, alongside eleven objectives. The theological affirmations include the church's concern for the entire person (including their moral, spiritual, political, and cultural conditions); that the church can and should be an instrument for social change; that "God's creation of Black persons is good and they are persons of worth and dignity"; that the Gospel of Christ has something to say to/from the individual and collective lives of Black people; and that Jesus Christ is a liberator and gave his life to "increase the love of God and neighbor."[45] These theological affirmations, though simple and often taken for granted in more recent theological conversations, represented much needed affirmations of Black Christians' ability to reflect on their experiences in conversation with the revelation of God. And while people of African descent had been doing theology for generations, it was during this mid-twentieth-century moment that many were articulating theological norms and convictions that affirmed who they were as blessed and beloved by God—not in spite of their Blackness, but because of and in conversation with the pride and beauty of being Black.

Stokes's objectives were equally expansive and radical in all that they proposed for Black church education. These included:

1. To study the dialogue in Black theology . . . in order to help persons become aware of God as revealed as Jesus Christ, The Liberator.
2. To understand other religious faiths of Black people—Islam, African traditional religions, humanism, and secularism.
3. To help Black people know who they are and what their human situation is in the American society.
4. To enable persons to investigate and evaluate historical Black religious experience, beginning with Africa, through slavery, into the contemporary urban society, and to seek its relevance for life today.
5. To help Blacks fulfill their liberating role as disciples of Christ in the world.
6. To share with White Americans, and all God's people, the God-given Black perspectives on the Christian faith.
7. To enable and equip Black children, Black youth, and Black adults to discover their divinely created human potential.
8. To utilize religious education as a major tool for liberation, freedom and justice in the American society.
9. To design a broad-based educational program that aims at helping Blacks remedy past deficiencies in American society and the Church . . .
10. To stimulate Blacks to engage in sharing, from the Black experience and perspective, meanings, values and purposes and power . . .
11. To equip Blacks with those skills and strategies that influence those responsible for today's critical decisions and choices, thereby controlling the present and creating the future Black Americans want.[46]

Her expansive objectives for Black church education reflect her likewise expansive vision of what religious education in general can and should do. They also help us to understand how Stokes was outlining a very wide and multidimensional program for religious education. Both in this article and in her work at various organizations, we note that what she proposed is much more than what most persons can ever dream of accomplishing. However, for Stokes all of these suggested objectives were not only possible but necessary. Stokes was clear that Black church education was not simply about helping people to regurgitate theological or historical truths. For Stokes, education was about the "survival and transformation that ameliorates those societal ills that Christian faith is committed to remedy."[47]

Stokes was also attentive to the need for concrete and actionable models for Black religious education, and she suggested the model of the "ethnic church school." She made parallels to Jewish religious instruction and models of religious education among Greek Orthodox Christians in the United States, but she also pointed to the ways in which a Black Church ethnic school would be designed to teach

> Black history, Black church history and contemporary issues viewed from the Black perspective. It would celebrate the genius of the Black experience, as expressed in the life of the individual, the Black family, and the Black Christian community. It would aim to develop creativity within its members, to express their religious insights through drama, music, dance, painting, poetry, and creative writing.[48]

Stokes proposed that the ethnic school model always include at least three curricula focusing on "formal course offerings" and content (what was historically treated as the sole curriculum), as well as a curriculum that deals with "social development," and a third that foregrounded "Black self-awareness and self-development" or what we might consider as the inner space of being a Black person.[49]

These objectives and proposals for change also indicate the other areas to which Stokes committed her life. For example, many people were surprised by her inclusion of other Black religions, but Stokes understood the interconnected nature of religious communities and traditions and was committed to interreligious study—particularly among African Americans—because she saw the ways that different religious groups were attempting to work for the liberation of Black people. Thanks to that recognition, she affirmed this work and conversation. Likewise, her focus on the history of Black people from Africa to the present remained a consistent thread throughout her models of religious education and her own research.

African-Centered Pedagogy and Scholarship

Religious educator Yolanda Smith described Stokes as a "gifted teacher" who implemented a "variety of teaching methods and techniques including discussion, experience, travel, and contextualized approaches to education. She believed that dialogue was a way to honor people's life stories and facilitate communication."[50] Smith also noted the ways in which Stokes was pioneering in her early African-centered pedagogy. For example, one of Olivia Pearl Stokes's early contributions to our understanding of the ways that Black religion, education, and social change intersect was in her emphasis on and interest in Africa and the connections of Africa with the educational and cultural projects of African Americans. Through her mother and her Abyssinian Church family, Stokes connected with African missionaries, and these early twentieth-century missionaries' letters and reports introduced her to life and culture in Africa. Even beyond learning about Africa from missionaries, Stokes recounts her multilayered connections with Africa and her political and social concerns. For example, she talked about a great aunt who was a "strong supporter of Marcus Garvey" and her early exposure to Garvey's "Back to Africa" movement.[51] Therefore, from her early childhood, she became a student of African culture and recognized why it was important for Black Americans to study African history.

Stokes was an early and committed pan-Africanist. Throughout her life, Stokes traveled widely throughout Africa, including leading several teaching trips there. Her educational methods included immersion trips and travel seminars. In part, she wanted students to encounter firsthand what she herself had experienced by traveling to Africa, in short, a world far beyond the racism and false images presented about Africa. In doing this work, Stokes was preparing many other generations of students and teachers to travel to Africa to learn from African teachers and leaders.

These travel experiences helped to recenter the contributions of Africans and to help African American and White educators understand what is possible when White supremacy is not the norm. Educator Cynthia Dillard, in her book *The Spirit of Our Work: Black Women Teachers (Re)member*, gives us a glimpse of what Olivia Pearl Stokes was attempting to help people experience by taking them to Africa. Dillard writes, "when Black women in the Black diaspora (re)turn to the continent of Africa . . . that . . . journey changes our lives from the inside out . . . it shifts our bodies, minds, and spirits."[52]

Indeed, most of Stokes's writings were on Africa, including books to teach even the youngest of children about Africa in a dignified way. Among them are *The Beauty of Being Black*[53] and *Why the Spider Lives in Corners: African Facts and Fun*.[54] Both of these were published while she was working with the National Council of Churches and with attention to the need to create more resources for Black churches and youth. She wrote them, she said, because she "became tired of black being considered a problem.... It just made me angry. I grew up and I wanted the White churchmen to consider me a person, not always a problem, but they just looked at every black person as a problem."[55] Stokes was attempting to correct years of negative images and education about Africa that came not only from White supremacist school structures but also from African American communities themselves.

Why the Spider Lives in Corners gave a very basic and fun set of facts about life in Africa but corrected the ways in which Africa had been described in Eurocentric terms. Even when writing for children, Stokes offers correctives and ways of centering Africa for a new generation. For example, the introduction of this book begins

> All human life probably began in Africa. . . . The discovery—or rediscovery—of Africa by White people started about the same time that Columbus discovered America, in 1492. For a long time people believed that nothing much had been going on in Africa until the white people got there. But the truth is that some splendid civilizations had come and gone long before 1492.[56]

Similarly, *The Beauty of Being Black* is a collection of stories and artwork from African artists and storytellers that Stokes helped to curate and share with a wider audience. Stokes included stories passed down as part of the rich oral traditions, poetry from African teenagers, as well as the work of more established poets. The rich and diverse collection was her attempt to invite people into this world, but also to honor and respect the wisdom and agency of Africans.

Stokes also wrote a book on *The Emerging Role of African Women*, highlighting the expanding leadership among African women and building more bridges between the work of African and African American women. Here again Stokes did research and interviewed African women leaders, giving voice to their experiences and struggles. She understood such interviews and such books that came out of them as a continued site of activism and advocacy for a larger pan-African community.

Stokes's interest in and commitment to Africa went beyond writing about Africa and introducing African Americans (and others) to Africa. She also helped to establish teacher-training programs in five African universities. Because of her work, the Ethiopian government invited her to serve as its

Minister of Education—an opportunity she declined.[57] In short, Stokes was building a legacy of teaching excellence that centered Africa not simply as an idea, but also as an actual place of learning and wisdom.

Stokes's Contributions to Black, Radical, Religious Education

In many ways, Olivia Pearl Stokes brings us full circle to the ways that early twentieth-century Black women educators dedicated their lives to transforming the world through religiously inspired education and civic engagement. Yet notice that Stokes's activism and contributions to radical Black religious education look very different from those of the other activist-educators discussed so far in this book. In part this is because she was the only self-identified professional religious educator and because her work was centered quite deliberately and single-mindedly in religious spheres. Unlike Burroughs and other Black women, Stokes did not launch large-scale clubs or movements for the empowerment of Black women or communities. Instead, her work centered on leadership development and the ways that churches (Black and White) could participate in developing leadership among "the masses of Black people."

While Stokes was not on the front lines of organizing for civic change (and indeed often chose paths of working with organizations and not against/outside of them to effect change), I propose her as an exemplar of Black radical religious education because she, along with her contemporaries like Grant Shockley, was one of only a handful of professional religious educators, and one among an even smaller number of Black religious educators attempting to help Black Christians, young and old, live into the radical implications Black liberation theologies.

As someone who came to learn about Black liberation theology only while at seminary, I know that Stokes's work (and that of others) was not immediately or fully received in most Black churches. Indeed, her contributions to the field of religious education and to the Black church have not received as much attention as those of some of her male counterparts who were both serving as pastors and in full-time teaching roles at seminaries and universities.[58] However, part of what inspired me about Stokes's work was her commitment to staying true to her faith convictions and a vision of educating for freedom and liberation that she lived every day and that would never allow her to "stand down," even—or perhaps especially—among her own people.

Likewise, her work still pushes radical progressive religious educators to imagine how we might educate persons toward/for liberation within and beyond the current structures and realities of Black religious life. As one who worked with and in Black and interracial Christian organizations, Stokes reminds us of another possibility of what Black religious and radical education can entail—and even how one must plan for and strategically implement it. Stokes concluded her vision of education in the Black church by noting that

> Change is uncomfortable and rarely welcomed. Usually it is resisted overtly or covertly. Therefore, it must be planned for if it is to occur . . . [but o] ur faith, our Black people and all God's created ones, require and demand that change come, and that this oppressive and unjust society become The Kingdom of God on Earth.[59]

In reflecting on Stokes's legacy, we affirm with her the difficulty of change, and we hope that we will be inspired to dream and implement visions of Black religious education that are comprehensive and attentive to the spiritual, historical, cultural, and psychosocial development and heritage of Black people.

8

Albert Cleage Jr.

June 13, 1911–February 20, 2000

An Impossible Conception

Rev. Albert Cleage Jr. (who later took the name Jaramogi Abebe Agyeman) unveiled a nine-by-eighteen-foot mural of a Black Madonna and child on Easter Sunday, March 26, 1967. The unveiling of the mural also marked the beginning of the *Black Christian Nationalist Convention* and what would later become a new denomination, the Shrine of the Black Madonna of the Pan-African Orthodox Churches. That Easter morning, Cleage reflected,

> We really don't need a sermon this morning. . . . We could just sit here and look at the Black Madonna and marvel that we've come so far . . . that we can conceive of the possibility of the son of God being born by a black woman.
>
> And that's a long way for us 'cause it wasn't so long ago when that would've been an impossible . . . conception because our idea of ourselves was so distorted. We didn't believe that even God could use us for His purpose because we were so low, so despised, because we despised ourselves.
>
> And to have come to the place where we not only can conceive of the possibility, but to have come to the place where we are convinced, upon the basis of our knowledge, of our historic study, upon the basis of all the facts . . . that Jesus was born to a black Mary; that Jesus, the Messiah, was a black man; [and] that the nation that he came to save was a black nation.[1]

Cleage was both launching a new movement and, in many ways, bringing together years of wrestling with his Christian faith and the oppression of Black people in the United States. He was pushing his congregation, the wider community of Detroit, and the nation to consider what it meant to see themselves as made in God's image, to live into this idea, and to launch a movement to educate other Black people to see and embrace this "impossible conception." Cleage was teaching his congregation and community through the unveiling

Teaching to Live. Almeda M. Wright, Oxford University Press. © Oxford University Press 2024.
DOI: 10.1093/oso/9780197663424.003.0009

of the image of the Black Madonna and Child. It was one of many radical lessons and pedagogical strategies that Cleage employed over the course of his ministry and life.

Cleage's theological vision and educational project are essential to our discussion of radical, religious activist-educators in the latter half of the twentieth century. He embodied radical Black religious education and was at the forefront of the transformations of Black religion and education that emerged during the civil rights and Black Power movements. Cleage was charting a more radical path for pastors who were interested in reimagining what Black churches could be about and was putting in place the type of religious education that integrated their commitments to Black liberation, African and African American culture, and Christian liberation theology. One might argue that Cleage was enacting the type of cultural and ethnic school model for which Stokes had called. However, Stokes and Cleage were working and developing their visions for Black church education in parallel and separate spaces. Nonetheless, both were indeed calling for a rethinking of Black Church education and even an expansion of the social, psychological, and political dimensions of Black religion and education. But there were some radical differences in their conceptions.

Cleage was also breaking ground in terms of creating, writing, and preaching a Black theology of liberation—not simply attempting to preach what had already been created in an academic school of theology. Cleage was not writing for the academy or even for a White audience.[2] Instead, he was writing quite deliberately for Black people, and he was doing so as a pastor—with a concern for what was immediately needed for the praxis of Black religion and social transformation. In fact, Cleage's first publication, *The Black Messiah* (1968), was a collection of twenty sermons, which he described as follows:

> The sermons included in [The Black Messiah] were preached to Black people. They are published in hope that they may help other Black people find their way back to the historic Black Messiah, and at the request of many Black preachers who are earnestly seeking ways to make their preaching relevant to the complex and urgent needs of the Black community.[3]

On that Easter Sunday morning, Cleage was launching a "black ecumenical movement." His theological positions, though still decidedly Christian, took on new meaning as he emphasized the "blackness" of the divine and of interpreting Jesus as a revolutionary figure, a Black Messiah. He also reinterpreted the Easter story and resurrection, so central to Christian identity:

> The resurrection which we celebrate today is the resurrection of the historic black Christ and the continuation of his mission. The church which we are building and which we call upon you to build wherever you are, is the church which gives our people, Black people, faith in their power to free themselves from bondage, to control their own destiny, and to rebuild the Nation—beginning with those individual followers of a Black Messiah who are ready to break the servile identification of the oppressed with their oppressor.[4]

Young Cleage: Foundations of Political and Religious Radicalism

Historian Angela Dillard rightly notes that "the only way to understand Reverend Cleage's political theology is to start with his biography."[5] Cleage's early life and education point both to inspirations for his radical religious and political vision and to paradoxes in his life and work. Cleage was born into a comfortably middle-class and close-knit family. His father, Albert B. Cleage Sr., was a medical doctor who had moved north from Tennessee (where he was born in 1883). The elder Cleage had been able to take advantage of many early educational opportunities, including graduating from Henderson Normal and Industrial College (1902), Knoxville College (1906), and Indiana School of Medicine (1910).[6] Rev. Cleage's mother, Pearl Reed Cleage, was born in Lebanon, Kentucky, in 1886, the daughter of a mulatto father and a "very fair [skinned]" mother.[7] Pearl and Albert Sr. met in Indianapolis, where he was studying and where she and her family were living after her oldest brother moved to Indianapolis to find work in 1888.[8] Pearl and Albert Sr. met at their church, United Witherspoon Presbyterian Church, in 1907 and were married about three years later.[9]

Albert Cleage Jr. was born on June 13, 1911, in Indianapolis while his father was interning at the city hospital. Albert Jr. was the oldest of what would become a family of seven children. From Indiana, Dr. Cleage first moved his growing family to Kalamazoo, Michigan, in 1912 to set up his private practice—and to be near other aunts, uncles, cousins, and extended family[10]—but later settled in Detroit because of the greater opportunities for them there. It was in Detroit that Dr. Cleage was appointed as the first Black city physician and helped to start Dunbar Hospital—a hospital for Blacks—in 1918 as a means of providing both better healthcare for Black patients and to training for Black doctors and nurses.[11]

None of these advancements and opportunities were without complications. Most accounts of Cleage's father include discussions of the controversies around his decision to start a colored hospital, as some thought such a decision would end efforts to integrate the rest of Detroit's hospitals fully.[12] Likewise, his appointment as the city physician by a White Republican mayor with rumored connections to the Klan and to organized crime angered White citizens and confused Black ones.[13] Dr. Cleage's successes and appointments also had both a positive and negative impact on young Albert, who recalled getting beaten up often as he walked home from school because of his father's position. More positively, he also recalled going on house calls with his father to "indigent" parts of the city, visiting not only Black neighborhoods but communities of ethnic Whites, including Polish and Irish communities.[14] Historian Hiley Ward describes how this early work left an impression on young Albert and his friends. Ward even posits that going on house calls was "a pastime that could stir a young black to empathy, and to social concern over injustices and inequities, and toward ministry and toward a militant black nationalist position."[15]

The young Cleage's mother was also a powerful force in his early life. Small wonder, as she was described as overseeing "every aspect of the children's lives from, their schooling to their choice of playmates . . . and . . . their religious education."[16] And while young Cleage's father was seen as a race man, advancing the causes of Black people in Detroit by his advocacy and living a respectable life, it can be argued that young Cleage learned many of his strategies of direct confrontation and protest from his mother. Pearl Reed Cleage took seriously her children's education and did not sit idly by when they experienced racism and second-class treatment in their predominately White schools. Instead, she worked to get the "Detroit Board of Education to hire Black teachers and provide a decent education to Black children."[17] Her daughter also recalled her "giving lectures on Black history" at an elementary school in their community.[18]

Education

Cleage's formal education in predominately White schools, with only a few other Black students, also shaped much of his early experiences and left an indelible mark on his life. For example, while attending Northwestern High School in Detroit, he had to fight against racism in classrooms where teachers forced Black children to sit in the back rows of classrooms and where racial prejudice prevented him from serving on the newspaper staff.[19] Later, Cleage drew on those high school experiences when he protested the ongoing racism and oppressive structures in the Detroit Public school system for another generation of students.[20]

However, upon graduating from high school, it was not yet clear that Cleage would pursue activism or ministry. Instead, he took a more circuitous path toward his ultimate vocation. Dillard describes his undergraduate education as "erratic," noting that he attended Wayne State University off and on from 1929 to 1938.[21] He had gone to Wayne State to study sociology and pursue a career in social work, but he also tried out an array of other passions and pursuits:

> From 1929–1931, [Cleage] ran a booking agency for small musical combos . . ., then [he was] executive secretary for the local NAACP. Cleage also tried his hand at a career as a drummer . . . he spent a great deal of time in the small jazz and blues clubs of Paradise valley.[22]

From 1931 to 1932, he studied sociology at Fisk University, before returning to Michigan and working for the Detroit Department of Health. He took more than ten years to complete his undergraduate degree, in part because of his increasing disillusionment with social work and social services' inability to transform or even address the conditions of Black people in the United States.[23] Even though he was now suspicious of social work, all of his formal higher education up to that point had steeped him in sociology and social psychological methods, methods Cleage later reflected on as being something else he had to "unlearn" as he attempted to help liberate Black people.

Cleage's Early Religious Life: "Apostle to the Youth"

Yet Cleage's academic pursuits do not convey a fraction of what helped to shape his sense of self or his later work as an activist, pastor, and educator. Cleage's early religious experiences help us to see yet another dimension of the budding militant and change agent. Cleage's mother fondly described his early attempts at preaching and sharing the stories of the Bible:

When he was a little boy, I always told stories—I took them through the Bible—Mary's flight into Egypt, and others. This day, he stood there, his eye level with the table: "Tell me a story," he said. "Not today, I am so busy," I said; "You tell me a story. . . . Sure you know stories," . . . [But] He didn't talk very plain. He began telling the whole story of Joseph, sold into Egypt. He dumbfounded me. The poor tiny boy held all that together in his mind.[24]

His mother also recounted occasions when young Albert would demand that she sit down to listen to him "make a talk." She described him standing on the stairs and mimicking what he must have observed his father doing as a lay leader in church or even his pastor. She described how he "talked and talked . . . and [how] the perspiration would run down."[25] His mother affirmed his youthful efforts, and while she did not directly say that she knew that young Albert was called to ministry as a young boy, she observed many things in him early on that were pointing toward his later calling and work.

His family also noted the ways that young Albert was never a happy-go-lucky child. Instead, his mother and sister noted that his early experiences of racism at school and even viewing pictures of lynching in the *Crisis* magazine had a profound and sobering effect on Albert. His mother recalled:

there was nothing funny when he was a small boy. . . . He was a serious little boy. He wore little white blouses and trousers, and was always with a book. . . . He was never happy-go-lucky. Why? That's the way God made him. . . . It might be that at a tender age when he should be happy, he saw practices concerning colored children and it took all the jolliness out of him.[26]

In part because they were in tune with his personality and experiences, people encouraged Cleage from an early age to be a leader in his faith and to be reconciled with being a "bookish" and sober young man. We have seen how Cleage's mother was significant in helping to shape Cleage in his faith and activism. But as Cleage grew, he also expanded the spheres of his religious life beyond his immediate family's influence. For example, while Cleage's parents had met at and helped to form Black Presbyterian churches, Cleage was much more ecumenical in his religious practice from his youth onward, and so during his high school years he participated regularly in many churches in the Detroit area. His later ministry was shaped by this affiliation with a wide variety of congregations and pastors.

Cleage named two pastors in particular who left a mark on his life. The first was Rev. Charles Hill, the pastor of Hartford Baptist Church. Cleage described him as being radical in his social action and protest but becoming "evangelical on Sunday morning."[27] Cleage's successor, D. Kimathi Nelson, described Cleage's disillusionment with Hill and other pastors like him a bit more bluntly, writing that Cleage "found them [Hill and others] to be embarrassingly schizophrenic on Sunday mornings when their radical and progressive social and political views took a back seat to the old time gospel."[28]

The second pastor to influence him particularly was Dr. Horace White, the pastor of Plymouth Congregational Church. He modeled for Cleage a clearer integration between one's social action and faith. Dr. White served on the Detroit Housing Commission and was involved in leading marches to "demand integration of city projects."[29] Cleage recounted that

> Horace White was concerned with the emerging labor movement and political action. He was liberal rather than radical, but he brought it into church. His was all one religion—weekdays and Sundays. This is also my preference—all one faith.[30]

Cleage was also an active member of the youth group at Plymouth Church and even served as an "assistant" in the youth ministry while he was a student at Wayne State. Cleage stated that "Whatever youth work they wanted done, I did," and so he led discussions and other programming for the "Pilgrim League of young adults."[31] Before this, Cleage had served as "chairman of a youth group at St. Cyprian's Episcopal Church" during high school.[32] Cleage's early ecumenical formation was often centered around programming for and with young people, and this was something that he took with him into his ministry, often studying ways of offering the best religious education for youth and creating models of comprehensive youth ministry.

In these early mentors and experiences of ministry, we see the foundations that helped Cleage establish his faith and that set the course of his ministry. Thus, it was not surprising that Cleage returned to his earlier experiences of religious communities and enrolled at Oberlin School of Theology after becoming disillusioned with social work and its ability to help Black people. While at Oberlin, he worked as a student pastor at Union Congregational Church in nearby Painesville, Ohio, implementing models of comprehensive youth ministry and putting into practice his significant "emphasis on religious education."[33] Dillard also argues that it was at Oberlin that he began to weave together his unique approach to theology, one that "integrated both intellectual and pragmatic dimensions" and that went far beyond social gospel approaches to religion.[34] Cleage was a budding practical theologian, always trying to make sense of the emerging neo-orthodox theology made popular by Reinhold Niebuhr and Karl Barth while also dealing with the sobering realities of the lives of Black people in the United States.

Cleage graduated from Oberlin in 1943, was ordained, and got married all in that same year. Cleage married Doris Graham, whom he met at Plymouth Church, and began his ministerial career as pastor of Chandler Memorial Congregational Church in Lexington, Kentucky. Cleage, however, only pastored in Kentucky for one year before being invited to serve as the interim copastor at the Fellowship of All Peoples in San Francisco, California, a collaboration between Howard Thurman, A. J. Muste, and Albert Fisk. It was an experiment in integrated religious community, a vision of a beloved community, at least from an integrationist's point of view. And even though Cleage was an interim pastor at Fellowship for only part of 1944, it appears that he was more than happy to leave, unimpressed by what he regarded as the contrived and artificial nature of the "experiment" at Fellowship. In fact, he stated,

> An interracial church is a monstrosity and an impossibility. . . . The whites who came, came as sort of missionaries. They wanted to do something meaningful, but this was not really their church. The blacks regarded it as experimental too, or were brainwashed to think that is was something superior.[35]

It is unclear how open Cleage was to a vision of interracial religious communities prior to going to San Francisco, but he accepted the opportunity and through it "soured" on the whole idea of an integrated religious community. Why? In part it was because of his experiences with his White copastor, Albert Fisk. Cleage, who never shied away from speaking out against injustices, was bothered by Fisk's "avoidance of such issues as Japanese internment and the treatment of Black soldiers and war workers."[36] Cleage found Fisk "well-meaning" but intent on avoiding any attention to racial tensions and power dynamics in his version of an ideal community—"his heaven."[37]

Cleage's ministry and education continued while he was in California. He entered the Graduate School of Religion at the University of Southern California (USC) in Los Angeles in order to explore visual education and filmmaking, interested in ways of using films as a means of religious education. He recalled, "I was interested in religious filming, in trying to find a way to touch the black man [sic] en masse."[38] Cleage even took a course on cinematography with Cecil B. DeMille, who directed the *Ten Commandments* (1923 and 1956) and other blockbuster movies, many with religious themes and storylines. Yet Cleage soon determined that he was being called to something different and decided not to commit three or four years to the doctorate in religion and visual education; "Other things were more pressing" for Cleage.[39]

Even throughout what might be characterized as his brief experience of higher education, Cleage was reflecting on the religious and political lives of Black people and attempting to develop the most innovative means of educating Black people about the truth of who they were and their faith. Because visual art, iconography, and representation played a central role in the launching of Cleage's Black Christian nationalist movement, I understand his coursework at USC and even the desire to study filmmaking as part of his attention to the importance of visual education in his religious pedagogy.[40]

From California, Cleage's ministry continued at St. John's Congregational Church in Springfield, Massachusetts. When he was appointed to St. John's in August 1945, local newspapers focused on Cleage's beliefs about religiously inspired social action and his commitments to working with children and youth.

The new pastor emphasizes that in his opinion the church has a profound responsibility for bettering the conditions under which people live. "Religiously I feel that preaching should be based upon the Bible in so far as possible, and at the same time should have significant current application to the problems of the world in which we live," he wrote. "I place considerable emphasis upon those aspects of the church program which touch children and young people."[41]

Cleage's emphasis on social ministry and youth were front and center during his time at St. John's. His biographer, Hiley Ward, received numerous testimonies from parents, fellow educators, and even youth themselves who were positively affected by Cleage's ministry there. At the same time, Cleage was heavily involved in civic affairs. As the chair of the local NAACP Redress Committee, Cleage led efforts to push city officials to hold public "hearings on police brutality cases against blacks, most of them teens."[42] Among other recollections of Cleage's civic work were that

- When two boys were beat up and came to him, [Cleage] gave them the last cents out of his pockets and got them home.
- The boys of the Jinx bar across the street from the church all said he was the only man they could call on day or night.
- When a family broke up, he kept the daughter, Carrie, in his own home.
- When one night . . . [Cleage] got a call from the police about two run-away girls; he went down there at once, brought them home, and got in touch with their parents.[43]

Cleage led efforts to provide enrichment opportunities for children and youth, taking youth on trips, making sure that they all had the money they needed on these trips, and even learning the basics of basketball in order to help youth learn the sport. Cleage's work in Massachusetts was not simply a steppingstone for his return to Detroit in 1950, but it did emphasize his life-long commitment to young people, even as his efforts changed and his more militant religiosity was fermenting.

Cleage had been hoping to get back to Detroit even before he came to St. John's. He finally returned there as pastor of St. Mark's United Presbyterian Church.[44] After he was appointed to St. Mark's, Cleage continued his work with the NAACP in Detroit and garnered positive responses in the local press for speaking out against "America's materialism" and for championing the causes of the underprivileged.[45] However, during this time period Cleage was still wrestling with what role the church should play in the struggle for Black freedom and liberation. Cleage also began running into conflicts with the Presbyterian leadership that "was doing everything in its power to dis-courage Cleage's political activism in the local NAACP."[46]

When his frustrations reached a breaking point, Cleage led a dissenting group of members to form a new congregation, St. Mark's Congregational Church. We can speculate about why Cleage did not simply resign or move to a different church. But given his long-held desire to plant his own church and in light of his later work in developing a new denomination, it is clear that Cleage understood this move to be the right one and in line with a larger vision for radical, religiously based change. This of course does not mean that Cleage was not remorseful about the process by which St. Mark's Congregational was formed.[47]

Cleage and his newly formed congregation purchased their own building in 1957 and took the name Central Congregational Church. It was here that Cleage finally began to put into practice his own theological and ministerial vision, with careful attention to the integration of theology and social activism in all aspects of the church's life. In describing his work at Central, Dillard writes,

> Central's blend of theology, social criticism, and community organizing attracted a large following of young professionals and residents from [the immediate area] and across the city during the late 1950s. Reverend Cleage was particularly proud of his youth ministry, which was reported to be the largest . . . in the area.[48]

Cleage was in tune with the younger generations of his community and attracting members from all over the city with his emerging work as a militant Black Christian nationalist. Cleage understood his ministry to go far beyond those of the people who were official members of the Central congregation and so implemented a "Parish Visitation Program" to visit families in the neighborhoods around the church. Cleage argued that the "half a million Black people in the five-mile radius surrounding the church" were all part of Central's parish and were thus included in the mission and responsibility of the church.[49] This was not only a savvy way to grow the congregation and improve community relations; it also reflected Cleage's understanding of the need to reorient society away from the rampant individualism in the United States and toward communalism in order to bring about true liberation.

With his radical ideas and many other talents, Cleage could easily have approached social change from any number of bases. But Nelson notes that "Like many before him, Cleage came to the conclusion that the church offered the only institutional framework that allowed progressive black leadership the relative freedom to explore real solutions to the problem of black oppression."[50] Besides, Cleage was not called only to be an activist: he was also an activist pastor and educator. For those reasons, Cleage was committed to building on the institutional and economic framework of the Black church and to restructuring the Black church to put the freedom and flourishing of Black people at its center. Therefore, in 1967 when Cleage unveiled the Black Madonna and child, he was setting the stage for what would become his most radical intervention—that of reimagining the Black church and bringing about his vision of nationalism, as a nation within a nation, complete with its own network of counterinstitutions controlled by Black people and for their flourishing.[51]

As his vision of the Black church continued to evolve, Cleage changed the name of Central Congregational, in 1970, to the Shrine of Black Madonna. From the unveiling in 1967 and the renaming in 1970, Cleage launched a new denomination and network of churches, the Shrines of Black Madonna of the Pan-African Orthodox Christian Church. The churches in the network are often simply referred to as *the Shrine*. This network grew to include shrines in Kalamazoo, Michigan, Atlanta, Houston, and a later expansion to South Carolina.[52]

Black Christian Nationalism and Education

Cleage begins his first published book, *The Black Messiah*, with a sermon entitled "Fear Is Gone." He starts with a passage of scripture from Genesis 1:27: "So God created man [sic] in his own image" and then expands on it, stating,

> This is the essential Christian message which gets so mixed up in the minds of people. God created us in his own image. We intend to live as beings created in the image of God, and everything we do in the church should be designed to help us live that way.[53]

Here, as we have seen elsewhere, Cleage was connecting the divine truth that Black people are made in the image of God with the work and programming of and in the Black church and the community. In this sermon he went on to argue that something had shifted in the United States, and that Black people were consequently no longer afraid of dying. By extension, they were also no longer afraid of demanding their freedoms. He preached,

> Why is fear gone? Fear is gone essentially because we are in the process of becoming a Black Nation, a nation that is as real as if it had a capital, a Congress and a president. We as a people are now dedicated to one purpose, freedom for black people.[54]

Through his sermon and book, Cleage disseminated the theological and practical ideas that form the basis of his understanding of Black Christian nationalism.[55] Cleage's version of nationalism is distinct from that of other thinkers at that point in the twentieth century (and before). For Cleage was not pushing for a separate sovereign entity or nation-state. Instead, he reflected on the lived realities of Black people in the United States, noting that

> I use the concept of a "nation within a nation" to describe the separation that's enforced on black people. . . . The white man has done too good a job. I was separated from the day I was born. . . . You can't ask me if I'm advocating separation . . . I just inherited it.[56]

Cleage therefore confronted those critical of his supporting Black Nationalist rhetoric, noting that Black nationalism was simply the result of years of segregation created by Jim Crow era laws. Black nationalism, he said, was also a shift away from the more celebrated and dominant idea of interracial unity and integration that so many people had championed just a decade earlier.

Cleage was offering Black people something different. For he insisted that Christian theology, specifically Black theology, could do much more than call for reconciliation (often at the expense of oppressed people, having to be in a relationship with their unreformed oppressors). By unveiling a Black Madonna and writing a theology of a Black Messiah, Cleage was in a variety of ways demonstrating his conviction that part of overturning the legacy of White supremacy in the United States and creating a truly free Black nation begins with learning and seeing the history, legacy, and divinity *of Black people*. Consequently, Cleage not only began to preach about a revolutionary Messiah who looked like Black people (and, as Cleage argued, was indeed a Black person); he also set about creating a church and ministry that centered Black people, their freedom, and self-determination.

Of course, not everyone got onboard. And while Cleage had aimed some of his harshest critiques at Black clergy who he felt were not working toward the liberation of Black people, he understood the role that many Black pastors and their churches had played in offering Black people an escape or a cathartic release in the face of daily affronts to their humanity. Cleage leveled his critique mainly at Black clergy who preached only or primarily about individual salvation.[57] Both socially and theologically, Cleage was suspicious of individualism. In his articulation of Black Christian nationalism, Cleage therefore foregrounded a more communal understanding of humanity and Christianity.

Numerous books could be written to explore the nuances of his Black Christian nationalism. But what was central to that project was education—and the process of transforming the minds of Black people.

So, Cleage set out to make this vision a reality, putting in place a plan and structures for bringing about this reorientation for education and for this turn from the individual to the communal. His second book, *Black Christian Nationalism*, outlines this plan, including the extensive religious education program of the Shrine of the Black Madonna.

Cleage begins *Black Christian Nationalism* (1972) with a powerful critique and discussion of the role of education in this project. For example, Cleage fervently criticizes the religious literature of both Black and White publishing companies, writing,

> It's become impossible for Black people to use Sunday school literature from white publishing houses. Literature from Black publishing houses is just as bad because it is a copy of the same material. Such is the persistence of white authority. When white publishing houses began to put Black pictures in every quarterly just to make it "respectable," this did not change the basic white orientation of the literature. Black church-school literature must teach Black children at all age levels that there is nothing more sacred than the liberation of black people. . . . There is no justification for a church-school lesson in a black church that does not combat the individualism of the white world. Black children must be taught that the communal life of Africa is essential for the survival of Black people.[58]

Cleage knew that merely adding a few images did nothing to alter the deep theological content or the impact of the educational efforts. And he was convinced that education—a decidedly and unabashedly Black education—was central to the Black liberation struggle, writing that "Nothing constructive can be accomplished until Black [people's] minds are transformed."[59] In describing the educational program developed at the Shrine of the Black Madonna in Detroit, he therefore carefully explained the necessary process:

> Black Christian Nationalism approaches Black liberation realistically. First, we must restructure the minds of Black people. We have developed a complicated training program (a Black educational process). . . . We have rediscovered the concept of Nation and African communalism, uniting all aspects of life in one total experience with power to hear and transform. . . . Step by step the old brain which the white man has ruined must be replaced by a new brain capable of absorbing new information, building a new self-image, and rejecting individualism and materialism.[60]

Cleage included in these education processes rational, emotional, and spiritual encounters and outlined a three-phase "training program" required for true liberation, the three phases being "creating the motivation to change, unlearning the old, and learning the new."[61] Cleage, along with his leadership teams of the newly formed *Shrines*, designed the Alkebu-Lan Academy, a school of Black studies, which replaced "the traditional church school and work[ed] with elementary and junior-high children and young people."[62] And while Cleage stressed the importance of teaching children from a very young age (and thus reducing the amount of "unlearning" that was required), the educational program was designed for all people who wanted to join the "Black Christian Nationalist movement."

The program for new members included twelve months of training in:

- KUANZA: (The act of beginning). Acceptance of BCN creed, covenant, pledge of loyalty, Baptism into the Black Nation.
- KUA: (The process of growing).
  o G—Training—three months of Black Group Dynamics
  o *Moja*—First level—three months—BCN Theology
  o *Mbile*—Second level—three months—BCN philosophy
  o *Tatu*—Third level—three months—BCN program
- KUANZISHA: (The initiation to full membership).
  o *Nne*—Fourth level—Assignment of program responsibilities.[63]

The basic training required members to commit significant time to studying and being in community with other members of the Shrine (as the community was called). This training structure reflected the seriousness with which Cleage approached the educative task, as well as his understanding that true transformation from years of miseducation and individualism takes time. Cleage argued that this re-education and transformation process would be more effective if members lived together, communally, and he worked toward models of this in the 1970s, one being Mtoto House.

Mtoto House: The Children's Community

As the Shrine of the Black Madonna began to expand its reach, other educational models and programs were also introduced to help believers live into their understandings of communalism. In particular, during the late 1970s and early '80s, Cleage and members of the Shrine created *Mtoto* House, the

Children's Community, as a kibbutz-style living and learning community in which the children of Shrine members were raised communally. They set up a series of "group houses" with a designated house parent that provided structure and nurture for small groups of children. Depending on the numbers of the children of a particular age in the community, the group houses included six to nine children, separated by gender in the older age groups.

The program began with a mission of helping to raise a better child—meaning of helping parents and children to overcome the traps of individualism by allowing even this most sacred responsibility of raising one's child to be entrusted to church leadership and oversight. As one can imagine, the idea of communally raising children created a stir and some parents resisted, particularly once the rule of seeing one's biological family only on Sunday afternoons was put in place. However, for others the creation of group houses was an extension of the communal ethic and living arrangements that many Shrine members had already established in Detroit, Atlanta, and Houston. Many of the members of the Shrine had already established informal communal childcare networks as the groups worked together to spread the reach and mission of the movement. Therefore, the creation of Mtoto house brought more formal structure and training for those who would commit to serving as house parents and leaders.

Dr. Shelley McIntosh (also known by her African name and her role in the church as Cardinal Monifa Imarogbe) describes in her book, *Mtoto House: Raising African American Children Communally*, both the challenges and joys of implementing the group house model, the impetus and theories guiding its creation, and the rituals that helped to shape the children's lives together.[64] McIntosh served initially as one of the house parents for the nursery program and later was promoted to the director of the youth programs for the Pan African Orthodox Christian Church. Cleage encouraged her to further her education in order to learn educational and developmental models for raising children. McIntosh noted European American thinkers such as Abraham Maslow, Lawrence Kohlberg, and James Fowler, alongside African American thinkers like Marcus Garvey, Cleage, and Carter G. Woodson, as shaping the theoretical pillars of the Mtoto House model.

McIntosh, alongside Cleage and others, developed the daily rituals and educational models for Mtoto House. For example, each day the children participated in a morning ritual. Once gently awakened by a house parent's greeting, they moved to an altar inside the apartment/house for their "First Observance." The idea of doing morning prayers or devotions with one's children is not unique to Mtoto House; however, the content was uniquely Afrocentric and reflected the mission to empower Black children. The Mtoto House ritual went like this:

> *Acknowledgment of God:* (Done by group leader or child).
> *Call:* O Holy and Powerful God, we acknowledge Your Presence. (All raise arms and lift heads upward as this is said.)
> *Response:* In You, we live, move, and have our being.
> (This call and response is done at least three times).
> *Meditation* (Focused breathing, guided by group leader or child, who says): We open ourselves to the experience of God through meditation . . . [65]

The meditation period was followed by an affirmation:

> *Call:* Like every child growing up in the Black Nation Israel, Jesus was taught The Covenant, the Law, and the Prophets.
> *Response:* Like Jesus, we accept the Covenant, the Law, and the Prophets as revelations of God, binding upon His Chosen People.
> *Call:* The Quest. Jesus sought the experience of God when he left Nazareth and walked the dangerous Jericho Road to Jerusalem to be baptized in the Jordan River where he heard the voice of God declare him to be the Messiah, and a dove lighting upon his shoulder symbolized the fact that he had received the Holy Spirit.
> *Response:* Like Jesus, we too, seek the experience of God . . . [66]

The morning meditation ritual ended with the children praying silently, and then saying as a group:

> Almighty God, please strengthen us to keep the Covenant, and strengthen us to keep our belief that we are Your Chosen Ones. . . . Please touch us with the Holy Spirit, making our group the New Messiahs, with power to liberate our people and to change the world. This we pray in the name of Jesus, the Black Messiah, Amen.[67]

This time of prayer affirmed that "prayer means to be in communion with God" and that the "incarnate energy" of the children could become one with the "Transcendent God" in and through the act of praying.[68]

At the conclusion of their morning observances, the children then took care of the rest of what might be considered more typical morning activities of washing up, dressing for school, making their beds, and cleaning up their communal living space. Before leaving their group house, the children recited the Alkebu-lan pledge:

> We are God's chosen children. We are black. We are good. We are proud. We are God's chosen ones. We love, we protect, we defend all of our Alkebu-lan brothers and sisters until the end. We are one. No one dare try to pull us apart or they will meet the power of Alkebu-lan. We are the best out of all the rest. We are God's chosen children. Let Alkebu-lan rise. Let the black nation live![69]

This morning ritual along with other daily rituals points to the ways that Mtoto House was attempting to offer daily affirmations of the children as being chosen by God and part of a Black nation, and even as empowered to "liberate" their people and change the world. McIntosh noted that she designed the daily rituals to "sharpen the children's perceptions of who they are and what they should strive to be."[70]

Yet even in the Mtoto House model, the school-aged children attended the local public schools, and therefore the Shrine was living into this idea of a "nation within a nation," with the intention that the students would know that while they were set apart, they were not completely isolated from the rest of American culture.[71] Instead, the house parents supplemented the education the children received in public schools and helped students to excel with a rigorous after-school program that included tutoring, enrichment opportunities, and summer programs—all steeped in African and African American history and empowerment.

The Mtoto House continued in the Shrine from 1981 through the early 2000s, and McIntosh was able to collect the reflections of children and youth who had grown up in the group houses during those years. While the reflections were not all positive or negative, what becomes clear from them is a general sense of the ways that the experiences left a lasting impact on the children and leaders of the group houses. Many of the adults found a sense of purpose and meaning in the unpaid work they were doing there. Many of the youth understood—even if only upon going to college or leaving the Shrine—the ways in which their identity and understanding of self were forever changed by living and learning communally, even if only for a few short years. Though some struggled to transition to other types of communities or even with whether they would remain as full-time workers or leaders in the Shrine, they all voiced their genuine appreciation for their house parents and their commitment to the collective work.[72]

In reflecting on the legacy of Mtoto House, it is also that Cleage, in reimagining what the Black church could be, centered the development of children and youth as part of this vision. In one of his sermons on "What can we give our youth?" in *The Black Messiah*, Cleage argued that he wanted to offer young people a *nation*. He wanted Black youth to have a place where they were valued, loved, and treated as human—with high expectations and sense of pride in themselves and their people. He saw this as a necessary corrective to the ongoing alienation young Black people were feeling from the larger White society. However, he also affirmed the leadership of young people and encouraged adults to be a nation, which supported youth in their efforts to effect change.

Even as *nationalist* language has been challenged, there is still a need for spaces and resources to empower young people and offer them opportunities to contribute to something in which they can believe. The ongoing indictment that Black churches are irrelevant to the struggles and lives of Black youth, along with the relative absence of Black religion in contemporary movements for social change, is a reminder that there might be more for us to learn from Cleage's call to give youth a nation to which to belong.

Contributions to Black Radical Religious Education

Cleage's first biographer described him as the "most hated man in Detroit" and noted that Cleage himself said that "you won't have any trouble finding my enemies."[73] Why was Cleage so despised? And why would he wear this as a badge of honor? In part, Cleage's particular approach to activism and social change was not the kind that had any patience or tolerance for social niceties, respectability politics, or any other attempts at working within current systems to effect change, particularly if they came at the expense of Black people's liberation and wholeness.

Yet Cleage was no enigma. He was the human result of living through decades of attempts at gaining civil rights and social change in the United States and growing more and more dissatisfied with the conditions of Black people. In short, Cleage reflected much of the late civil rights era transitions to Black Power and the general recognition that the civil rights movement had not brought about the types of change for which even moderate Black leaders were hoping.

More enigmatic about Cleage are the innovative ways in which he approached Black Christianity. Instead of jettisoning any connection to the Christian church—as other Black radicals called for—or even participating in a project that might be seen as continuing a tradition of attempting to work toward some universal Christian vision, Cleage's theology and activism evolved to include an approach to social change that was strategically pro-Black.

In *The Black Messiah*, Cleage pointed to the ways in which his theological ideas about blackness and the divine intertwined with religiously inspired social change. Cleage offered a different perspective on radicalism. He was not pushing for the transformation of American society as a whole; instead, he was nationalist in his philosophy and program. He wanted to create alternative, self-supporting structures for Black people in the United States, or what he called a nation within a nation. If taken seriously, his work in establishing the Shrines of the Black Madonna can be understood as pushing Black Christianity and education to embrace different emphases regarding what was included in theological and religious education, and as empowering Black children and people to see themselves in/as the divine. This again was a proposition already called for generations earlier, but one that Cleage put into practice in some unique ways.

Beyond his radical ideas, Cleage also stands out among the activist-educators in this book because of his religious praxis and the ways in which he built a radical educational model in Black churches with the specific goal of reimagining them. While most of the other activist-educators explored in this book were living at the intersections of religion, education, and social change primarily in their roles as activists or as educators, Cleage entered this work as a radical pastor. And even as we might contrast Cleage and Lawson because of their opposing views on nonviolence and what transformation looks like, there are also parallels in their work. They were both keen theological minds that both theorized about the liberation of Black people and recruited people to do the work.

Cleage also contributed to our understanding of Black radical religious education because he was one of the first Black pastors of the later twentieth century who was committed to preaching a theology that not only included

Black Power but also centered it. Indeed, the distinguished academic Black theologian Dr. James Cone wrote in his autobiography that Cleage was the only preacher he had ever heard preaching in a way that was "unashamedly and unapologetically black."[74]

Even as his contemporaries and later generations struggled to embrace many of the more nationalist aspects of Cleage's theology and the teachings of the *Shrine of the Black Madonna*, Cleage has left an indelible mark on Black theological and religious education by reminding us of

- The power of images in our educational efforts and in the formation/ transformation of our minds and spirits;
- The power of naming and seeing the divine in Black people and in the ability of Black children to be able to transform their worlds;
- The power of intentional and rigorous educational efforts in the formation of revolutionary change; and
- The power of communalism and collective work in religiously inspired social change in the United States.

As we have seen with many of the other activist-educators, their activism remained a lifelong calling and did not simply fade away after a time. Likewise, Cleage's revolutionary message and ministry continued throughout his long life. And while his status as the "most hated man in Detroit" or even his work in local political efforts took a quite different shape from those of other activist-educators, Cleage remained committed to the cause of Black liberation and flourishing.

Later in Cleage's life his theological vision continued to evolve, as did his approach to religious radicalism and educating for social change. Some describe the evolution in his theological vision as embracing a more metaphysical turn, or even mysticism—seeing "the experience of God and love as the basis of revolutionary transformation and a program for self- and communal actualization as ultimately more important than institutional strategies."[75] Both Cleage's evolution and his contribution to Black religious radical education can be summarized in his own words, from a 1980s poem:

> [...]
> As we feel today,
> So men felt 2,000 years ago
> Until a child

> Created out of the very substance of God
> Discovered his inner Divinity
> And changed the world.[76]

For Cleage, change and liberation had to include complete transformation of religious and social worlds. However, we also note his emphasis on the radical psychological transformation that is included in a process of discovering one's "inner Divinity." Thus, his understanding of a radical messiah included one who came to remind all of their inner Divinity as well:

> "What I do you can do, and even more.
> The Kingdom of God is within you."
> So every town and Ghetto
> Is Bethlehem.
> And every child born of a Black Madonna
> Is a new MESSIAH . . .
> Only waiting to discover
> His inner Divinity.[77]

Conclusion

Looking Back to Move Forward: Reclaiming the Revolutionary Tasks of Black Religious Education

Third Thursdays are sacred. This past year, I was privileged to be a part of a monthly online *Sisters in Education Circle (SIEC).* On the third Thursday of each month, we would log on, and we would breathe a collective sigh because of the privilege of being with each other and of knowing that even if just for a few hours, someone else understood some of the joys and struggles of being a Black teacher and of continuing in the Black activist-educator tradition. The group consisted of forty to sixty Black women educators who are working in public and private institutions, teaching at the elementary, high school, and collegiate levels. I began this book by reflecting on Rita Pearson's Ted Talk and her legacy as a Black activist-educator, and during SIEC I found myself coming back, not only to Pearson's talk, but to the work of so many other activist-educators. See, I love teachers, and I really love Black women activist-educators. But part of me had forgotten how tangible the energy and creativity are when I enter a room (even virtually) with so many brilliant and creative Black teachers. Thus, third Thursdays became sacred space and time for me to reconnect with actual teachers, with the legacies of Black teachers, and with my identity as an activist, religious educator. These gatherings made me reflect on my years of teaching middle school math and science in Cambridge and Boston—and of even more years of teaching Sunday school, youth group lessons, and Bible studies (all before and even alongside of my work as a professor and academic practical theologian).

Dr. Akosua Lesesne started SIEC as a retreat for Black women educators after years of experiencing despair at what she observed taking place in too many higher-level conversations about the education of Black children. She wanted to honor the wisdom that Black teachers have when it comes to teaching and caring for Black children, wisdom that is often overlooked or discounted in policymaking decisions. Lesesne repeatedly affirms both that she "trusts Black women" and that "Everything I've ever needed to know

Teaching to Live. Almeda M. Wright, Oxford University Press. © Oxford University Press 2024.
DOI: 10.1093/oso/9780197663424.003.0010

about teaching I learned from a Black woman."[1] Likewise the SIEC norms honored and valued Black educators. Group norms included the reminder that "we treat each other as sacred (because we are)." This was coupled with the folk wisdom that "you're not going to treat me any old kind of way."

SIEC was also a sacred time because Lesesne curated each Zoom session as sacred space. We began with two primary rituals: sharing music and creating an altar or table of remembrance. The music began with the short refrain from Walela, a Cherokee women's group:

> Is everybody here?
> Has everybody got a place to hide?
> Is everybody safe and warm inside?[2]

As this evocative refrain played in the background, sisters gathered and greeted each other. They welcomed new folks and shared their appreciations for the beauty of the space. Other songs also played in the background including Patti Labelle's "You Are My friend" (which Lesesne designated as the official SIEC song) as well as others that varied from month to month. Each of these songs was an affirmation of the type of community that we were creating, and they "set the atmosphere" for the time to come.

The altar or table of remembrance also invited participants into the space, to focus on the ancestor on whom the "sister elder" educator was going to be reflecting during that session. The virtual altar always featured a candle and picture of the ancestor, lovingly arranged, and "pinned" in the Zoom screen. The ancestors being remembered included some of the African American women activist-educators included in this book, such as Septima Clark, and others who could easily have been added to this text, such as Mary McLeod Bethune, Mary Ellen Pleasant, Ruby Middleton Forsyth, Virginia Estelle Randolf, and even literary greats such as Ntozake Shange, Paule Marshall, and Toni Morrison. Each session was expertly led by "sister elders" throughout the year, including by Gloria Ladson Billings, Cynthia Dillard, Lisa Delpit, Yolanda Sealey-Ruiz, Rachel Harding, Monica George-Fields, Joyce King, Itihari Toure, Gloria Boutte, Debra Watkins, and Katura Jenkins-Hall, among so many others. Each of the sister elders is an expert in her own right, with decades of teaching wisdom and rigorous scholarship to her name; however, what stood out most to me during these sessions was their unfailing commitment to loving Black people, loving their students, and loving other Black educators. These elders shared stories of growing up and how they entered the teaching profession, of the ways in which they were often not seen, heard, or valued, at least at first. They even told of the many ways that they had to take risk and create something new for Black children and themselves. These innovative interventions included alternative schools and pedagogies.

As I tried to soak up as much of their wisdom as possible and to store the collective spirit and energy of each sacred Thursday, I remember also hearing and sitting with the ways in which each of these sister elders and other teachers connected to the spirit and the divine in their work. The SIEC group reminded me of the past and current ways that Black teachers have been and continue to be religious and spirit-led activist-educators. While SIEC is not a sectarian group and does not advocate for any particular religious or spiritual practice or confession, there was something important about the ways in which the space was open to the influence and expression of spirituality and religious practices among its members. So often, public spaces, particularly public educational spaces, are antagonistic to spirituality and religion, but in SIEC the Black women educators both were respectful of individual freedoms and acknowledged a collective cultural heritage that for so many of us includes robust spirituality and religious practices and communities. The faith and spirituality expressed in SIEC was an expansive and inclusive one that went far beyond any one religious tradition, but it included respect for ancestors and a genuine love of all people, and it centered the worth and dignity and stories of Black children.

Our sacred Thursday gatherings also reminded me that the stories I was exploring among these twentieth-century activist-educators were not exceptional. Western scholarship tends to privilege stories that traffic in the idea that "no one has ever done this before and could ever do it again." But in SIEC, there was a collective wisdom expressed by Gloria Ladson Billings as she described the work and legacy of "ordinary Black women" who have always known how to "make a way out of no way." There was a collective sense of the ways in which they knew collectively as educators what it was like to have to do the seemingly impossible and to draw on the resources of the spirit, their ancestors, and themselves in order to effect change in the lives of entire communities of Black people. Listening to the shared wisdom of the sister elders in SIEC also reminded me of the many Black teachers and activists throughout the twentieth and twenty-first centuries who embodied the best of the Black teaching tradition and the extraordinary work of Black religious activist-educators. These SIEC women reminded me to reflect on the ways of being that have persisted among Black educators, in part because the work of reflecting and remembering was essential to sustaining ourselves.

I remember thinking as I sat in one of the earlier SIEC gatherings that Lesesne's intervention was building community for Black women educators to strategize and connect. But as the year went on, I recognized that perhaps even more important was how she was creating space to help us to reconnect with the Spirit of God and our ancestors, who partner with us in the work of educating children and transforming the world. She was calling us to *re-member*—to reconnect with our spirit, to see the divine in our students, and to feel the transforming power of God in our ongoing work of *teaching to live.*

As SIEC sister elder and educator Cynthia Dillard reminds us in *The Spirit of Our Work: Black Teachers (Re)member*, such *(re)membering is not optional*, particularly for Black teachers.[3] Remembering, according to Dillard, includes "looking forward and backward, to engage our cultural memories to produce new space in which we all might live more fully."[4] The previous chapters in this book have been an exercise in remembering—looking backward at the legacies and lessons of some of the greatest religious activist-educators of the twentieth century. It has also a been a call to re-member—to put ourselves and our work back together and to look forward toward a vision of what is possible for spirit-led and religiously inspired activist-educators today (and in the future).

Looking Backward: Radical, Black, Religious Activist-Educators

To be certain, the work of looking backward and forward is not isolated or even sequential. Instead, in looking backward at these twentieth-century exemplars, we simultaneously catch a glimpse of a way forward. In truth, across each of the extraordinary individual educators, we see collective characteristics and embodied wisdom. Each of these educators were *combating entrenched anti-black racism and White supremacy in their daily lives, but also through their approaches to teaching/learning*. It cannot be overstated how intractable racism was during the early and mid-twentieth century (nor how it persists still today). Many of the educators had to confront racist educational systems head on, battling like Cooper to have the right to teach Black students both college preparatory courses and industrial education, or like Clark, who had to make do without the most basic of supplies for her segregated classroom. Other educators battled racism by working within the segregated worlds created by White supremacy to cultivate greatness and educational opportunities within Black enclaves. With the exception of Cleage, Stokes, and Lawson, all of the educators taught in legally segregated schools. However, like so many Black teachers, they used these segregated enclaves to instill a sense of pride into Black students and to teach both academic subjects and information required to survive in the United States and to fight oppressive structures. Likewise, Burroughs and Cleage used the resources of Black churches and denominations to create programs for Black students, run and controlled by Black people. And yet others, like Stokes and Lawson, fought racism through direct action—working with and often despite larger interracial religious coalitions.

Intricately connected to combating racism was the work of countering the long and insidious history of *mis-education* in the United States. *Mis-education*, the term coined by Carter G. Woodson, emphasized the ways in which education could be a tool of both liberation and oppression. Thus, the activist-educators in this book had to fight the ways in which education was being and had been used to continue inscribing values of the dominant group, to the detriment of Black people (and other oppressed groups). Mis-education was designed to drive a chasm between so-called educated Black people and their own community. Thus, Woodson and many of the educators in this book noted the ways that education was never neutral. Rather, if Black students imbibed the negative messages about themselves, it could be more detrimental than liberative. Therefore, given the history of educational inequities in the United States, these teachers were working to help children and adults succeed in schools and systems that were not designed to support them. They strategized to help their students counter both mis-education and a lack of educational opportunities. While Woodson in particular was criticizing mis-education in formal educational arenas, Ida B. Wells used the power of the press as an educator to launch an antilynching campaign that was rooted in countering the mis-education and misinformation spread about the causes of lynching. The erroneous information had been widely believed by White and Black people in America, namely, that Black men were lynched for raping White women. Wells systematically proved how false this rationale was. Even late into the twentieth century, educators like Cleage noted the many lessons that they had to unlearn (and help others unlearn) in order to be fully committed to the liberation of Black people.

Fighting racism, White supremacy and mis-education also included a core commitment to *affirming the worth of Black people*. These activist-educators were transforming lives because at their core they believed in the value, dignity, and humanity of Black people. This most basic belief, however, remained radical and elusive for some or even much of their (and our) lifetime. In other words, it cannot be assumed that even those charged with teaching Black students actually and fully believed in both their right to be educated and their *ontological somebodiness*.[5] At times even a few of the educators in this text trafficked in elitism and paternalism with regard to their work with and among the masses of Black people. However, even against elitist backdrops, all of the educators were committed to Black people and honored the contributions of Black people to society and their own lives—and thus saw them as worthy of being studied and educated. Both Cooper and Du Bois, and so many others alongside of them, did groundbreaking research and even charted new fields of study because of the ways that they took seriously the lives and worth of Black people—and our ability to tell our own stories—and to be worthy of systematic and rigorous intellectual studies. They affirmed the value of Black people as intellectuals, creating information and ideas and studying them. Similarly, educators like Clark left a legacy of "trusting the people," and of seeing even illiterate formerly enslaved persons as leaders and experts in transforming their communities and in organizing others for change. Burroughs similarly saw even the so-called menial work of women domestic laborers as valuable and thus designed her school to train this cadre of leaders for service both in their churches and communities.

In this book, I have carefully attended to the intersections of religion, activism, and education in the lives and work of these activist-educators. And as I've noted throughout, there was no single way that they all embodied this intersection. Part of why I included each of the educators I did in this book was because of the different perspectives they represented and the ways in which they expanded our conversations about religion, education, and social change. However, even across this diversity, there is a general and collective openness to the ways that religion(s) and spirituality function for Black people and in concert with Black radical education. Even in those we might consider to be the least religious, like Du Bois, we also see an intersection of his understanding of the importance of religion in the lives of Black people and his work to transform how Black people were researched and educated. Likewise, we also see an expansion beyond practical categories of "social gospel Christianity" or even liberation theology to see ways of being religious that are both pragmatic and exhibit an unwavering faith in God, themselves, and the people. Each of the activist-educators, regardless of their religious affiliation or even the evolution of their religious thought and practices, throughout their lives exemplified a tremendous faith. This faith sometimes included orthodox Christian theology and the practices of institutional Christianity, and at other times it included a healthy disdain for institutional religion. Their faith was not simply in God or some type of divine energy (though most of the educators professed a strong faith in God to work on their behalf): their faith also included faith in themselves. Many of the activist-educators were just confident (or foolish) enough to believe that the work that they were attempting could be accomplished. Even in the face of many setbacks and failures, these activist-educators embodied perseverance and hope. The grit of Ida B. Wells in the face of getting death threats and being slandered; of Nannie Helen Burroughs in the face of multiple attempts by her own denomination to take over her school; and of Septima Clark, who had to fight sexism and racism even in civil rights organizations, all stand in this long tradition of Black educators who had to continue believing in the rightness of their cause and in their ability to make a difference (or complete the tasks before them).

Part of their faith in themselves and in the people was the recognition that their work and the educational opportunities that they were offering were part of a *futuring project*. I am indebted to Andre Gilford, one of my students, who helped give me language that helps to encapsulate the hopeful and even eschatological nature of the work of these activist-educators. Gilford, in our seminar on Black Religion and Radical Education, named the work of so many African American teachers as a "futuring" project. The language of *futuring* is helpful because it reminds us of the ways that Black teachers, particularly activist teachers, have been involved in projects that attempt not only to help Black people live now, but also to "give them hope and a future."[6] Teaching to live was not only a call to offer people survival skills (even though those were/remain important); part of the need to help people learn to survive and learn how to live is also so that they actually have a chance to see and live into a future. Therefore, the activist-educators were committed to helping Black people see a future, one better and more hopeful than the limits of their current reality. By daring to educate Black women and girls alongside of boys, Cooper was helping women to see and live into a different future. By training college students in nonviolent social change, Lawson was helping an entire generation of young Black people see and live into a different future. Collectively, the work of religious activist-educators is that of helping Black people to hold onto hope and prepare for a future that is currently unimaginable or unattainable.

One of the other remarkable qualities that I noted both in selecting these activist-educators and in reviewing the myriad lessons from their lives is the way that even as they grew older these teachers continued to be activists and advocates for social change. I was impressed by the longevity of many of them (from Anna Julia Cooper to Du Bois and Clark, Olivia Pearl Stokes, and Lawson living well into their eighties and nineties). I noted this in part because I never take for granted the ability of Black people and particularly Black activists to live long and full lives. That is a gift that is too often taken away from Black people (because of the effects of the intersections of racism and health disparities). But even for those who did not live as long (such as Wells), I noted that throughout their lives they continued to work, grow, adapt, and pursue their passions/justice. An urgency remained in them throughout their lives. They recognized that their calling to educate and to fight injustices did not retire; if anything, it only evolved as they grew older and as they began to be more generative in their efforts to cultivate change in a younger generation. This ongoing zeal made me question whether it was because of their faith (in God, themselves, and their work) that they were able to sustain the long callings of their activism and work. Indeed, for many like Cooper, Wells, Burroughs, Clark, and Lawson, their faith in God was part of the sustaining power of their work. And even for activists like Du Bois and Cleage, there was a fire that burned in them that did not ever allow them to turn away from fighting injustices—even if/as they moved out of the public eye later in their lives. Connected to this ongoing and lifelong commitment to social transformation, these activist-educators in fact not only worked for change but also became *movements*.

These radical educators were called and compelled to respond to the injustices around them, and therefore they became advocates and sources of change within dysfunctional societies and educational systems. These educators moved beyond teaching prescribed "content" to their students. Educators like Cooper and Clark also spent time working with parents and training and encouraging other teachers. It is rare that a radical educator keeps their resources, skills, frustrations, or concerns to him/herself. Instead, either formally or informally, they become sources of change. Septima Clark was fired from her public school teaching job because she refused to give up her membership in the NAACP, but I daresay she was a threat beyond her NAACP membership. Getting fired propelled her to keep working, and it was via the Tennessee Highlander School and later the Southern Christian Leadership Conference's (SCLC's) Citizens Education Training Program that she more formally began training other teachers. She recruited unlikely and previously untrained community members to become teachers and leaders. Likewise, Burroughs, via her *Worker Magazine* and Woman's Convention, trained and helped new missionaries and educators stay committed to the tasks assigned to them. Each of the religious activist-educators inspired and led movements for social change that went far beyond their lifetime and individual work.

Looking Forward: Reclaiming the Revolutionary Tasks of Religious Education

Looking backward at the collective work of these activist-educators helps us to begin to reimagine how we might continue in their legacy and transform what it means to be a religious activist-educator in the future. As I researched each of these activist-educators and focused more carefully on their early childhood and religious formation, I kept returning to questions of how each of them was shaped in faith and learned to listen to (or at least stumbled upon) their lifelong commitment to working to transform the world. And here again we saw a variety of "call narratives" and early faith formation, from Cooper and Du Bois's early connection to local Episcopal and Congregational churches that helped sponsor their education, to Wells and Clark, whose social life and church work were intricately connected and who worshiped across denominational lines, to yet others like Lawson and Cleage, whose faith formation was both institutional and directly connected to the faith of their parents, primarily their mothers. These early narratives remind us to advocate not only that families and churches mentor young people in single or narrow ways, but also for entire congregations and families to return to the work of surrounding generations of young leaders and helping to support their endeavors at every turn.

It should go without saying that congregations and families still have an important role to play in the continued viability of religious communities and in helping new generations answer a call to faithful service. But for so many years it has felt as if many Black churches have too readily given up hope in the face of trends toward religious decline. Instead of seeing this as a call to innovate, too many have floundered in their commitment to nurturing the spiritual lives of young African Americans. To be fair, this book is not a systematic study of religious education or faith development in contemporary Black churches, and thus I reserve my fuller assessment of religious education in Black churches for a different book.[7] And yet, embedded in the lives of the religious activist-educators are experiences that remind us of what is possible in Black religious communities.

I have often looked beyond Black church education as a site of transformative education and as the catalyst for liberative pedagogy in new generations. I have researched people and movements at the intersections of religion, education, and social change, who are often not directly situated within religious communities. And I continue to affirm the ways in which we learn from exemplars both within and outside of traditional religious communities. However, I have also begun to wrestle more seriously with this question: Can Black churches still be part of the development and mentoring of generations of religiously inspired activist-educators? And while I would love to offer a resounding yes, the best that I can offer is *maybe*. My questions about the role of institutional Black religion in the future project of activist-education depends on the willingness of churches to adapt and to partner with youth and young adult activists in ways that they have never imagined before. For example, churches must take seriously the suspicions and distrust that many youth and young adults (and their parents) have of institutions in general, and to decenter and rethink the hierarchical and often rigids ways in which institutions have worked in the past. Again, there is a lesson to be learned here from the activist-educators who even generations before had to launch out and create their own clubs, conventions, schools, and coalitions to support their work and movements. Even in the past, congregations did not necessarily lead the charge. But they helped to support the work with space, resources, and theological and moral grounding. Therefore, my lingering questions are less about whether congregations can get into (back into) the business of nurturing activist-educators and more about what types of education and formation are required. For example, the stories of the activist-educators in this book invite us to remember and consider anew the *revolutionary* nature of education, and specifically religious education. bell hooks's description of her early experiences of teaching and learning also reflects the legacy of these activist-educators in Black communities, when she wrote, "For black folks teaching—educating—was fundamentally political because it was rooted in the anti-racist struggle. Indeed, my all-black grade school became the location where I experienced learning as revolution."[8] The idea of learning as revolution is at the center of the lives of activist-educators, but I was also left wondering: What would it look like for kids to experience education as revolutionary, as a practice of freedom in both public schools and religious educational settings? What would it look like for every teacher to see their work as a sacred calling and education as a practice of liberation and freedom? What would it look like for congregations and religious communities to commit to the educational and social needs of children and families as an integral part of their spiritual development and wholeness? And what would it mean for us to have a wider and more expansive vision and understanding of the sacred task of education and transformation, particularly religious education that goes beyond learning facts about one's religious tradition to educating for the wholeness and flourishing of all people?

Of course, the pragmatist in me always looks for ways of implementing these radical visions. Many of the educators in this book, like Olivia Pearl Stokes, can help us here, particularly with her detailed outline of the ethnic school model as a means of implementing revolutionary education in Black churches. In addition to Stokes' work, I recognize that embracing the revolutionary dimensions of religious education also requires creating educational curriculum and spaces that are rich in a womanist communal ethic, one that centers the well-being and flourishing of Black people (children, youth, and women in particular). This model also counters the theological parochialism that has become so dominant, and that has prompted so many Black people to question the liberative possibility of the Black church.

Radical Black religious education must be decidedly innovative in both content and methods. In a recent conversation, SIEC director, Akosua Lesesne, reminded me of the importance of being intentional about educational design, alongside rich content. Education is not simply pouring information into empty vessels. Since it is formative and transformative, any vision of radical Black religious education must attend to *how* we invite new generations into shared work and commitment. This builds directly on the innovation of educators in the past and present. For example, it remembers the innovative methods of Lawson and Clark, who not only had to center the work of laypeople and women and students but also had to rethink how education took place and where. In each case they were conducting religious education and education for social change in unexpected places. They were also reminding learners of the revolutionary nature of Jesus, and how God was involved in their struggles for freedom and was supporting them to fight on. As such, when we embrace the revolutionary or radical dimension of religious education in this century, we must also reimagine how we invite and inspire others into the collective reflection on how God is showing up in their current struggles for freedom.

Therefore, radical Black religious education not only attends to the content of womanist and Black liberation theology (as written by other scholars), but it must also invite new generations into womanist theological reflection whereby the work of "naming God" and seeing the divine for oneself is not limited to academic theologians.[9] Indeed, describing how God is moving has never has been limited to academic theology. Part of reclaiming the revolutionary nature of radical Black religious education entails reminding Black people of their roles in testifying to who God is and how God is moving in their lives.

When I envision education that helps create new generations of religiously inspired activists, I do not ask simply whether religious education should be political and revolutionary. Instead, I see the need for Black churches and communities to embrace the radical and revolutionary work already taking place among activists and educators and to walk with them in ways that seek to learn and create space for ongoing transformation and spiritual renewal for both religious communities and activists. In summary, I see the need for us to heed Carter G. Woodson's wisdom, that "Real education means to inspire people to live more abundantly, to learn to begin with life as they find it and make it better . . . "[10]

Notes

Introduction

1. See Pierson's obituary, https://www.legacy.com/us/obituaries/houstonchronicle/name/rita-pierson-obituary?pid=165784768. At the time of her death, Pierson was still educating and was embarking on a community-wide antipoverty and education program. See Hollie O'Connor, "Waco Poverty Expert Rita Pierson Dies," *Waco Tribune-Herald*, June 29, 2013. Updated July 15, 2020.
2. See Karen Baker-Fletcher, *A Singing Something: Womanist Reflections on Anna Julia Cooper* (New York: Crossroad Publishing, 1994).
3. These critiques included more extreme attempts to call the Black Lives Matter movement anti-Christian (see, for example, https://decisionmagazine.com/the-stated-goals-of-black-lives-matter-are-anti-christian/ (accessed September 11, 2021), as well as conversations and reports that name the increasing numbers of nonaffiliated Black youth/young adult activist and the more inclusive and decentralized leadership in the movement as a marker of distinctiveness from the civil rights movement of the mid-twentieth century. (See Emma Green, "Black Activism, Unchurched?," *Atlantic Magazine*, March 22, 2016, https://www.theatlantic.com/politics/archive/2016/03/black-activism-baltimore-black-church/474822/.)
4. This work was not an attempt to ignore or refute the possibility of Black activism apart from religious communities and particularly apart from the Black church. Indeed, there is a long and rich legacy of activism in the African American community that does not center the Black church, and many scholars have problematized the narrow centering of the Black institutional church in the civil rights movements, among them Barbara Savage. Rather, this work was an attempt to offer resources for Black people in search of and in conversation with an ongoing tradition of religious, activist education and to explore the ways that there is continuity between the twentieth-century educators and the work of Black teachers and activist-educators today—even in relationship to conversations of faith.
5. See Barbara Savage, *Your Spirits Walk beside Us*, (Cambridge, MA: Harvard Press, 2008), 2–12. See also Kenneth Hill, *Religious Education in the African American Tradition* (St. Louis, MO: Chalice Press, 2007). Hill goes further to note that liberation theology remains a minority theology among Black Christianity in the United States. Regardless of the traction of Black liberation and womanist theologies in academic circles, they have not made the same lasting and continued impact in local congregations and communities. Alongside the reality that Black liberation theology is not (and never has been) the dominant theology among African American Christians is the ongoing conversation about the increasing numbers of youth and

young adults (of every race) who are not affiliated with religious organizations. While the data is somewhat less detrimental for African Americans, there have been several reflections on whether, how, and why radical social change among this generation of Black young people is no longer connected to their religious communities/churches (see *Atlantic* article by Green, "Black Activism, Unchurched").

6. Savage, *Your Spirits*, 11.

7. See Almeda Wright, *The Spiritual Lives of Young African Americans* (New York: Oxford University Press, 2017), 160–166.

8. This phrase, however, is somewhat redundant given the long history of religion, education, and activism connecting in the lives of Black teachers.

9. Audrey Thomas McCluskey, *A Forgotten Sisterhood: Pioneering Black Women Educators and Activists in the Jim Crow South* (New York: Rowman and Littlefield, 2014).

10. Ibid., 1.

11. Ibid., 7.

12. Ibid. However, not all teachers were organizers or even activists. For many, teaching was one of the few professions open to Black women. Some therefore regarded teaching as an opportunity for self-advancement with little regard for the larger society, and even in others it bred elitism and created schisms between this educated elite and the masses of Black people.

13. See Almeda Wright, "Unknown, but Not Unimportant! Reflecting on Teachers Who Create Social Change," *Religious Education* 111, no. 3: 262–268, doi: 10.1080/00344087.2016.1172861.

14. bell hooks, *Teaching to Transgress* (New York: Routledge, 1994), 2–3. She notes that this education was in direct opposition to the education she received in White-dominated schools, where the White teachers were invested in teaching/reinforcing White supremacy.

15. McCluskey, *A Forgotten Sisterhood,* 1.

16. McCluskey uses the phrase *activist educator* sporadically throughout the book (see p. 16) but does not offer a precise definition of the idea. However, I emphasize her research in the way that I employ the term *activist-educator*, because of her recognition of these Black women educators' counterhegemonic work and understanding of education as a path to freedom, while also noting (in passing) the importance of their faith in God and themselves in order to make it work.

17. There are also many examples of the complicated and compromised connections between religion, education, and social change. In truth many of the early discussions of what role(s) religion could play in education or in social transformation particularly for African Americans were those of concern and a general fear that religion was not necessarily or primarily a support in the educational achievements of Black people. Many early Black elites named a contentious relationship between Black religion and political life as well. See Barbara Savage, *Your Spirits Walk beside Us* (Cambridge, MA: Harvard, 2008), and Gary Dorrien, *The New Abolition: W. E. B. Du Bois and the Black Social Gospel* (New Haven, CT: Yale, 2015).

18. Given my interest in the work of educators and the role of education in social change, I noted the strong educational leanings of early denominational leaders and the

interconnected histories of establishing churches and social aid societies and schools in the eighteenth and nineteenth centuries.

19. Gayraud Wilmore, *Black Religion and Black Radicalism* (Maryknoll, NY: Orbis Press, 1998), ix.

20. In many ways, Wilmore was responding to a centuries-old question renewed in the rise of the Nation of Islam and a more secular Black Power/Black Nationalist movement of "how Black people could embrace the religion of their oppressors?" For many, the question of how one could be Black and Christian was real and pressing, as Christianity had been (and continues to be) connected to White supremacist, Eurocentric, and nationalist strands that were used to oppress (and definitely not to liberate Black people).

21. Gayraud Wilmore, *Black Religion and Black Radicalism*, vii.

22. See Gary Dorrien, "What We Don't Know about Black Social Gospel: A Long-Neglected Tradition Is Reclaimed," *Religion Dispatches*, November 9, 2015, accessed May 23, 2016, http://religiondispatches.org/what-we-dont-know-about-black-soc ial-gospel-a-long-neglected-tradition-is-reclaimed/. This of course resonates with the findings of Savage noted earlier, and even the work of scholars such as Gary Dorrien, who outlines a history of the Black Social Gospel in the early twentieth century, which includes figures like Du Bois, Ida B. Wells, and Nannie Helen Burroughs. But even in classifying them as part of a Black social gospel movement, he is not easily able to codify their diverse religious beliefs and practices. Neither does Dorrien argue that these proponents of a Black social gospel were ever in the majority among Black Christians. Instead, he calls them *embattled minorities* (Dorrien, "What We Don't Know about Black social gospel"). See also Dorrien, *The New Abolition*.

23. See Almeda M. Wright, *The Spiritual Lives of Young African Americans* (New York: Oxford University Press, 2017), 104–106, for my fuller exposition of the role of womanist theology and methods in my research. See also Delores Williams, *Sisters in the Wilderness* (1993; repr. Maryknoll, NY: Orbis Press, 2003), and

    Linda E. Thomas, "Womanist Theology, Epistemology, and a New Anthropological Paradigm," *Cross Currents 48*, no. 4 (Summer 1998), http.://www.aril.org/tho mas.htm.

24. See Carl A. Grant, Keffrelyn D. Brown, and Anthony L. Brown, *Black Intellectual Thought in Education: The Missing Traditions of Anna Julia Cooper, Carter G. Woodson, and Alain LeRoy Locke* (New York: Routledge, 2016), xix.

25. For example, most theories and philosophies of education ignored the contributions of Black teachers and intellectuals well into the twentieth century. Toward the end of the century, some scholars and schools of education began to attend more carefully to the writings of figures like Du Bois and Booker T. Washington, but most were not included as part of a wider canon for teaching and learning in America. See Grant et al., *Black Intellectual Thought*, for a larger discussion of the marginalization of Black intellectual thought in education.

26. See Mary C. Boys, *Educating in Faith* (Lima, OH: Academic Renewal Press, 1989), 8–11.

27. Boys, *Educating in Faith*, 6–7. She further breaks down each of these foundational questions to explore more carefully everything from revelation (How is God revealed?) to conversion, faith and belief, theology, culture, and the goal of education.

She also wrestled with questions of knowledge (What does it mean to know?), how social sciences factored into the theorizing of religious education, theorists' understanding of curriculum and teaching, and the vision of society toward which each theorist was educating.

28. Allen Moore, ed., *Religious Education as Social Transformation* (Birmingham, AL: Religious Education Press, 1989), 1–10.

29. Moore, *Religious Education as Social*, 7. Coe's work is also highly connected with educational philosopher John Dewey, among others. Mary Boys also describes the connection between Coe's understanding of religious education and the work of Paulo Freire. She points to the ways that both Coe and Freire, in very different historical and political contexts, affirm the work of education in transforming the world. See also George Albert Coe, *What Is Christian Education?* (New York: Scribner, 1929); and Horace Bushnell, *Christian Nurture* (New Haven, CT: Yale University Press, 1967).

30. This critique does not dismiss the usefulness of her typology, but I am pointing to the lack of engagement with African Americans and many other marginalized communities in even the most comprehensive surveys of the field of religious education and its development over time in the United States. For example, there is a need to ask: Do we see a social thrust in religious education in African American communities? Would we have named it as such? Do many of the religious activist-educators explored in this work, such as DuBois, Wells, and Nannie Helen Burroughs, count as part of this social religious education tradition? Would any of the Black clubwomen, who are calling for both religious reform and social and individual uplift, count?

31. Hill, *Religious Education in the African*, 5.

32. For example, at early points in American religious history most schools constituted a type of religious education in that most were created for the training of (male) ministers, and it was only later in the education of Black people that vocational/skills-based schools and curriculum were created. But in the earliest models of formal education in the United States (or the early colonies) all education was a type of religious instruction/formation. Explicit religious instruction often continued to be a central part of the curriculum even when different types of schools emerged.

33. This quote is taken from James Cone's book blurb and review for Charles R. Foster and Fred Smith, *Black Religious Experience: Conversations on Double Consciousness and the Work of Grant Shockley* (Nashville, TN: Abingdon Press, 2003).

Section I

1. See Kevin K. Gaines, "Racial Uplift Ideology in the Era of 'the Negro Problem,'" Freedom's Story, TeacherServe®, National Humanities Center, accessed August 18, 2021, http://nationalhumanitiescenter.org/tserve/freedom/1865-1917/essays/racialuplift. htm, for a helpful discussion of the idea of racial uplift during the post–Civil War era. Gaines offers a helpful critique of the elitist tendencies of the ideology of racial uplift. However, in this chapter I am also pointing toward the ongoing externally imposed

effects of anti-Black racism and oppression that required Black people throughout the twentieth century (and beyond) to have to tell their own stories and to counter the effects of racist histories and ideologies on themselves and others.

Chapter 1

1. Anna J. Cooper, "Sketches from a Teacher's Notebook: Loss of Speech through Isolation (1923?)," in *The Voice of Anna Julia Cooper*, ed. Charles Lemert and Esme Bhan (New York: Rowman & Littlefield, 1998), 225.
2. A. J. Cooper, "Sketches," 226.
3. Ibid.
4. Louise Daniel Hutchinson, *Anna J. Cooper: A Voice from the South* (Washington, DC: Anacosta Neighborhood Museum of the Smithsonian Institution, 1981), 89.
5. Hutchinson, *Anna J. Cooper*, 89. *Southland* was one of the first publications for which Cooper wrote. Cooper described it as the "first Negro magazine in the United States." The editor of Southland, Rev. Joseph C. Price, was the President of Livingston College in North Carolina (an African Methodist Episcopal Zion college).
6. Ibid., 3.
7. Ibid., 14.
8. Ibid., 20. See also her own account of entry into the school.
9. Ibid.
10. Ibid.
11. Some records note that she would have started school at nine and thus would have been teaching since then. Cooper in her own words writes that she began teaching at the age of eight. (See ibid., 20.)
12. See Hutchinson for much of this background information. Cooper recounts the joys of teaching her mother the subtle differences between letters, such as b, f, and l.
13. Hutchinson, *Anna J. Cooper*, 21.
14. Anna J. Cooper, "The Higher Education of Women," in *A Voice from the South, 1892* (Mineola, NY: Dover Thrift Editions, 2016), 34–35.
15. A. J. Cooper, "Higher Education," 34–38. Cooper continues this section by appealing to the Black ministers to commit to supporting women's education: "Now this is not fancy. It is a simple unvarnished photograph, and what I believe was not in those days exceptional in colored schools, and I ask the men and women who are teachers and co-workers for the highest interests of the race, that they give the girls a chance! . . . if there is an ambitious girl with pluck and brain to take the higher education, encourage her to make the most of it. Let there be the same flourish of trumpets and clapping of hands as when a boy announces his determination to enter the lists; . . . let money be raised and scholarships be founded in our colleges and universities for self-supporting, worthy young women, to offset and balance the aid that can always be found for boys who will take theology."
16. Note that Cooper does not raise any objection to men being the only ones allowed into the ordained clergy positions.

17. A. J. Cooper, "Higher Education," 25. Here Cooper writes of a feminine ingredient or flavor that religion, science, art, and economics have all needed.

18. Brittney Cooper, *Beyond Respectability* (Chicago: University of Illinois Press, 2017), 3. Cooper echoes my contentions that we do a disservice to Black women's contributions to the intellectual and "canon"-building work of early twentieth-century Black intellectuals if and when we only look at what could be published or what book-length works were produced by Black people during this time period. While it is important to esteem Du Bois and Woodson, among others, for the types of larger histories of the race they produced or called for, we cannot pretend that Black women were not contributing to the intellectual work, the study, and discussion of race questions/issues that mattered to people of color just based on the difficulties sexism presented in terms of the types of work they could produce/get published and the places we typically look for Black intellectual theories. Brittney Cooper writes that "if we actually want to take Black women seriously as thinkers and knowledge producers, we must begin to look for their thinking in unexpected places, to expect its incursions in genres like autobiography, novels, news stories, medical records, organizational histories, public speeches, and diary entries . . . " (B. Cooper, *Beyond Respectability*, 12.)

19. A. J. Cooper, "The Status of Women in America," in *A Voice from the South*, 60. These dualisms take place in both "Womanhood: A Vital Element" (1886) and "The Status of Woman in America" (1892) and reflect more of the dominant thinking regarding the inherent, natural nature of the genders as well as her observations of the way that male dominance has led to cruelty and unmitigated greed and acquisition, which could have been tempered by women's interventions and perspectives.

20. A. J. Cooper, "The Status of Women in America," 66–67.

21. Ibid.

22. Many readers and scholars note the difference in tone of Anna Julia Cooper's writing and some of her male contemporaries, including many of Du Bois's essays. For example, Du Bois's experience growing up surrounded by a White gaze and always feeling that he had to compete or that he was deemed as coming up short pushed him to write poignantly (but negatively) about his experiences as a Black man in America—describing the warring in his spirit. Meanwhile Cooper wrote of being educated in North Carolina, in a Black school where her major points of contention were the limits that men (White and Black) attempted to put on her regarding what educational trajectories she could pursue. And even in this setting, we can look at Cooper's larger community and the ways that historians describe the zeal and fervor with which the Black community was pursuing education and voting rights during the Reconstruction era. Thus, we see in Cooper's writings, which were both earlier than Du Bois and from a very different social location, a celebration of the giftedness and gift of women (and all people) to participate in advancing society.

23. A. J. Cooper, "Womanhood: A Vital Element in the Regeneration and Progress of a Race," in *A Voice from the South*, 5. Earlier in this essay she also notes the way Christ serves as the foundation of all justice and progressive ideals that society could even attempt to conceive of: "Christ gave ideals not formulæ. The Gospel is a germ requiring

millennia for its growth and ripening. . . . With all the strides our civilization has made from the first to the nineteenth century, we can boast not an idea, not a principle of action, not a progressive social force but was already mutely foreshadowed, or directly enjoined in that simple tale of a meek and lowly life. The quiet face of the Nazarene is ever seen a little way ahead, never too far to come down to and touch the life of the lowest in days the darkest, yet ever leading onward, still onward, the tottering childish feet of our strangely boastful civilization" (Cooper, p. 5).

24. A. J. Cooper, *Voice*, 5.

25. A. J. Cooper, *Voice*, 18–19.

26. A. J. Cooper, *Voice*, 18.

27. Baker-Fletcher, *A Singing Something*, 42.

28. A. J. Cooper, "On Education," in *Voice*, 250.

29. She had a small stint teaching at Wilberforce College and serving as the President of Frelinghuysen University, a small collection of schools dedicated to teaching adult learners in Washington, DC (see Hutchinson, *Anna J. Cooper*, 155–173). Cooper also helped form a Sabbath school at St. Augustine's. There is little information available on this school. I, however, note this too as an example of Cooper's commitment to teaching youth and adults. Indeed, the creation of a Sabbath school for poor Black children (and adults) was radical and an important part of her early teaching work.

30. A. J. Cooper, "On Education," 250.

31. Hutchinson, *Anna J. Cooper*, 53–57. From 1901 to 1906 Cooper was principal of M Street School. She introduced a college preparatory curriculum, which led the school to become accredited by Harvard (for the first time). They also placed students at schools like Harvard, Yale, Radcliffe, Dartmouth, Amherst, Oberlin, and Brown. She was ousted from this position by the predominately White DC school board, in large part because they did not appreciate the international attention she gained from a French researcher named Klein, who identified M School as the best in DC. They also did not agree with the college preparatory curriculum and favored vocational education for Black students instead, which she opposed, noting the diversity among Black students, wanting to offer the widest curricular offerings possible. The larger context around this controversy also includes Du Bois coming to give a speech at M Street School during the 1902–1903 academic year, in which he criticized the practices around the country of attempts to "restrict the curriculum of colored schools" (Hutchinson, 69). This is included in the newspaper accounting of the controversy and connects Du Bois's speech with an inquiry made by Dr. Atwood, a Black citizen in attendance, who wanted to see if this kind of restriction was taking place in DC. This call for an investigation of course unsettled many in power and also contributed to Cooper's removal.

32. Hutchinson, Anna J. Cooper, 68.

33. Ibid.

34. Ibid., 155.

35. A. J. Cooper, "On Education," 258.

36. Baker-Fletcher, 57.

37. Ibid.

38. See Baker-Fletcher and Hutchinson's discussions of Coopers debates with Rev. Francis Grimke and Cooper's disagreements with him on particular interpretations of scripture and theological standpoints (Baker Fletcher, 57–60).

39. See Baker-Fletcher, 65. She writes of Cooper, "To claim that Black people were created in the image of God undoubtedly sounded as radical to the ears of many White Americans then as the Black liberationist claim that God is Black sounds to many White people today" (Baker-Fletcher, 65).

40. This is important to point out, because it prompts us to explore when and how Cooper began to articulate this type of radical theology, which Baker-Fletcher names as influenced by the social gospel. I actually see influences on Cooper's theology and thought far beyond the "White social gospel" and see her also contributing to what Gary Dorian and others have outlined as a Black social gospel strand, without moving away from the pious practices of Black women's spirituality. See Almeda Wright, *The Spiritual Lives of Young African Americans* (New York: Oxford University Press, 2017), 186–92, for a fuller discussion of this.

41. A. J. Cooper, *Voice*, 3. The larger context of her thoughts is quoted here: "It is true the spirit of Christianity had not yet put the seal of catholicity on this sentiment. Chivalry, according to Bascom, was but the toning down and softening of a rough and lawless period. It gave a roseate glow to a bitter winter's day. Those who looked out from castle windows reveled in its 'amethyst tints.' But God's poor, the weak, the unlovely, the commonplace were still freezing and starving none the less in unpitied, unrelieved loneliness. Respect for woman, the much lauded chivalry of the Middle Ages, meant what I fear it still means to some men in our own day—respect for the elect few among whom they expect to consort. The idea of the radical amelioration of womankind, reverence for woman as woman regardless of rank, wealth, or culture, was to come from that rich and bounteous fountain from which flow all our *liberal and universal ideas*—the Gospel of Jesus Christ" [emphasis added].

42. Lemert and Bhan, *Voice*, 19.

43. Ibid., 344.

44. See Shirley Moody-Turner, " 'Dear Doctor Du Bois': Anna Julia Cooper, W. E. B. Du Bois, and the Gender Politics of Black Publishing," *MELUS 40*, no. 3 (2015): 47–68, http://www.jstor.org/stable/24570162, for a powerful discussion of the ways that Cooper struggled to get her work published and the ways she reached out to DuBois, both for help and in critique of his work as an editor.

Chapter 2

1. Du Bois, *Souls of Black Folks* (Mineola, NY: Dover Publications, 2016), 52.

2. Du Bois, *Dusk of Dawn (the Oxford W. E. B. du Bois)* (New York: Oxford University Press, 2007), 16.

3. See Reiland Rabaka. "W.E.B. Du Bois's Evolving Africana Philosophy of Education," *Journal of Black Studies 33*, no. 4 (March 2003): 399–449, https://doi.org/10.1177/0021934702250021, for a discussion of Du Bois's educational philosophy that centers on his "Talented Tenth" essay.

4. Others also often refer to Du Bois's collection of essays (W. E. B. Du Bois, *The Education of Black People, Ten Critiques, 1906–1960*, ed. Herbert Aptheker (New York: Monthly Review Press, 2001), which he was never able to publish while alive, for his most complete thoughts on education and critiques of higher education for Black people.

5. However, Du Bois names the evolution of many of his elitist educational theories as he revised his vision of the "Talented Tenth" in 1948 and notes further the power of the masses (thanks in part of Marxist critiques) to move agendas forward on their own and because of their mass numbers).

6. I want to emphasize how I am situating Du Bois religiously/spiritually, even as others might want to look for a more directly or explicitly institutionalized religious value or system. His impact is also explicitly religious in terms of how he informs the disciplines. I am careful not to overstate or overemphasize any formal or institutionally affiliated religiosity in Du Bois, but I also do not shy away from naming the spiritual and religious values that he demonstrated (even as he evolved away from formal religious affiliation and participation).

7. Book review of *The Souls of Black Folks*, by W. E. B. Du Bois, University of Massachusetts online exhibit, http://scua.library.umass.edu/exhibits/dubois/page5.htm, accessed August 17, 2021.

8. Du Bois's life and scholarship remain a source of inspiration and reflection for me because of the ways he was able to capture the experiences of so many African Americans and other people of color living in predominantly White spaces and confronting daily the effects of White supremacy. For example, one of his most frequently analyzed ideas is that of *double consciousness,* by which he named the mental gymnastics that many Black people undertake to hold together their identities as Black and American. Even as we might hope that an experience of "twoness" would end or for our identities as Black and American not to feel contradictory and at times completely incompatible, Du Bois's discussion of double consciousness still speaks to generations of people and scholars. It has provoked many of us to think again about the psychological toll (and at times trauma) associated with being Black in the United States, or, more correctly stated, the toll associated with anti-black racism and White supremacy that is entrenched in the U.S. landscape.

9. Du Bois, *Dusk*, 5.

10. Du Bois, *Dusk*, 5.

11. Ibid.

12. Ibid., 6.

13. Ibid., 6.

14. Others, like Carter G. Woodson, took up the project of researching and cataloging Black people's history and lives with even more vigor.

15. Du Bois, *Dusk*, 8.

16. Ibid., 15–16.

17. Ibid., 16

18. Du Bois's father's family, in particular his grandfather Alfred Du Bois Sr., also has interesting connections to the Episcopal church in New Haven. He was part of a group of Black people agitating and protesting racism in the Episcopal church there and for the formation of a Black Episcopal community, St. Luke's. While this offers some interesting contexts for Du Bois's familial religious orientation, Du Bois was clear that his father's family had little direct contact and influence on young Du Bois.

19. Du Bois, *Dusk*, 5.
20. Herbert Aptheker, ed., "Introduction," in *W. E. B. Du Bois, Prayers for Dark People* (Amherst: University of Massachusetts Press, 1980), vii.
21. Ibid.
22. Ibid., viii.
23. Du Bois, *Dusk*, 16
24. Ibid.
25. Ibid., 17.
26. Ibid., 32
27. Ibid.
28. Aptheker, *Prayers*, 33.
29. Ibid., 58.
30. Ibid., 21.
31. Ibid., ix.
32. This is not to say that Du Bois's larger project of systematically studying the lives of Black people and noting the accomplishments of a group that was newly freed was not conducted to benefit the conditions of the masses of Black people. However, I am noting that Du Bois's approach to improving the education/lives of the masses of Black people was an indirect one. In part, this indirect work informs many of his larger ideals such as the idea of the "talented tenth" or the ability of creating an educated Black elite that would then take on the work of educating the rest of the Black community.
33. http://scua.library.umass.edu/duboisopedia/doku.php?id=about:philadelphia_Negro&do=show, accessed June 27, 2018.
34. http://www.webdubois.org/wdb-AtlUniv.html#primary.
35. Ibid.
36. Zuckerman, xv–xvii.
37. Ibid., xvi.
38. Du Bois, *An Autobiography of W. E. B. Du Bois*, 1940, 220, quoted in Les Back and Maggie Tate, "For a Sociological Reconstruction: W.E.B. Du Bois, Stuart Hall and Segregated Sociology," *Sociological Research Online* 20, no. 3 (August 2015): 155–166, doi:10.5153/sro.3773. They write, "But in the violent years at the end of the century one incident had a lasting effect on Du Bois's faith in the role of science and reason in achieving social progress. It involved the plight of an illiterate Black farm labourer in Georgia called Sam Hose. Sam Hose had killed his White employer, Alfred Cranford, and was accused of assaulting Cranford's wife." Du Bois committed to paper the appropriate evidence and mitigating circumstances of Hose's crime. In *The Autobiography of W.E.B. Du Bois*, he describes, "I wrote out a careful and reasoned statement concerning the evident facts and started down to the Atlanta Constitution Office, carrying in my pocket a letter of introduction to Joel Chandler Harris. I did not get there. On the way news met me: Sam Hose had been lynched, and they said his knuckles were on exhibition at a grocery store farther down Mitchell Street along which I was walking. I turned back to the University. I began to turn aside from my work" (1940; 222). This experience brought home the barbarism of White supremacy.

He could not be a detached or even "contemptuously fair" social scientist while people like Sam Hose were being lynched, brutalized and starved. The research he was conducting constituted "so small a part of the sum of occurrences"; it was too far from the "hot reality of real life." . . . For a fuller accounting of Du Bois's shift from his almost naive belief in what Alfred Young calls "emancipatory social science," see Alford A. Young et al., *The Souls of W. E. B. Du Bois* (New York: Routledge, 2006), https://doi.org/10.4324/9781315631981.

39. Phil Zuckerman, "Introduction," in *The Negro Church*, ed. W. E. B. Du Bois (Oxford: AltaMira Press, 2003), vii.

40. It is important to acknowledge that this was a massive ethnographic project, and thus Du Bois employed several students and other scholars in the field, including some of the earliest women sociologists.

41. Du Bois, *The Negro Church*, 208.

42. Ibid., 189.

43. Instead of lambasting the churches for not teaching Black youth the importance of moral goodness (as the essence of religion), we might hope that Du Bois would simply note the diversity of beliefs among African American Christians. However, it was more in line with the scholarship of his time to offer one universalizing perspective of what Christianity should be, even in the face of empirical data that reminds us that there are many different understandings of the religion and its priorities among Christians. It is also interesting to me that a century later, another sociologist, Christian Smith (*Soul Searching*) critiques the religious beliefs of U.S. teens for focusing primarily on "being good" and "having a good life." In some ways, more of the country shifted to or embraced Du Bois's assessment of what religion should be about, and generations later the critique arises that this is problematic as well. In part this reminds me of the positionality of the researchers and interpreters to the data. Particularly with relationship to religion, what the researcher holds to be essential to religion/Christianity automatically shapes their findings about how religion should function in people's lives. The prior beliefs of the researcher often do not allow the narratives of participants, particularly children and youth, to speak authoritatively about their faith. Often the religious ideas and beliefs of children and youth are immediately deemed insufficient or as an indication of some shortcoming in their upbringing or religious formation.

44. The idea that religious education only focuses on Christian nurture is also a particularly limited view of what religious education and formation entailed historically and today.

45. Scholars such at Barbara Savage argue that Du Bois's criticisms of the Black church (along with those of Woodson) shaped the discourse around the Black church for decades, both positively and negatively. Savage points mostly to the negative impact of Du Bois's criticisms in that it became the taken-for-granted paradigm of the Black church and shaped conversations about the Black church being more of a hindrance to political and social engagement among Black people, instead of a help. Thus, many generations of scholars after Du Bois did not fully appreciate or even see the ability of

the Black church to be the incubator for the mid-twentieth-century civil rights movement in the United States. See Barbara Savage, *Their Spirits Walk beside Us.*

46. Du Bois, *The Negro Church*, p. xii.
47. A larger discussion of Du Bois's work as the editor of the *Crisis* magazine and his contributions to the expansion of Black art and culture in this role as editor is beyond the scope of this chapter but is a crucial part of Du Bois's commitment to helping Black people tell and celebrate their own stories (and to move beyond seeing themselves as mere recipients of cultural, religious expressions).
48. Du Bois, *The Education of Black People*, 195.

Section II

1. Ida B. Wells-Barnett quoted in Emilie M. Townes, "Living in the New Jerusalem: The Rhetoric and Movement of Liberation in the House of Evil," in *A Troubling in My Soul*, ed. Emilie M. Townes (Maryknoll, NY: Orbis, 1993), 86.
2. Burroughs' desire to establish a school also had a great deal to do with "self-determination" and wanting to be able to control the curriculum and administration of her school, while many other schools "for" Black youth and girls were still controlled by White benefactors and public educational boards.

Chapter 3

1. Ida B. Wells, *Crusade for Justice: The Autobiography of Ida B. Wells*, ed. Alfreda M. Duster (Chicago: University of Chicago Press, 1970), 298–299.
2. Many other activists and educators at the turn of the twentieth century were also Sunday school teachers and prided themselves in their commitment to organizing educational opportunities for newly freed Black children and adults.
3. Wells, *Crusade for Justice*, 298–299.
4. Ibid., 299.
5. Ibid.
6. Ibid., 299–305.
7. Miriam Decosta-Willis, ed., *The Memphis Diary of Ida B. Wells.* (Boston: Beacon Press, 1995), 128–129. See also Emilie Townes, "Because God Gave Her Vision: The Religious Impulse of Ida B. Wells-Barnett," in *Spirituality and Social Responsibility: Vocational Vision of Women in the United Methodist Tradition*, ed. Rosemary Skinner Keller (Nashville, TN: Abingdon Press, 1993), 141.
8. Mia Bay, *To Tell the Truth Freely: The Life of Ida B. Wells* (New York: Hill and Wang, 2009), 10.
9. Emilie Townes, *Womanist Justice, Womanist Hope* (Atlanta: Scholars Press, 1993), 109.
10. Miriam Decosta-Willis, ed., *The Memphis Diary of Ida B. Wells* (Boston: Beacon Press, 1995), 132–133.

11. Ibid., 128–129. Much of what we know about Wells's religious life and her experiences as a Sunday school teacher is found in her personal diaries, of which there only remains a small set from 1885 to 1887 (but it is likely that she kept diaries for much longer periods). Because of the nature of journals, these writings are not as polished as her published pieces, but they afford us a particularly personal glimpse into her struggles and strivings.

12. Ibid., 142.

13. Ibid., 129.

14. See Linda O. McMurry, *To Keep the Waters Troubled: The Life of Ida B. Wells* (New York: Oxford, 2000), 13. McMurry writes, "In part, Wells was greatly influenced by the Northern White Methodist Episcopal missionaries who taught her at Rust College, the common name of the school that was established to teach newly freedmen and women in Holly Springs, Mississippi. Rust was 'strongly tinged with evangelical Christianity.' Students were required to attend daily chapel, weekly prayer meetings, and church on Sunday. W. W. Hooper, who became president of Rust while Ida was a student, was remembered as a religious man who 'prayed in chapel with his eyes open and would call your name when he got through if you didn't behave.' Such an environment reinforced the religious training Ida received at home" (p. 13). Wells also excitedly recounted in her diaries going to hear Dwight Moody and other traveling revivalists preach.

15. Decosta-Willis, *The Memphis Diary*, 128.

16. Wells, *Crusade for Justice*, 9.

   According to the history of the school (https://www.rustcollege.edu/about-rust-college/history/), "Rust College was established in 1866 by the Freedman's Aid Society of the Methodist Episcopal Church. Its founders were missionaries from the North who opened a school in Asbury Methodist Episcopal Church, accepting adults of all ages, as well as children, for instruction in elementary subjects.... In 1870, the school was chartered as Shaw University, honoring the Reverend S.O. Shaw, who made a gift of $10,000 to the new institution. In 1892, the name was changed to Rust University to avoid confusion with another Shaw University. The name was a tribute to Richard S. Rust of Cincinnati, Ohio, Secretary of the Freedman's Aid Society. In 1915, the title was changed to the more realistic name, Rust College."

17. Wells, *Crusade for Justice*, 9.

18. Ibid.

19. Ibid.

20. Bay, *To Tell the Truth*, 10

21. Ibid., 16.

22. Ibid., 17.

23. Mia Bay, *Afterwords on CSPAN*, https://www.c-span.org/video/?284872-1/afterwords-mia-bay, aired March 26, 2009.

24. Wells, *Crusade for Justice*, 31.

25. Ibid.

26. It's interesting that we have to re-emphasize and reclaim Ida B. Wells's legacy as a teacher and educator. In part this deals with the reality that the object of Wells's activism and protest was primarily antilynching work, separation/segregation in public spaces (such as the train), and Black economic empowerment (as a site of White people's ire). Others whom we claim as educators or even radial educators (but who only taught formally for a few years) were also protesting injustices in the educational arena and calling for improved practices and policies there. Others still benefited from elite higher education—to which Wells never had access. This is in contrast to many others, such as Woodson, who only taught a few years formally. Woodson and Du Bois stayed connected to academia and were trained academics, whereas Wells was not—thus the need to reclaim her ongoing educative work/impact.

27. Wells, *Crusade for Justice*, 22.

28. Ibid.

29. Ibid.

30. Ibid., 23. *The Living Way* was started in 1874, and Wells recounts Rev. R. N. Countee asking her to write for it.

31. Ibid.

32. Ibid., 35. Wells notes that she became editor of the *Freespeech* in 1889. Her other co-owners were Rev. F. Nightingale, "pastor of the largest Baptist church in town," and J. L. Fleming (p. 35). It is amazing to me both that she would take on owning and editing a newspaper at such a young age and in spite of the financial risk and investment. It also speaks to her reputation as a writer and journalist that she would both be invited and included on equal footing with these local leaders and businessmen. There is also something important to attend to with the ongoing intersection of religion and religious organizations and leadership with the Black newspapers and communities during the late nineteenth century (and beyond). For Wells it was a natural arrangement that the pastor of one of the largest Black Baptist churches would also run a newspaper and thus could sell papers to his membership.

33. See Burnis R. Morris, *Carter G. Woodson: History, the Black Press, and Public Relations* (Jackson: University Press of Mississippi, 2017), 5–7. In particular, Morris offers a helpful chart of the many newspapers that Woodson read at Oliver Jones's tearoom in the 1890s (the illiterate coal miner) and explores the long-standing role of the press in Woodson's early formation and his later ability to promote and popularize Black History.

34. This connection between education and a Black-controlled weekly also points to a larger connection with the establishment of Black publishing houses/bodies, often religious presses at the same time as (or soon after) the establishment of independent Black denominations. See Kenneth Hill, *Religious Education in the African American Tradition* (St. Louis, MO: Chalice Press, 2007).

35. See Mia Bay, ed., *Ida B. Wells: The Light of Truth* (New York: Penguin Books, 2014), 218–219. In this work, Wells is also departing from her earlier writings and many of the writings of women during the nineteenth century, as she is not simply attempting to offer a female perspective or a perspective based in female moral authority. Instead, in the book *Red Record: Tabulated Statistics and Alleged Causes of Lynching in the*

United States, 1892–1894, she gives statistics and figures to illuminate the realities of lynching.

36. See Bay, *To Tell the Truth*, 45–58, for a fuller account of Wells's lawsuit of the Chesapeake, Ohio and Southwestern Railroad, after being asked to leave the "ladies' car" of the train in 1883. Wells initially won her suit in a lower court, only to have it overturned on appeal and with the growing push of segregation.

37. See Jennifer Sandlin, Michael O'Malley, and Jake Burdick, "Mapping the Complexity of Public Pedagogy Scholarship 1894–2010," *Review of Educational Research* 81 (2011): 338–375, https://doi.org/10.3102/0034654311413395.

38. Mai-Anh Le Tran, *Reset the Heart: Unlearning Violence, Relearning Hope* (Nashville, TN: Abingdon Press, 2017), 15–16.

39. Ellen Carol Dubois, "Raking Muck," *New York Times*, February 14, 1999, https://www.nytimes.com/1999/02/14/books/raking-muck.html.

40. She was giving up the newspaper that Ferdinand Barnett co-owned. Wells had bought a share from him before they were married. So, she was giving up not simply writing for newspapers, but also running one.

41. Wells, *Crusade for Justice*, 226–227.

42. Ibid.

43. Bay, *The Light of Truth*, 433

44. Bay, *To Tell the Truth*, 192.

45. Ibid, 316.

46. Ibid., 10.

47. Ibid., 7.

48. Ibid., 9.

49. Wells, *Crusade for Justice*, 415. See Bay, *Tell the Truth*, 315–316, for a fuller description of Wells-Barnett's references to Isaiah 62:6–9 and the Lord calling for watchmen on the walls to never let down their guard and to a sermon by abolitionist Wendell Phillips.

50. Ida B. Wells died of kidney disease on March 25, 1931, at the age of 68, in Chicago, Illinois. She once said, "I felt that one had better die fighting against injustice than to die like a dog or a rat in a trap" (https://www.biography.com/authors-writers/ida-b-wells).

Chapter 4

1. Opal Easter, *Nannie Helen Burroughs* (New York: Garland Publishing, 1995), 67.

2. Easter, *Nannie Helen Burroughs*, 67–68.

3. Nannie Helen Burroughs, "How the Sisters Are Hindered from Helping," in *From National Baptist Convention, Journal of the Twentieth Annual Session of the National Baptist Convention, Held in Richmond, Virginia, September 12–17, 1900* (Nashville, TN: National Baptist Publishing Board, 1900), 196–197. See also Graves, 25–26, in Kelisha B. Graves and Nannie Helen Burroughs, *Nannie Helen*

Burroughs: A Documentary Portrait of an Early Civil Rights Pioneer, 1900–1959 (Notre Dame: University of Notre Dame Press, 2019), muse.jhu.edu/book/66677.

4. Graves and Burroughs, *Nannie Helen Burroughs*, 24. Graves describes this as Burroughs's first public speech, and while I am certain that it is the first that we have record of, Burroughs had been active in her local church and writing and working for the Christian Banner long before her speech at 21 years old. This early church work and her cultivation of relationship within the denominational leadership paved the way for her to even have the opportunity to address the men and clergy at the national denominational meeting. We have to recognize the ways that other churchwomen both had to put their faith in Burroughs and must have already had evidence of her public speaking skills.

5. Cooper was addressing the Episcopal clergy in 1886, a little over a decade before Burroughs's address at the National Baptist Convention.

6. Evelyn Brooks Higginbotham quoted in Barbara Ransby, *Ella Baker and the Black Freedom Movement: A Radical Democratic Vision* (Chapel Hill: University of North Carolina Press, 2003), 14.

7. Higginbotham, *Righteous Discontent* (Cambridge, MA: Harvard University Press, 1994), 217.

8. Ibid.

9. Ibid.

10. Easter, *Nannie Helen Burroughs*, 25.

11. Sources note that John Burroughs either died or abandoned his family around the time Jennie decided to move to Washington, DC. See Graves and Burroughs, *Nannie Helen Burroughs*, xxii. Here, Graves notes the peripheral nature of John Burroughs in Nannie's life.

12. For a helpful discussion of Burroughs's early education in Washington, DC, see Shantina Shannell Jackson, "'To Struggle and Battle and Overcome': The Educational Thought of Nannie Helen Burroughs, 1875–1961" (Ph.D. diss., University of California, Berkeley, 2015).

13. McCluskey, *A Forgotten Sisterhood*, 103.

14. Easter, *Nannie Helen Burroughs*, 26.

15. Higginbotham, *Righteous Discontent*, 218.

16. Savage, *Your Spirits Walk beside Us*, 165. See also Easter, *Nannie Helen Burroughs*, 26. Easter notes that Burroughs was not able to get work as a domestic science teacher in Washington, DC, or at Tuskegee, though she wrote to Booker T. Washington there seeking employment. Easter does not discuss the underlying causes of Burroughs's inability to get a teaching job but notes the impact of this on Burroughs and notes this in light of the limited employment opportunities for Black women during the 1890s.

17. Earl L. Harrison, *The Dream and the Dreamer: An Abbreviated Story of the Life of Dr. Nannie Helen Burroughs and Nannie Helen Burroughs School at Washington, DC* (Washington, DC: Nannie Helen Burroughs Literature Foundation, 1956), 9–10. See also Easter, *Nannie Helen Burroughs*, 26, 57.

18. Easter, *Nannie Helen Burroughs*, 27

19. Ibid.

20. Ibid.

21. Graves and Burroughs, *Nannie Helen Burroughs*, xxiv.

22. Jackson, "To Struggle and Battle," 31: "Nannie relocated to the bustling city of Louisville in 1897. That year, the Christian Banner, the Baptist newspaper she worked for, moved its offices to Louisville. The move coincided with the Foreign Mission Board of the NBC relocating from Richmond, Virginia. Rev. L. G. Jordan, Nannie's employer, also made the journey. Once in Louisville, Nannie joined a growing population of influential and educated Black Baptists charged with coordinating the activities of over two million Baptists throughout the United States."

23. Easter, *Nannie Helen Burroughs*, 58.

24. Ibid.

25. See Ibid., 27–31, for fuller accounts of the many women who had attempted to organize a separate national Woman's Convention for years, starting as early as 1890 and getting nominal support in 1895. These women struggled against the rampant patriarchy and sexism of the male conventions and "parent bodies." The women also had to struggle because the men knew their power and the strength of their financial contributions and services and did not want to relinquish control of them and their money by allowing the development of a separate Women's Convention.

26. Ibid., 59.

27. Ibid., 60–62.

28. Ibid.

29. Even though the school opened debt-free, it experienced financial instability throughout its existence, in part because of Burroughs's vision for the school and her desire to add new buildings to the existing campus over the years.

30. McCluskey, *A Forgotten Sisterhood*, 1.

31. Ibid.

32. Easter, *Nannie Helen Burroughs*, 58. See also E. A. Wilson, *History of the Woman's Convention 1900-1955*, 1955, Burroughs Papers, Library of Congress.

33. Nannie H. Burroughs, "The Colored Woman and Her Relation to the Domestic Problem," in *The United Negro, His Problems and His Progress: Containing the Address and Proceedings of the Negro Young People's Christian Congress, Held August 6-11, 1902*, ed. Irvine Garland Penn and John Wesley Edward Bowen (Atlanta: D. E. Luther Publishing, 1902), 324–329. See also Graves and Burroughs, *Nannie Helen Burroughs*, 27–31.

34. She noted (somewhat pejoratively) that with other immigrant labor options many White families would not see the need to employ Black women.

35. Nannie H. Burroughs, "The Colored Woman and Her Relation to the Domestic Problem," 324–329. See also Graves and Burroughs, *Nannie Helen Burroughs*, 27–31.

36. Easter, *Nannie Helen Burroughs*, 63.

37. Ibid.

38. Nannie Helen Burroughs, "With All Thy Getting," *Southern Workman* 56, no. 7 (July 1927): 299–301. See Graves and Burroughs, *Nannie Helen Burroughs*, 54.

39. See Easter, *Nannie Helen Burroughs*, 89n28. There, Opal references a 1956 souvenir booklet from the dedication of a new dormitory.

40. Victoria W. Wolcott, "'Bible, Bath and Broom': Nannie Helen Burrough's National Training School and African-American Racial Uplift," *Journal of Women's History* 9, no. 1 (Spring, 1997): 88–110, 88, https://www.proquest.com/scholarly-journ als/bible-bath-broom-nannie-helen-burroughs-national/docview/203245730/se-2?accountid=15172.

41. Ibid., 91.

42. Sarah D. Bair, "Educating Black Girls in the Early 20th Century: The Pioneering Work of Nannie Helen Burroughs," *Theory and Research Education 36*, no. 1 (Winter 2008): 18. See also Nannie Helen Burroughs Papers, Library of Congress (NHB Box 311). A review of lesson plans and exam questions shows a broader array than even this list. The actual courses and exam titles included: Millinery, Rhethoric, Grammar, Social Ideals / Social Services courses (which included theology, OT history, and accounts of the life of Jesus), Chemistry, Physiology, Algebra, Commercial Mathematics, Latin, French, Music, Ancient History (Rome and Greece), Current History, England's History, among others.

43. Bair, "Educating Black Girls," 18. See also Nannie Helen Burroughs Papers, Library of Congress (NHB Box 311).

44. Burroughs, "With All Thy Getting," 299–301. See Graves and Burroughs, *Nannie Helen Burroughs*, 54–55.

45. Bair, "Educating Black Girls," 19.

46. Ibid.

47. Ibid.

48. See Higginbotham, *Righteous Discontent.*

49. Evelyn Brooks-Higginbotham, "Religion, Politics, and Gender: The Leadership of Nannie Helen Burroughs," *Journal of Religious Thought 44*, no. 2 (Winter/Spring 1988), 12.

50. NBC, *Journal of the Twenty-fifth Annual Session of the National Baptist Convention and the Sixth Annual Session of the Women's Convention, Held in Chicago, IL. October 25–30, 1905* (Nashville, TN: National Baptist Publishing Board, 1905), 270.

    See also Evelyn Brooks-Higginbotham, "Religion, Politics, and Gender." Does this statement about streetcars set her and Wells, who came to "fame" and to her own voice protesting the injustices people of color experienced on public railcars, at polar opposites? In some ways, yes; their approaches/responses to the ills Black people faced in the early twentieth century differed, but there was an eerily similar attention to the domestic sphere/home as the place of utmost importance, educationally, ethically, and religiously. Both placed incredible weight (and blame) at the feet of Black women and mothers—while simultaneously calling out injustices and generations of oppression.

51. Higginbotham, *Righteous Discontent*, 152.

52. Ibid., 151.

53. Ibid., 152.

54. Higginbotham, "Religion, Politics, and Gender," 15.

55. Ibid., 16.

56. Ibid., 17.

57. https://cfshrc.org/article/justice-for-all-the-womanist-labor-rhetoric-of-nannie-helen-burroughs/.

58. Easter, *Nannie Helen Burroughs*, 105.

59. Nannie Helen Burroughs (1879–1961), Miss Nannie H. Burroughs, President, Nat'l. League of Rep. Colored Women, ca. 1920s, reproduction from lantern slide, Nannie Helen Burroughs Papers, Prints and Photographs Division, Library of Congress (130.07.00); National League of Republican Colored Women, Colored Women in Politics Questionnaire, completed by Elizabeth Jeter Greene, New London, CT, ca. 1920, Nannie Helen Burroughs Papers, Manuscript Division, Library of Congress (130.06.00). See also https://www.loc.gov/exhibitions/women-fight-for-the-vote/exhibition-items/.

60. Ibid.

61. Graves and Burroughs, *Nannie Helen Burroughs*, 115–118.

62. Ibid., 117.

63. Ibid. See also Burroughs, "Ballot and Dollar Needed to Make Progress, Not Pity," *Pittsburg Courier*, February 17, 1934, 2.

64. From LOC (Library of Congress) Finding Aid. In her 1902 corresponding secretary's report to the Woman's Convention, Burroughs emphasized the need for Black Christian women to have access to literature and teaching materials in order to prepare themselves to be leaders in the churches and organizations. On behalf of the Woman's Convention she assumed the task of making literature available, writing many of the publications herself. When the Woman's Convention did not have its own publications on requested subjects, Burroughs often purchased the required material from trade publishers and had it forwarded to subscribers. In 1934, with the assistance of Una Roberts Lawrence and the Woman's Missionary Union, she relaunched *The Worker* as a missionary magazine and teaching tool. She edited the magazine from 1934 until her death in May 1961, increasing its quarterly circulation from 375 to over 100,000.

65. LOC Finding Aid.

66. Ibid.

67. *The Worker: A Missionary Quarterly*, Volume 1: No. 1 (1934), Nannie Helen Burroughs Papers, Library of Congress.

68. Ibid.

69. Ibid.

70. *The Worker: A Missionary Quarterly*, Volume 13: No. 66. (1950), Nannie Helen Burroughs Papers, Library of Congress.

71. Ibid. (1950), Nannie Helen Burroughs Papers, Library of Congress. The editorial is somewhat confusing, and I do not fully know the larger discourse she is responding to, but the volume is published at the end of 1950 in a time of conversations about the importance of desegregation and efforts for Black people to assert themselves for equal rights.

72. Nannie Helen Burroughs Papers, Library of Congress (NHB Box 47), Letter from Mary E. Robinson, October 16, 1957.

73. Nannie Helen Burroughs Papers, Library of Congress (NHB Box 47).

74. Savage, *Your Spirts Walk beside Us*, 166.

Section III

1. Though focusing on only Clark and Lawson does make for a more manageable and focused chapter, this does not indicate that Clark or Lawson was working in isolation or without the assistance of many different teachers and leaders. This chapter could have included any number of Clark's colleagues in the Citizenship Education program, such as Dorothy Cotton, Andrew Young, Bernice Robinson, or any of the other community teachers who were trained to teach across the South. Likewise, in this chapter I mention but could have discussed at greater length the cadre of student leaders that Lawson trained in nonviolence and who began training others across the South, leaders such as Diane Nash, John Lewis, and many others. Likewise, each of these figures and stories is not complete without the work of activist and community educators like Ella Baker and Fanny Lou Hamer.

Chapter 5

1. Katherine Charron, *Freedom's Teacher: The Life of Septima Clark* (Chapel Hill: University of North Carolina Press, 2009), 3. Charron writes, "Our perception of the black freedom struggle changes when we place the worldview and deeds of black women activist educators such as Septima Clark at the center. . . . No longer does the black church stand alone as the primary institutional base for the civil rights movement; the schoolhouse—often the *very* same building—becomes an equally important site."

2. David P. Levine, "The Birth of the Citizenship Schools: Entwining the Struggles for Literacy and Freedom." *History of Education Quarterly* 44, no. 3 (2004): 388. Andrew Young states, "If you look at the black elected officials and the people who are political leaders across the South now, it's full of people who had their first involvement in civil rights in the Citizenship Training Program" (Levine, 388). The Citizenship Schools adult education program began in 1958 under the sponsorship of Tennessee's Highlander Folk School and under leadership of the Southern Christian Leadership Conference (SCLC) in 1961. When the project ended in 1970, approximately 2,500 African Americans had taught basic literacy and political education classes for tens of thousands of their neighbors.

3. Septima Clark and Cynthia Brown, *Ready from Within* (Trenton, NJ: Africa World Press, 1999), 103–106.

4. Clark with Brown, *Ready from Within*, 106.

5. Ibid., 107.

6. Ibid.

7. Ibid.

8. Ibid., 103.

9. Ibid., 117. See also Charron, *Freedom's Teacher*, 26–28. In particular, Clark's father (Peter Porcher Poinsette) was born to an enslaved mother (who was likely raped, as Poinsette never spoke of a father) and only moved to Charleston after the end of the Civil War. As a former enslaved person, he was not welcomed by the free Black people already living in Charleston and who were fearful of losing their status with the influx of newly freed persons from the plantations and rural areas of South Carolina. Clark's mother, Victoria Warren Andersen, however, was born free in Charleston in 1870, and later her family moved to Haiti, taking a risk on a better life in a free and independent Haiti.

10. Clark's initial attempts to use Black professional teachers in some of her organizing did not work because of these class differences and the mistrust on both sides. Clark often spoke of the ways that some of the rural workers and families on John's Island didn't trust outsiders (even from the city of Charleston) because they feared (rightly) that many in Charleston would look down on them and treat them disrespectfully. Clark also remarks on her growth in this area, which empowered her to work across lines of differences for decades to come (see Clark with Brown, *Ready from Within*, 103).

11. Jacquelyn Hall, Oral History Interview with Septima Clark, *Southern Oral History Program*, July 25, 1976, p. 1. Transcript of Interview with Clark by Jacquelyn Hall for Southern Oral History Program, Charleston, South Carolina, July 25, 1976 (accessed March 19, 2021). See also Clark with Brown, *Ready from Within*, 98. Here Clark names her first segregated public school as Mars Street School (and the one for White children as Mary Street School).

12. See Hall, Oral History. Clark in particular notes that her teachers at Avery wanted her to attend Fisk University when she finished at Avery, but Clark did not consider this because she was afraid that her mother would work herself too hard trying to make the monthly boarding fees (even if Clark got a scholarship to attend). The realities of their working-class life and the fact that each of Clark's siblings also worked to contribute to their family limited what Clark was able to do educationally. Thus, Clark started working as a teacher at eighteen years old and wasn't able to complete her undergraduate degree until years later in 1942.

13. Clark with Brown, *Ready from Within*, 117.

14. Ibid., 98.

15. Charron, *Freedom's Teacher*, 36.

16. Ibid.

17. Clark with Brown, *Ready from Within*, 97.

18. Ibid.

19. Charron, *Freedom's Teacher*, 34. See also Clark with Brown, *Ready from Within*, 96.

20. Clark with Brown, *Ready from Within*, 35–36.

21. In addition to the NAACP and PSTA discussed in this chapter, Clark was also member of the South Carolina Federation of Colored Women's Clubs, the YWCA, the Gamma

Xi Omega Chapter of Alpha Kappa Alpha Sorority Inc., and later the Highlander Folk School.

22. Charron, *Freedom's Teacher*, 117.

23. Ibid., 119.

24. In particular, Clark inviting Elizabeth Warring (the wife of a Charleston judge who had been instrumental in ruling in favor of Black people to vote in Democratic primaries and other issues) to speak was also a turning point in her leadership and activism—signaling her understanding of the importance of interracial collaborations (and the need for White allies to support the work).

25. Charron, *Freedom's Teacher*, 132.

26. Clark with Brown, *Ready from Within*, 35–36. See also Charron, *Freedom's Teacher*, 116–144, chapter on Clark's political training ground.

27. Septima Poinsette Clark, "Champions of Democracy," SCLC papers, undated, Box 542, Folder 12. See also Clark's Notes for Talks, 1974, Septima Clark Papers, Avery Research Institute, Box 3, Folder 26 (p. 4 of outline).

28. The definition of improvise includes both (1) to speak or perform without preparation OR (2) to make or create (something) by using whatever is available (see dictionary.com).

29. Clark's Notes for Talks, 1974, Septima Clark Papers, Avery Research Institute, Box 3 Folder 26 (p. 4 of outline). This includes an outline of her discussion of culture of Sea Island and the educational efforts. She herself calls the strategies of Black teachers improvisational.

30. Ibid., on civil rights struggle, and Life in Sea Islands; with program regarding latter talk at Howard University.

31. It is also not completely reactionary; it requires studying and gathering information prior to arriving, to know how to proceed. Clark discussed how in the moment they came up with strategies that they tested out (not knowing if they would work), but that later became the foundation of much of their educational successes.

32. Levine, "The Birth of the Citizenship Schools," 405–406.

33. bell hooks, *Teaching to Transgress* (New York: Routledge, 1996), 2–5.

34. Charron, *Freedom's Teacher*, 230. Clark credits Myles Horton (founder of Highlander Folk School) for his patience and work in winning over Jenkins to a more people-centered form of leadership and education: "Clark respected Jenkins and did not want him to think her a meddler. However, she also felt that he assumed a 'preacher' role at community meetings, and on more than one occasion, she had seen Jenkins talk so long that the people walked out. She and Horton worked patiently with him [Jenkins]."

35. Charron, *Freedom's Teacher*, 230.

36. Avery Institute, Box 8, Folder 2. Clark's correspondence as training supervisor, Citizenship Schools, regarding administration of program, recruiting students, etc., around the South, 1961–1967, and undated. This records Clark calling out Aaron Henry, James Bevel, and Amzie Moore.

37. Avery Institute, Box 8, Folder 2.

38. The quotation was sent out in a printed greeting card from Clark. In an unpublished article J. Douglas Allen-Taylor notes that sending out preprinted Christmas cards to hundreds of friends was a common practice of Clark. This card was from December 1975. The complete quotation helped to summarize her "philosophy of work" and

read, "The greatest evil in our country today is not racism, but ignorance . . . I believe unconditionally in the ability of people to respond when they are told the truth. We need to be taught to study rather than to believe, to inquire rather than to affirm." See http://www.safero.org/articles/septima.html (accessed June 18, 2021).

39. Exceptions to the trends to focus primarily on Clark's work as an educator and activist include Rosetta Ross, *Witnessing and Testifying: Black Women, Religion, and Civil Rights* (Minneapolis, MN: Fortress Press, 2003), 51–89.

40. Septima Poinsett Clark, "Citizenship and Gospel," *Journal of Black Studies 10*, no. 4 (June 1980): 461–466, https://doi.org/10.1177/002193478001000408, 463.

41. Ibid., 463.

42. Ibid.

43. Ibid.

44. Clark's Correspondence, Avery Institute, Box 8, Folder 2: Undated Reports, pp. 3–4 of report, "Report from a Refresher Course Meeting at Dorchester Community Center, McIntosh, GA, June 16–18, 1961." The reports include updates on getting schools started and operating the schools. In one of her field reports, under the heading of OPPOSITION, she types, "Opposition: Churches—bribery of ministers—There is a minister who is taking free shirts, etc. from White businessmen, and is discouraging his congregation from boycotting the stores. You don't know how nonchalant some of those ministers are, if it isn't something to give them more money in their pocket. There's something like 75 ministers in Savannah, and we get cooperation from about 3." The *Summary of Progress* is also interesting as it outlines the particulars of who is working with the schools and what types of opposition they are encountering as well. From her autobiography, she also notes that she often encountered resistance and some hesitation from pastors and leaders, as they did not want to upset the respected status quo and White businessmen who often gave them gifts or favors. She vividly recounts a fear of missing out on the annual anniversary gift of a new suit, if these clergy ever dared to publicly support voter registration or the citizenship schools. However, her faith at the intersection of God, people, and social change did not render Clark blind to the corruptions within religious leadership, nor did this corruption stop her from taking risks to continue the work she felt called to do. Like so many other activist religious educators we've explored in this book, Clark unapologetically called out the corruption and resistance to social change from within religious communities.

45. Eugene Walker, Oral History Interview with Septima Poinsette Clark, July 30, 1976, Interview G-0017.

46. Clark's Correspondence, Avery Institute, Box 8, "Folder 2: Undated Reports," pp. 3–4 of report; "Report from a Refresher course meeting at Dorchester Community Center, McIntosh, GA, June 16–18, 1961."

47. Clark's Correspondence, Avery Institute, Box 8, "Folder 13: Note cards regarding talks on non-violence," undated.

48. SCLC papers, Box 545, folder 10, "Philosophy of the Movement." Clark references Peter's words in Acts 5:29. The larger context is the persecution of Peter and some other apostles (and later placing them in jail) as they are teaching about Jesus (after being warned not to). The full quotation is: "We must obey God rather than any human authority" (NRSV).

49. We hear rhetorical echoes of or precursors to King's letter from a Birmingham jail, and to others who look toward a higher authority in the face of unjust civic laws.
50. Here also I note echoes of this faith in radical democracy in later educational theorists like Henry Giroux.
51. Howard Thurman, Baccalaureate Address at Spelman College, May 4, 1980, as edited by Jo Moore for *The Spelman Messenger* 96, no. 4 (Summer 1980): 14–15.

Chapter 6

1. Lawson's role as an educator is not limited to his work during the civil rights movement. He continued teaching and training university students across the country in the history, philosophy, and strategies of nonviolence but also trains community organizers and unions about how to effect large-scale change through nonviolence.
2. Kent Wong, Ana Luz Gonzalez, and James Lawson Jr., eds., *Nonviolence and Social Movements: The Teachings of Rev. James M. Lawson Jr.* (Los Angeles: UCLA Center for Labor Research and Education, 2016), 3.
3. See David Halberstam, *The Children* (New York: Fawcett Books, 1998), 138.
4. Kent Wong et al., *Nonviolence and Social Movements*, 6.
5. Michael K. Honey, *Love and Solidarity: James Lawson & Nonviolence in the Search for Workers Rights* [film] (Reading, PA: Bullfrog Films, 2016), http://docuseek2.com/cart/product/1101.
6. Ibid.
7. Ibid. Lawson tells this account often as the beginning of his journey of nonviolence. There are other videos and accounts of this as well that offer greater details. See also Wong et al., *Nonviolence and Social Movements*; Veena Howard, "Nonviolence as Love in Action: James Lawson's Transforming the Promise of Jesus' Love into a Practical Force for Change," *Practical Matters Journal 13* (Summer 2020).
8. Honey, *Love and Solidarity*.
9. My gut reaction to hearing this approach is to think it was somewhat naive and dangerous (based on our experiences today), but that was how his mind was working and how as a young boy he shifted his approaches to the ongoing racism around him.
10. See Halberstam, *The Children*, for more of the backstory. See also Wong et al., *Nonviolence and Social Movements*. Lawson was very well educated and attended Baldwin Wallace College (in Ohio), where he continued to practice nonviolence and began to read the biography of Gandhi. He was arrested for not heeding the draft and had to serve thirteen months in prison. Many of his peers appealed to their status as students to avoid the draft. Not so Lawson. He objected to the war on moral and religious grounds. He was a budding pacifist and paid the price for his beliefs and values. But as we will see, it was the beginning of him also living in a strategy of nonviolent resistance. Rather than avoid jail or getting arrested, he embraced those measures, regarding them as furthering his cause and raising awareness of the injustices that were/are so pervasive in the United States and world.

11. *James Lawson: Reflections on Life, Nonviolence, Civil Rights, MLK, United Methodist Videos*, January 12, 2017, https://www.youtube.com/watch?v=zc7wg41lUM4. Lawson often recounts his mother's influence on his early understanding of nonviolence and commitment to finding a different way of handling conflict and racialized hate.

12. *James Lawson: Reflections on Life.*

13. Ibid.

14. Howard, "Nonviolence as Love in Action," 1–26.

15. Ibid., 5.

16. Dennis Dickerson, "James M. Lawson, Jr.: Methodism, Nonviolence, and the Civil Rights Movement," *Methodist History 52*, no. 3 (April 2014): 168. Dickerson is reflecting on a letter where Lawson described his religious influences while serving his prison sentence for opposing the Korean War and refusing the draft.

17. Dickerson, "James M. Lawson, Jr.," 168.

18. Interview with James Lawson, 1 of 4. Directed by Nelson, Stanley. WGBH Educational Foundation, 2017. https://video.alexanderstreet.com/watch/interview-with-james-lawson-1-of-4.

19. Howard, "Nonviolence as Love in Action," 5. Howard is quoting from a recent interview with Lawson.

20. Dickerson, "James M. Lawson, Jr.," 175–77.

21. Halberstam, *The Children*, 41–47.

22. Honey, *Love and Solidarity.*

23. Ibid. Quote from Kent Hong.

24. Honey, *Love and Solidarity.*

25. While I reference and build on the steps and stages of nonviolent campaign that Lawson teaches in his workshops, in this section I am more intentionally looking at how he teaches people and how he brings them into this work and to a better understanding of the principles and practices of nonviolence.

26. An open forum like a congregation would often have too many people or the potential for too much to be shared.

27. See Interview with James Lawson, 1 of 4.

28. Ibid.

29. Ibid.

30. Honey, *Love and Solidarity.*

31. Halberstam, *The Children*, 60.

32. Halberstam wrote, "Sometimes when he [Lawson] taught about the evils of segregation it was as if these terrible things were happening to other people in some distant land, not to them right here in Tennessee. They were all accustomed to spellbinding preachers, men who as they reached the climax of their sermons became louder and more passionate. Lawson was completely different; as he reached a critical point, he became cooler and more careful, and sometimes they had to strain to hear him" (p. 60).

33. Ibid., 60–61.

34. Almeda Wright, *The Spiritual Lives of Young African Americans* (New York: Oxford, 2017), 110–112.

35. James M. Lawson, Jr., "Nonviolence: A Relevant Power for Constructive Social Change, Lawson Papers," FOR III, Nonviolence Workshops, 1958 Folder, Box 38, Special Collections and University Archives, Vanderbilt University.

36. However, the students that Lawson did recruit were "easy to recruit" as noted by one of the early participants, because they were all more than aware of the indignities that they were suffering and the injustices surrounding them. I contrast this with some of the other movements for change and educational strategies employed by other critical educators, such as Freire, in that much of the work that Lawson was doing with his students was not about critical consciousness raising. Most of the students were well aware of the systems and structures they were facing. Instead, he was training them (and in a sense raising their awareness) to see their collective, nonviolent power. Lawson notes in his work with students in Arkansas (part of the Little Rock 9) that he had to work to teach these students that while they were being told "not to fight back," he was actually advocating and trying to teach them and others how *to fight back non-violently* (Interview, American Experience).

37. Diane Nash quoted in Wong et al., *Nonviolence and Social Movements*, 54.

38. Halberstam, *The Children*, 61.

39. Ibid.

40. Ibid.

41. Ibid., 62–63.

42. It was the wives of local clergy who shared their accounts and experiences of the indignities they experienced as they attempted to shop in downtown Nashville. While most accounts of Lawson's work in Nashville focuses on the students he trained, he initially started meeting and training other pastors and their wives. He started meeting with groups of thirty to sixty people at local churches in the Nashville community (see Howard, "Nonviolence as Love in Action," 7). From these early meetings and assisted by listening to the women students in his later weekly workshops, Lawson began to hone in on the target/object of their direct action.

43. Lawson continued this type of radical pedagogy and cultivated other strategies for nonviolent change and resistance as he continued his work with labor unions (as offered to the labor unions in Los Angeles in the 1980s): "So I suggested among other things, go to them. So you get them to talk about their situation. And you work with that person until that person then is really talking freely with you, and is beginning to share with other workers—and with all sorts of other people—his own scene. There has to be deep preparation in nonviolent struggle, because they have to understand the strategic value of goals which are measurable and attainable as a way of corralling all your resources and not getting confused, and not allowing the nature of the struggle to move you off-goal . . . off-target (Honey, *Love and Solidarity*).

44. This was similar to the color caste system Clark experienced in Charleston.

45. Howard, "Nonviolence as Love in Action," 11.

46. Cf. reference to the work of Augusto Boal who talks about theater and his concept of *Theatre of the Oppressed* as rehearsals for the revolution.

47. Howard, "Nonviolence as Love in Action," 12.

48. Ibid.
49. Halberstam, *The Children*, 79.
50. Deborah Mathis, "The Rev. Lawson on Human Endeavors for Hope and Change," Minds of the Movement blog, International Center on Nonviolent Conflict (ICNC), January 15, 2018, bit.ly/RevJLicncBlog.
51. Ibid.
52. Interview with James Lawson, 1 of 4.
53. *James Lawson: Reflections on Life*.
54. For examples of Clark's frustration with different activist see Avery Institute, Box 8, Folder 2, Clark's correspondence as training supervisor, Citizenship Schools, regarding administration of program, recruiting students, etc., around the South, 1961–1967 and undated. Clark wrote, "I think that the staff of the SCLC working with me in the CEP feels that the work is not dramatic enough to warrant their time. Direct action is so glamorous and packed with emotion that most young people prefer demonstrations over genuine education." Likewise, Lawson was a vocal critique of the gradual and indirect strategies of older civil rights organizations like the NAACP.
55. Honey, *Love and Solidarity*.

Section IV

1. Barbara Savage, *Your Spirits Walk beside Us* (Cambridge, MA: Harvard University Press, 2008), 2.
2. See Gayraud Wilmore, *Black Religion and Black Radicalism* (Maryknoll, NY: Orbis Press, 2003), for a helpful retracing of this rich legacy.
3. Cf. Delores Williams, *Sisters in the Wilderness*; bell hooks, *Teaching to Transgress*.

Chapter 7

1. Olivia Pearl Stokes, "Education in the Black Church: Design for Change," *Religious Education 69*, no. 4 (1974): 433–445, at 439.
2. It is not clear when the first doctoral degrees in religious education began, in part because of the ongoing connections between education and religion well into the mid-twentieth century.
3. Cole Arthur Riley, *This Here Flesh* (New York: Convergent, 2022), 3.
4. Black Women Oral History Project, Interviews, 1976–1981, Olivia Pearl Stokes, OH-31, Schlesinger Library, Radcliffe Institute, Harvard University, Cambridge, MA, pp. ii and 4. Persistent link: http://nrs.harvard.edu/urn-3:RAD.SCHL:10048765.
5. Ibid., 3.
6. Ibid.
7. Ibid.
8. Ibid., 4.

9. Ibid., 16 (see also p. 46).

10. Ibid., p. 10.

11. For a larger discussion of the ways that urban congregations adapted during the Great Migration, see Albert Raboteau, *Canaan Land: A Religious History of African Americans* (New York: Oxford University Press, 2001), 84–85.

12. Oral History, 12.

13. Ibid., 13.

14. Ibid., 17.

15. Ibid., 9.

16. Ibid., 13.

17. Ibid., 10.

18. Ibid., 14.

19. Ibid., 15.

20. Ibid., 19. Stokes worked at the Baptist Education Center from 1941 to 1952, since she was nineteen years old.

21. Oral History, 19.

22. See Charles R. Foster and Fred Smith, *Black Religious Experience: Conversations on Double Consciousness and the Work of Grant Shockley* (Nashville, TN: Abingdon, 2003), 153.

23. Oral History, 20.

24. Ibid.

25. Ibid., 24.

26. Ibid.

27. Ibid.

28. Ibid., 22.

29. Ibid.

30. Ibid.

31. Ibid., 56.

32. Ibid.

33. Ibid., 29–30.

34. Ibid., 29.

35. Ibid., 30.

36. Ibid., 57.

37. I wonder, however, why Stokes—with her background in theology and her strong opinions on what theology was and was not—did not in her projects articulate a Black theology (or even a Black woman's theology). Instead, Stokes focused on educational models for Black theology and on the development of children and youth.

38. Oral History, 57.

39. Stokes, "Education," 433–445.

40. Ibid., 434.

41. Ibid., 436.

42. Ibid., 439.

43. Ibid., 437. See also "The Mission of the Church from the Black Perspective," unpublished statement from the August 1969 Krisheim Conference on "The Educational

Role of the Black Church in the '70s." Department of Educational Development, National Council of Churches, New York.

44. Stokes, "Education," 436–437. See also "The Mission of the Church from the Black Perspective."

45. Stokes, "Education," 437.

46. Ibid., 437–438.

47. Ibid., 438.

48. Ibid., 440–441.

49. Ibid., 439–440.

50. Yolanda Smith, "A Spirituality of Teaching: Black Women's Spirituality and Christian Education" (unpublished Religious Education Association paper), 2007.

51. Oral History, 5.

52. Cynthia Dillard, *The Spirit of our Work: Black Women Teachers (Re)member* (Boston: Beacon Press, 2022), xiii. See also https://www.theskanner.com/news/northwest/32928-black-scholar-cynthia-dillard-in-as-new-dean-of-seattle-univers ity-s-college-of-education. In this interview, Dillard describes the value of immersive pedagogy, writing, "it was the Black women who I think had the most to say about the kind of teacher education that would really be useful and helpful if you really wanted to center Blackness, and you wanted to center all the other intersections as well. So that's what this book is about, it's just beautiful stories of Black women who spent a bunch of time in Ghana with me. And they (had the opportunity for) critical study about that place, and about those heritages, and they spent time watching teachers who have never been displaced from their own heritage and culture, and children who were the same . . . they probably learned more about teaching and learning in those five or six days that they spent in schools in Ghana than they probably have learned in their entire teacher education. Partly because (they were observing) just masterful teachers who were not working against these questions of marginality, and not working against these questions of not being centered. Not working against not having a history book. That experience helped them to then come back to create different kinds of conditions for education at multiple levels here in the United States."

53. Olivia Pearl Stokes, *The Beauty of Being Black: Folktales, Poems, and Art from Africa* (New York: Friendship Press, 1971).

54. Olivia Pearl Stokes, *Why the Spider Lives in Corners: African Facts and Fun* (New York: Friendship Press, 1971).

55. Oral History, 38.

56. Stokes, *Spider*, 8.

57. Oral History, 21.

58. In part, I wonder about whether she would have had a larger hearing or impact had she in fact been a man (she asked this same question in her 1979 oral history interview). This is not to say that her work does not affirm her power as a woman; it simply acknowledges the ways that sexism and patriarchy were at play in her life and in the lives of so many Black women educators.

59. Stokes, "Education," 445.

Chapter 8

1. Excerpts and paraphrases from Dr. Cleage's sermon on March 26, 1967. Transcript at http://www.theyearofrestoration.org/Jaramogi-Abebe-History.html. Video: https://www.youtube.com/watch?v=Cb77sUDHMh8 (accessed June 20, 2015).

   I also do not know if there was an intentional play on words in Cleage's sermon, where he articulates this as an "impossible conception" and paralleled with the traditional naming of Jesus's birth to the Virgin Mary as the "Immaculate Conception."
2. Cone and Cleage are not known as collaborators, etc., but they were definitely aware of each other's work.
3. A. Cleage, *The Black Messiah* (Trenton, NJ: Africa World Press, 2017), 9.
4. Hiley Ward, Prophet *of the Black Nation* (Boston: The Pilgrim Press, 1967), 7–8.
5. Angela Dillard, *Faith in the City: Preaching Radical Social Change in Detroit* (Ann Arbor: University of Michigan Press, 2007), 239.
6. Ward, *Prophet*, 35. See also Dillard, *Faith in the* City, 239–241.
7. See K. Cleage, *Finding Eliza*, online archives at https://findingeliza.com/archives/264 (accessed April 26, 2022), and Ward, *Prophet*, 38.
8. K. Cleage, *Finding Eliza*.
9. Ibid. See also Ward, *Prophet*, 38.
10. Ward, *Prophet*, 35.
11. Dillard, *Faith in the City*, 240. See also Earl Fisher, *The Reverend Albert Cleage Jr. and the Black Prophetic Tradition: A Reintroduction of The Black Messiah* (New York: Lexington Books, 2021), 1.
12. See Angela Dillard, *Faith in the City*, 240, and Ward, *Prophet*, 39. Ward writes, "there was a lot of argument about starting it [the hospital], but he [Dr. Cleage] insisted on a colored hospital where he could be treated with dignity."
13. Ward, *Prophet*, 39–42.
14. Dillard, *Faith in the City*, 241.
15. Ward, *Prophet*, 40.
16. Dillard, *Faith in the City*, 241.
17. Ibid., 238–241. See also Albert Cleage, "What's Wrong with Our Schools," *Illustrated News*, February 12, 1962; Ward, *Prophet*, chap. 5, "The Monster Schools."
18. Dillard, *Faith in the City*, 238.
19. Ibid., 241.
20. A. Cleage, "What's Wrong with Our Schools." Dillard and others also noted the irony of Cleage later founding his own newspaper and advocating as many other activists had to for Black-owned and controlled news outlets in order to advance the work of Black people.
21. Ward adds that Cleage's undergraduate education spanned thirteen years, from 1929 to 1942 (Ward, *Prophet*, 53). Cleage did not earn his BA from Wayne State until 1942, after he had already started graduate classes at Oberlin Theological Seminary. Cleage was only four language credits shy of his undergraduate degree requirements.
22. Dillard, *Faith in the City*, 242.
23. Ibid.

24. Ward, *Prophet*, 46.

25. Ibid.

26. Ibid., 45.

27. Ibid., 42.

28. D. Kimathi Nelson, "The Theological Journey of Albert B. Cleage, Jr.," in *Albert Cleage Jr. and the Black Madonna and Child*, ed. Jawanza E. Clark (New York: Palgrave McMillian, 2016), 23.

29. Ward, *Prophet*, 42.

30. Ibid.

31. Ibid., 51–52.

32. Ibid., 51.

33. Dillard, *Faith in the City*, 243.

34. Ibid.

35. Ibid., 245. See A. Cleage, "New-Time Religion," in *The Black Messiah*, 110.

36. Dillard, *Faith in the City*, 245.

37. Ward, *Prophet*, 55.

38. Ibid., 56.

39. Ibid.

40. The commissioning of murals and religious icons is not unique to Cleage, but it is interesting that he understood the importance of changing not only theology to reflect Black people and their liberation struggles, but also the images of the divine.

41. "St John's Church Elects Rev Albert Cleage Pastor," *The Springfield Republican*, August 29, 1945, p. 1. See also https://findingeliza.com/archives/1209 (accessed May 3, 2022).

42. Ward, *Prophet*, 56.

43. Ibid., 57–58.

44. Wanting to plant a church in Detroit, even before he came to St. Johns, Cleage had written to his family about the idea and was searching for a building when he was called to St. John's. Cleage's early letter noted that he was open to being supported in a local church plant by either the Presbyterians (his family's denomination) or the Congregational church—the church he was ordained in.

45. Dillard, *Faith in the City*, 250.

46. Ibid.

47. Ibid.

48. Ibid., 251.

49. Ibid.

50. Nelson, "Theological Journey," 23.

51. In 1968 Cleage gives back grant and turns more inward, Dillard argues, signaling another move in his radical evolution—turning away from the "limelight" and focusing on the work of building his organization and allowing that work to be his most powerful lesson for/to the world.

52. The expansion to South Carolina included the purchasing of a large acreage farm, *Beulah Land Farm*, which was part of Cleage's vision for helping Black people create means of economic and even agricultural independence.

53. A. Cleage, *Black Messiah*, 11.

54. Ibid.
55. Cleage's second book *Black Christian Nationalism*, published in 1972, continues the themes explored originally in the *Black Messiah* (1968) and outlines the structure of his program of Black Christian Nationalism—or of enacting the teachings of Black Liberation theologies.
56. https://www.pbs.org/thisfarbyfaith/people/albert_cleage.html (accessed May 1, 2022). See also Ward, *Prophet*.
57. Ward, *Prophet*, x. This also connected with Cleage's dislike of the Pauline epistles and theology. He instead placed greater emphasis on the Hebrew prophets and Jesus—and the revolutionary communalism that he saw there.
58. A. Cleage, *Black Christian Nationalism*, xxxv.
59. Ibid., 210.
60. Ibid., 211–212.
61. Ibid., 212.
62. Ibid.
63. Ibid., 213. Italics and capitalization original. The program also included additional training for shrine leadership and ordained clergy.
64. Shelley McIntosh, *Mtoto House: Vision to Victory, Raising African American Children Communally* (New York: Hamilton Books, 2005).
65. McIntosh, *Mtoto House*, 38–39.
66. Ibid.
67. Ibid.
68. Ibid., 39.
69. Ibid., 40.
70. Ibid.
71. One of the discussions about the strengths and weaknesses of the program, a generation later, reflected on the ways that totalizing effects of the program did not permit students who may have benefited from public school–based extra curriculars from attending (things such as band, sports, or even clubs). See Shelley McIntosh, *Mtoto House*, 127.
72. See McIntosh for a fuller discussion of the reflections of the children and staff of Mtoto House. There were some significant critiques from youth about the relationships they did not get to fully cultivate with their biological parents, as well as other intersecting critiques about the ways that staff early on left their own jobs or educational pursuits in order to commit to "building a nation."
73. Ward, *Prophet*, ix.
74. James Cone, *Said I Wasn't Gonna Tell Nobody* (Maryknoll, NY: Orbis, 2018), 14. Cleage was somewhat critical of the academic turn in Black theology and argued that Black theology, once it was embraced and deemed acceptable by White academic institutions, would lose its power to help Black people. While I am not certain that this is an all-out critique of the direction/evolution of Black theology as an academic discipline, Cleage understood his project to be specifically about working with and for Black people and for their transformation. Cone also argued that that he knew that "Black Power advocates, like Stokely Carmichael, and militant black ministers, like

Albert Cleage, had no interest in debating White religious scholars or well-schooled White ministers," but that Cone did (Cone, 9). Thus, each was undertaking a very different, but necessary, project.

75. Dillard, *Faith in the City*, 247.
76. Quoted in ibid., 248. For the full text of the poem, see also "The BCN Message and Mission: Revolutionary Transformation," and "Messiah," in *10th Anniversary of Shrine #10: National Tribute to Jaramogi Abebe Agyeman* (n.p., June 1987).
77. Ibid.

Chapter 9

1. Akosua Lesesne, "Sisters in Education Circle," 2021–2022, Virtual Sister Circles flier.
2. "Is Everybody Here," Walela Walela, ℗ 2002 Triloka Records, ℗ Indieblu Music, https://www.youtube.com/watch?v=8FuUVCLK-w4.
3. Cynthia Dillard, *The Spirit of Our Work: Black Women Teachers (Re)member* (Boston: Beacon Press, 2022), 175.
4. Ibid., 176.
5. See Almeda M. Wright, *The Spiritual Lives of Young African Americans* (New York, Oxford, 2017), 226–228, for a fuller discussion of the idea of *ontological somebodiness*.
6. Paraphrase of Jeremiah 29:11.
7. See Almeda M. Wright, *Spiritual Lives*, for a fuller discussion of some of the trends within the Black church educational curriculum and preaching, as it connects with the development of Black youth.
8. bell hooks, *Teaching to Transgress*, 2.
9. See Delores Williams, *Sisters in the Wilderness* (Maryknoll, NY: Orbis Press, 2003), 22–29. Here Williams explores the idea of Black women naming God, and naming where they see God in their own lives is more fully in her discussion of Hagar's journey in the wilderness and her ability to name God through her experience and tradition, and not through the tradition of her slaveholders, Sarai and Abram.
10. Carter G. Woodson, *Miseducation of the Negro* (Chicago: African American Images, 2000 [1933]), 59.

Bibliography

Addison, Meeke. "The Stated Goals of Black Lives Matter Are Anti-Christian." *Decision Magazine*, September 11, 2021. https://decisionmagazine.com/the-stated-goals-of-black-lives-matter-are-anti-christian/

Aptheker, Herbert, ed. *Prayers for Dark People by W. E. B. Du Bois*. Amherst: University of Massachusetts Press, 1980.

Bair, Sarah D. "Educating Black Girls in the Early 20th Century: The Pioneering Work of Nannie Helen Burroughs." *Theory and Research Education* 36, no. 1 (Winter 2008): 9–35.

Bay, Mia, ed. *Ida B. Wells: The Light of Truth*. New York: Penguin Books, 2014.

Bay, Mia. *To Tell the Truth Freely: The Life of Ida B. Wells*. New York: Hill and Wang, 2009.

Boys, Mary C. *Educating in Faith*. Lima, OH: Academic Renewal Press, 1989.

Burroughs, Nannie H. "Ballot and Dollar Needed to Make Progress, Not Pity." *Pittsburg Courier*, February 17, 1934.

Burroughs, Nannie H. "The Colored Woman and Her Relation to the Domestic Problem." In *The United Negro, His Problems and His Progress: Containing the Address and Proceedings of the Negro Young People's Christian Congress, Held August 6–11, 1902*, edited by John W. E. Bowen and I. Garland Penn. Atlanta: D. E. Luther Publishing, 1902.

Burroughs, Nannie Helen. "With All Thy Getting." *Southern Workman* 56, no. 7 (July 1927): 299–301.

Bushnell, Horace. *Christian Nurture*. New Haven, CT: Yale University Press, 1967.

Charron, Katherine. *Freedom's Teacher: The Life of Septima Clark*. Chapel Hill: University of North Carolina Press, 2009.

Clark, Septima Poinsett. "Citizenship and Gospel." *Journal of Black Studies* 10, no. 4 (June 1980): 461–466. https://doi.org/10.1177/002193478001000408.

Clark, Septima, and Cynthia Brown. *Ready from Within*. Trenton, NJ: Africa World Press, 1999.

Cleage Jr., Albert. *Black Christian Nationalism: New Directions for the Black Church*. Detroit, MI: Luxor Publishers of the Pan-African Orthodox Christian Church, 1987.

Cleage Jr., Albert. *The Black Messiah*. Trenton, NJ: Africa World Press, 2017.

Cleage Jr., Albert. "What's Wrong with Our Schools." *Illustrated News*, February 12, 1962.

Coe, George Albert. *What Is Christian Education?* New York: Scribner, 1929.

Cone, James. *Said I Wasn't Gonna Tell Nobody*. Maryknoll, NY: Orbis, 2018.

Cooper, Anna J. "On Education." In *The Voice of Anna Julia Cooper*, edited by Charles Lemert and Esme Bhan, 248–258. New York: Rowman & Littlefield, 1998.

Cooper, Anna J. "Sketches from a Teacher's Notebook: Loss of Speech through Isolation." In *The Voice of Anna Julia Cooper*, edited by Charles Lemert and Esme Bhan, 224–229. New York: Rowman & Littlefield, 1998.

Cooper, Anna J. *A Voice from the South*. Mineola, NY: Dover Thrift Editions, 2016.

Cooper, Brittney. *Beyond Respectability*. Chicago: University of Illinois Press, 2017.

Decosta-Willis, Miriam, ed. *The Memphis Diary of Ida B. Wells*. Boston: Beacon Press, 1995.

Dickerson, Dennis. "James M. Lawson, Jr.: Methodism, Nonviolence, and the Civil Rights Movement." *Methodist History* 52, no. 3 (April 2014): 168–186.

Dillard, Angela. *Faith in the City: Preaching Radical Social Change in Detroit*. Ann Arbor: University of Michigan Press, 2007.

Dillard, Cynthia. *The Spirit of Our Work: Black Women Teachers (Re)member*. Boston: Beacon Press, 2022.

Dorrien, Gary. *The New Abolition: W. E. B. Du Bois and the Black Social Gospel*. New Haven, CT: Yale, 2015.

Dorrien, Gary. "What We Don't Know about Black Social Gospel: A Long-Neglected Tradition Is Reclaimed." *Religion Dispatches*, November 9, 2015. http://religiondispatc hes.org/what-we-dont-know-about-black-social-gospel-a-long-neglected-tradition-is-reclaimed/.

Du Bois, Ellen Carol. "Raking Muck." *New York Times*, February 14, 1999. https://www. nytimes.com/1999/02/14/books/raking-muck.html.

Du Bois, W. E. B. *An Autobiography of W. E. B. Du Bois*. 1940. Quoted in Les Back and Maggie Tate, "For a Sociological Reconstruction: W.E.B. Du Bois, Stuart Hall and Segregated Sociology," *Sociological Research Online* 20, no. 3 (August 2015): 155–166, doi:10.5153/sro.3773.

Du Bois, W. E. B. *Dusk of Dawn (the Oxford W. E. B. du Bois)*. New York: Oxford University Press, 2007.

Du Bois, W. E. B. *Souls of Black Folks*. Mineola, NY: Dover Publications, 2016.

Du Bois, W. E. B. *The Education of Black People, Ten Critiques, 1906–1960*. New York: Monthly Review Press, 2001.

Du Bois, W. E. B., ed., *The Negro Church*. Oxford: AltaMira Press, 2003.

Easter, Opal. *Nannie Helen Burroughs*. New York: Garland Publishing, 1995.

Fletcher, Karen Baker. *A Singing Something: Womanist Reflections on Anna Julia Cooper*. New York: Crossroad Publishing, 1994.

Foster, Charles R., and Fred Smith. *Black Religious Experience: Conversations on Double Consciousness and the Work of Grant Shockley*. Nashville, TN: Abingdon Press, 2003.

Gaines, Kevin K. "Racial Uplift Ideology in the Era of 'the Negro Problem.'" Freedom's Story, TeacherServe®, National Humanities Center. Accessed August 18, 2021. nationalhumanitiescenter.org/tserve/freedom/1865-1917/essays/racialuplift.htm.

Grant, Carl A., Keffrelyn D. Brown, and Anthony L. Brown. *Black Intellectual Thought in Education: The Missing Traditions of Anna Julia Cooper, Carter G. Woodson, and Alain LeRoy Locke*. New York: Routledge, 2016.

Graves, Kelisha B., and Nannie Helen Burroughs. *Nannie Helen Burroughs: A Documentary Portrait of an Early Civil Rights Pioneer, 1900–1959*. Notre Dame: University of Notre Dame Press, 2019. muse.jhu.edu/book/66677.

Green, Emma. "Black Activism, Unchurched?" *Atlantic Magazine*, March 22, 2016. https://www.theatlantic.com/politics/archive/2016/03/black-activism-baltimore-black-church/474822/.

Halberstam, David. *The Children*. New York: Fawcett Books, 1998.

Hall, Jacquelyn. Oral history interview with Septima Clark. Southern Oral History Program. July 25, 1976. https://docsouth.unc.edu/sohp/playback.html?base_file=G-0016&duration=03:46:55.

Harrison, Earl L. *The Dream and the Dreamer: An Abbreviated Story of the Life of Dr. Nannie Helen Burroughs and Nannie Helen Burroughs School at Washington, DC*. Washington, DC: Nannie Helen Burroughs Literature Foundation, 1956.

Higginbotham, Evelyn Brooks. Quoted in Barbara Ransby, *Ella Baker and the Black Freedom Movement: A Radical Democratic Vision*. Chapel Hill: University of North Carolina Press, 2003.

Higginbotham, Evelyn Brooks. "Religion, Politics, and Gender: The Leadership of Nannie Helen Burroughs." *Journal of Religious Thought* 44, no. 2 (Winter/Spring 1988): 7–22.

Higginbotham, Evelyn Brooks. *Righteous Discontent*. Cambridge, MA: Harvard University Press, 1994.

Hill, Kenneth. *Religious Education in the African American Tradition*. St. Louis, MO: Chalice Press, 2007.

hooks, bell. *Teaching to Transgress*. New York: Routledge, 1994.

Houston Chronicle. "Rita Pierson Obituary." July 12, 2013. https://www.legacy.com/us/obituaries/houstonchronicle/name/rita-pierson-obituary?pid=165784768.

Howard, Veena. "Nonviolence as Love in Action: James Lawson's Transforming the Promise of Jesus' Love into a Practical Force for Change." *Practical Matters Journal* 13 (Summer 2020): 1–25.

Hutchinson, Louise Daniel. *Anna J. Cooper: A Voice from the South*. Washington, DC: Anacosta Neighborhood Museum of the Smithsonian Institution, 1981.

Jackson, Shantina Shannell. 2015. "'To Struggle and Battle and Overcome': The Educational Thought of Nannie Helen Burroughs, 1875–1961." PhD diss., University of California, Berkeley.

Mathis, Deborah. "The Rev. Lawson on Human Endeavors for Hope and Change." *Minds of the Movement* (blog). International Center for Nonviolent Conflict. January 15, 2018. bit.ly/RevJLicncBlog.

McCluskey, Audrey Thomas. *A Forgotten Sisterhood: Pioneering Black Women Educators and Activists in the Jim Crow South*. New York: Rowman and Littlefield, 2014.

McIntosh, Shelley. *Mtoto House: Vision to Victory, Raising African American Children Communally*. New York: Hamilton Books, 2005.

McMurry, Linda O. *To Keep the Waters Troubled: The Life of Ida B. Wells*. New York: Oxford, 2000.

Moody-Turner, Shirley "'Dear Doctor Du Bois': Anna Julia Cooper, W. E. B. Du Bois, and the Gender Politics of Black Publishing." *MELUS* 40, no. 3 (2015): 47–68. http://www.jstor.org/stable/24570162.

Moore, Allan, ed. *Religious Education as Social Transformation*. Birmingham, AL: Religious Education Press, 1989.

Morris, Burnis R. *Carter G. Woodson: History, the Black Press, and Public Relations*. Jackson: University Press of Mississippi, 2017.

Nelson, D. Kimathi. "The Theological Journey of Albert B. Cleage, Jr." In *Albert Cleage Jr. and the Black Madonna and Child*, edited by Jawanza Eric Clark, 21–38. New York: Palgrave McMillian, 2016.

O'Connor, Hollie. "Waco Poverty Expert Rita Pierson Dies." *Waco Tribune-Herald*. Last updated July 15, 2020. https://wacotrib.com/news/education/waco-poverty-expert-rita-pierson-dies/article_061caec4-7b48-58d5-9a97-d287fa7e6ec8.html.

Rabaka, Reiland. "W.E.B. Du Bois's Evolving Africana Philosophy of Education." *Journal of Black Studies* 33, no. 4 (March 2003): 399–449. https://doi.org/10.1177/0021934702250021.

Raboteau, Albert. *Canaan Land: A Religious History of African Americans.* New York: Oxford University Press, 2001.

Riley, Cole Arthur. *This Here Flesh.* New York: Convergent, 2022.

Ross, Rosetta. *Witnessing and Testifying: Black Women, Religion, and Civil Rights.* Minneapolis, MN: Fortress Press, 2003.

Sandlin, Jennifer, Michael O'Malley, and Jake Burdick. "Mapping the Complexity of Public Pedagogy Scholarship 1894–2010." *Review of Educational Research* 81 (2011): 338–375. 10.3102/0034654311413395.

Savage, Barbara. *Your Spirits Walk beside Us: The Politics of Black Religion.* Cambridge, MA: Harvard Press, 2008.

Smith, Yolanda. "A Spirituality of Teaching: Black Women's Spirituality and Christian Education." Unpublished *Religious Education Association* paper, 2007.

Stokes, Olivia Pearl. *The Beauty of Being Black: Folktales, Poems, and Art from Africa.* New York: Friendship Press, 1971.

Stokes, Olivia Pearl. "Education in the Black Church: Design for Change." *Religious Education* 69, no. 4 (1974): 433–445.

Stokes, Olivia Pearl. *Why the Spider Lives in Corners: African Facts and Fun.* New York: Friendship Press, 1971.

Thomas, Linda E. "Womanist Theology, Epistemology, and a New Anthropological Paradigm." *Cross Currents* 48, no. 4 (Summer 1998): 488–499.

Thurman, Howard. Baccalaureate Address at Spelman College, May 4, 1980. *The Spelman Messenger* 96, no. 4 (Summer 1980): 14–15.

Townes, Emilie. "Because God Gave Her Vision: The Religious Impulse of Ida B. Wells-Barnett." In *Spirituality and Social Responsibility: Vocational Vision of Women in the United Methodist Tradition*, edited by Rosemary Skinner Keller, 139–164. Nashville, TN: Abingdon Press, 1993.

Townes, Emilie M. "Living in the New Jerusalem: The Rhetoric and Movement of Liberation in the House of Evil." In *A Troubling in My Soul*, ed. Emilie M. Townes, 78–91. Maryknoll, NY: Orbis, 1993.

Townes, Emilie. *Womanist Justice, Womanist Hope.* Atlanta: Scholars Press, 1993.

Tran, Mai-Ahn Le. *Reset the Heart: Unlearning Violence, Relearning Hope.* Nashville, TN: Abingdon Press, 2017.

Ward, Hiley. *Prophet of the Black Nation.* Boston: The Pilgrim Press, 1967.

Wells, Ida B. *Crusade for Justice: The Autobiography of Ida B. Wells.* Chicago: University of Chicago Press, 1970.

Williams, Delores. *Sisters in the Wilderness.* Maryknoll, NY: Orbis Press, 2003.

Wilmore, Gayraud. *Black Religion and Black Radicalism.* Maryknoll, NY: Orbis Press, 1998.

Wilson, E. A. *History of the Woman's Convention 1900–1955.* Burroughs Papers. Library of Congress, Washington, DC.

Wolcott, Victoria W. "'Bible, Bath and Broom': Nannie Helen Burrough's National Training School and African-American Racial Uplift." *Journal of Women's History* 9, no. 1 (Spring, 1997): 88–110. https://www.proquest.com/scholarly-journals/bible-bath-broom-nannie-helen-burroughs-national/docview/203245730/se-2?accountid=15172.

Wong, Kent, Ana Luz Gonzalez, and James Lawson Jr., eds. *Nonviolence and Social Movements: The Teachings of Rev. James M. Lawson Jr.* Los Angeles: UCLA Center for Labor Research and Education, 2016.

Woodson, Carter G. *Miseducation of the Negro*. Chicago: African American Images, 2000 (1933).

Wright, Almeda. *The Spiritual Lives of Young African Americans*. New York: Oxford University Press, 2017.

Wright, Almeda. "Unknown, but Not Unimportant! Reflecting on Teachers Who Create Social Change." *Religious Education* 111, no. 3 (2016): 262–268. doi: 10.1080/00344087.2016.1172861.

Young, Alfred A., Jerry G. Watts, Manning Marable, Charles Lemert, and Elizabeth Higginbotham. *The Souls of W. E. B. Du Bois*. New York: Routledge, 2006. https://doi.org/10.4324/9781315631981.

Index

For the benefit of digital users, indexed terms that span two pages (e.g., 52–53) may, on occasion, appear on only one of those pages.